The Fugitive Chemist

Abedawn Khalaf

الشمري
Alshimery
Press

Published in 2019 by Alshimery Press

ISBN Paperback: 978-1-9161368-0-9
Ebook: 978-1-9161368-1-6

A CIP catalogue copy of this book can
be found in the British Library.

Published with the help of Indie Authors World

I would like to dedicate this book to my family and everyone I have
met over the years who helped motivate me and
inspired me throughout my life's journey.

Acknowledgements

I would like to thank my wife, family and friends, both here in the UK and back in Iraq, for their support throughout the years. I also want to thank Christine McPherson for her help in editing this book. Naturally, above all, I wish to thank Kim and Sinclair Macleod without whom this book would not have got to the publishing stage.

Foreword

Dr Abedawn Khalaf – an appreciation by Professor Colin Suckling

Just over 30 years ago my erstwhile colleague, Dr George Proctor, introduced me to Abed Khalaf who was about to take on the role of the synthetic chemist in a project aimed at the discovery of catalytic antibodies. Once in a while in a scientific career, someone comes along who makes a real difference to progress and success; Abed was one such person and undoubtedly the most significant one in my career. In 1989 catalytic antibodies was a hot field of research and Abed turned out to be the right man at the right time. We were able to obtain a small number of catalytic antibodies and evaluate their properties. The opportunity that most fully and most extensively brought Abed's chemical and organisational skills into play, however, arose in 1993 when we began a project funded by Proteus Molecular Design into DNA minor groove binders intended for use as anti-infective drugs in human medicine. Abed became a key person in a team of chemists synthesising bespoke minor groove binders according to designs from Proteus, from which we learned concepts, skills, and techniques relevant to what was to become the primary field of our collaboration. After a short period of reflection to avoid conflicts of interest after that project ended, Abed, Professor Roger Waigh and I began what has now become known as the Strathclyde Minor Groove Binders (S-MGB) project, a project that has now become a project of international significance.

The central idea of the S-MGB project was that we could design, synthesise, and demonstrate the activity of minor groove binders active against almost any infectious agent (bacterium, fungus, parasite etc.) because they all contain DNA and by careful structural variation select compounds that are selective with respect to the host, be it human or animal. The importance of this idea has increased hugely since with the public and political recognition of the significance of antimicrobial resistance. More than anyone else in the synthetic chemistry community, Abed contributed over a period of more than 20 years to S-MGBs to the point at which we have active S-MGBs being investigated for development in four continents, Africa, India, South America, and Europe. Abed's contribution was immense because he made first most of the candidate compounds at Strathclyde. The most advanced compound is now in a phase 2 clinical trial in the hands of our partner company, MGB Biopharma for the treatment of Clostridium difficile infections.

Abed also contributed hugely over these years to the formation of undergraduate and postgraduate students in our laboratories. Nothing was ever too much trouble and he was always calmly and politely able to help. There can be few chemists who at their retirement can rightly say to themselves that they have contributed directly not only to a healthier world but also to the competences of those who will make their contributions in the future. I count myself to be very fortunate to have had such an all-round splendid colleague and friend for so many years.

Colin Suckling, OBE, DSc, FRSE
July 2019

Prologue

Life just does not follow a straight line. There are always problems, diversions, going forwards and falling backwards, as well as unforeseen and unexpected events which have the possibility of making life more complicated, more exciting, or incredibly frightening at times. However, the majority of us just have to take these events in their stride and say, "*C'est la vie.*"

From the beginning of my childhood, life seemed normal to us and everyone around us. Our parents did their best to nurture us, clothe and feed us, encourage our education, and try to keep us on the right path. As children, we gratefully accepted what was handed out to us.

My adolescence was more challenging. I had my own thoughts and ambitions and I was determined to achieve everything I could, but then the circumstances that surrounded me presented a mountain to climb.

After university, I had to endure eighteen months of national service which, like everyone else, I loathed. Iraq was ravaged with many years of war with its nearest neighbour, Iran, and it was inevitable that I would be sent to fight in the conflict at some stage.

Having the courage and determination to move on to fulfil my ambitions and desires in life led me to Scotland to study for two postgraduate degrees, and during that time I was extremely lucky to meet the woman of my dreams, who has been my wife for all these years.

Unfortunately, financial problems led to us travelling to Iraq and straight into the ongoing eight-year war with Iran. As an army reservist, I was posted to Erbil in Kurdistan, in the far north of Iraq. That part of the country was politically unstable; on one hand there were Kurdish factions that were fighting with each other, and on the other hand, Iranian fighter jets were bombing the area practically every single day.

As much as we loved the city of Erbil and the natives (Kurdish, Turkman, Arabs and others), life became intolerable for everyone in that part of the world, and especially for my wife and children. But when we decided to return to the UK, there were several obstacles which complicated matters.

While Carol was forced to fight her way through bureaucracy and paperwork to travel to Britain with our two children, my exit proved even more complicated. With a colleague, I escaped from an army training camp and began an arduous, harrowing, and at times dangerous, two-month journey over mountains and across several borders, overcoming language problems and visa difficulties, before finally and miraculously reaching the UK.

On my return to Britain, I worked as a postdoctoral research fellow at the University of Strathclyde in Glasgow, and was involved in many research projects, mostly in the field of medicinal chemistry. During the course of my research work, five patents were published, two of which were licensed to a pharmaceutical company. One of the drugs has now reached Phase II clinical trials as an antibiotic specifically for the treatment of the bacterial infection Clostridium Difficile.

Although I had to retire from work due to ill health in 2017, I hope I have made a small contribution to society and to humanity through the research work that I undertook.

This is my story...

Chapter 1

From the Beginning

I was born in the year 1952 in Karbala, Iraq, but unfortunately, I do not know the exact date of my birth and neither do any of my relatives. To me, that is a great pity; like everyone, I would like to know my exact date of birth. All I know is that I was the second youngest of six children, and was born at some point during the holy month of Ramadan in 1952.

When the very first government census was conducted during early 1960, the government decided to split those people who did not have an accurate date of birth (i.e. without a proper birth certificate) into two separate categories, according to roughly in which half of the year they were born. So, people who were told they were born in the first half of the year were given an official date of birth as the 1st of January that year; those born in the second half of the year were given the official date of birth as the 1st of July in that year. On top of this, most people born before the census were given the year of birth depending on whichever major events occurred around the time of the child's birth. For example, if a child was born during an eclipse of the moon or if there were exceptionally heavy rainstorms around the time of their birth in any given year, then the authorities would be able to roughly calculate the year of birth from records of when these events happened.

In my case, as I was believed to have been born during the second half of the year, my date of birth was officially registered as 1st July, 1952.

My father, Ibrahim Khalaf, always believed that all the family should stay together in the same house, no matter what happened. So I grew up in a three-bedroomed house that also had a very small box room. My parents slept in one bedroom, my two brothers and I in another, and my three sisters slept in the other bedroom. My grandmother, Sofia (my father's mother), who was already very old when I was born, slept in the small box room. Her husband died before I was born, and I do not know anything about him.

I cannot remember much about my grandmother Sofia, only that she was very, very old when she died, and nobody in the family seemed to have even one single photo of her! I do remember being very upset and crying profusely when she died, and I recall the mullah (holy man) coming to our house the night it happened. He sat in the room beside her coffin and recited from the Holy Koran all that night. The next morning, official criers (women who are paid to cry and mourn at funerals) came to the house to weep beside her coffin. The house was full of people, and eventually they carried the coffin to the mosque. Following this, the family was in mourning for three days.

Only a few days after her funeral, my father demolished the small box room and gave all my grandmother's belongings to the very poor people of our town.

My grandmother, Kefaya Jasim Al-Ta'i (my mother's mother) [01.07.1883 - 06.05.1981]. It is hard to believe that she was aged 98 when she died, as the mortality rates were bad for Iraqis then.

This is the only photograph I have of my Grandmother Kefaya (my mother's mother). I took this photograph myself in 1980.

She was married to Saeed Abbas Al-Kalash, who is believed to have been of Greek origin. She always told me that her husband was a very tall man – from her description he must have been around six foot six inches (approximately 1.98 metres) tall – Caucasian, blue-eyed, with sandy blond hair. I believe this account of him, because all my uncles and aunts were very tall and fairly white-skinned. Searching through the internet years later, I found the surname 'Kalash' associated with people who had migrated from Greece and settled in modern-day Turkey, Iraq, Iran, and Pakistan. Perhaps, and this is only a hypothesis, they came as part of the invading army with Alexander the Great.

My parents were both born in the city of Babylon and, after their marriage, they moved to the holy city of Karbala, which is only 42 kilometres west of Babylon. Both my parents were from farming families.

My father, Ibrahim, was born in 1905, but, naturally, did not have a birth certificate or any other official record of any sort to prove his year of birth. He had been married twice before: his first marriage did not work out as planned, and ended in divorce; his second wife, according to him, died of an unknown illness. My siblings and I are therefore the children from his third marriage. There were six of us in total, three boys and three girls, and I was the second youngest of the family.

Our house was in an alley with three other houses and a hamam (a public bath). The alley itself was only about one-and-a-half metres wide and about ten metres in length. I can clearly remember the main street. In the mornings, it changed from a mere street to a vibrant vegetable market, with two butchers' shops, one at either end of the road. Naturally, there was no room for cars or bicycles to go through, since the traders used to assemble their goods slap-bang in the middle of the street as well as on the two pavements, leaving only a narrow path for pedestrians and shoppers to walk past.

The hamam, which was right next door to our house, was divided into two sections – one part for men, the other for women. From the roof of the house, I could see the dome-shaped roofs and the chimney, which continuously spewed black fumes. The smell used to vary every now and then, and it was much later before I understood why the odour changed so much. The owner of this public bath – a man of Iranian extraction, who only ever employed other Iranians – used to collect old clothes, tyres, and papers, and he burned these as fuel to heat the water.

There was a seemingly endless collection of ropes tied from one roof dome to the other, and there were always a variety of different coloured towels draped over the ropes; these towels belonged to the establishment and were not for personal use by the staff. When I went there every week for a bath, it was always very hot, and there were benches for people to sit on and small marble sinks for mixing the hot and cold water together.

I used to get a great thrill from using the swimming pool there. It was always lovely and warm and had so many steps leading down to it. I would hang onto the railings near the shallow end to watch the proceedings. After the bathers came out of the baths, they would be given a towel to dry themselves, which they would just drop on the floor and leave for the assistant to pick up afterwards.

Our house, which was in an area called Al Abbasia Al Shirkea (which means to the east of the grave of Imam Abbas), consisted of a courtyard and two bedrooms on the ground floor. There was also a big bedroom on the first floor, which was occupied by my brothers and me until my older brother, Ali, got married. Then it was solely for him and his wife. Ali married our cousin, Kathiyma, who was one year older than him. I was told that this was not an arranged marriage as such because they loved each other and wanted to be married. According to my mother, Kathiyma had been orphaned when she was only a very little girl. So, on their marriage, my father partitioned off our parents' bedroom to make a smaller bedroom for my brother and me. Later on, as a teenager, I converted the courtyard into a small garden.

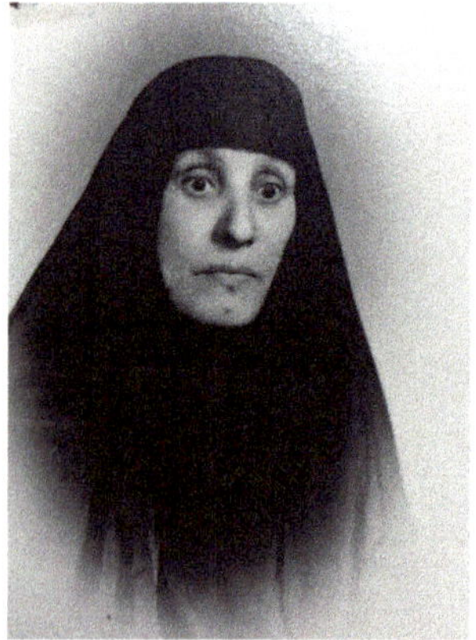

My mother in her younger years – date unknown.

My Mother Bedria (01-07-1922 to 13-07-1988).

My father, Ibrahim (01-07-1905 to 03-03-1983) – photo taken in the 1970s.

My mother once told me that my parents had previously owned a date-palm farm, and had kept a donkey in the house as a means of transport. For as long as I can remember, my family had always kept either a live goat or a live sheep in the courtyard. I clearly recall that at one stage there was a fairly young ewe that gave birth in the courtyard, and I took it upon myself to help her look after the baby lamb for many months. I was heartbroken and cried my eyes out when my parents informed me one day that, as we were very poor and struggling for money, they had decided to sell the baby lamb to raise some money. Soon afterwards, a buyer came for the lamb, and when he put it down on the ground to pay the money, the lamb came running over to me straight away. I was heartbroken to have to part with him.

The butcher who lived at the top end of the street had his own flock of sheep and would bring them into the street every afternoon to feed them. He used to put several metal basins in the middle of the street, which he would fill with barley or other seeds. My sister, Raskiyah, and I would go and pick up whatever barley or seeds were left over after the sheep were taken away and use whatever we gathered to help feed our own chickens, which we kept in a cage on the flat roof of the house.

I started at Al Ezza (which means 'pride') primary school when I was six years old. The school was not very far from our house, so my siblings and I used to walk to and from there on school days (Saturdays to Thursdays). As we were fairly poor, I must have looked peculiar wearing my traditional Dishdasha (a long-sleeved robe worn by men from the Arabian Peninsula which usually came down to the ankles), tucked inside my trousers or my shorts. It looked as if I had a very fat waist and very thin legs. Even then, the children from richer families wore more Westernised clothes, but we were of a lower standard.

I really enjoyed my time at school, because I loved learning something new every day. I always came out in the top percentile of the class and earned a number of certificates, which my family kept for many years. When we started learning the English language, the first lesson we had was to repeat words after the teacher, like 'saucer' and 'bicycle'. It is so clear in my mind how we used to shout the spelling of the word bicycle and making it rhyme (B-I-C-Y-C-L-E) while banging on the tables in front of us.

The only thing I was not good at was sport. I could run pretty fast, but I was dreadful when it came to football, basketball, and other physical exercises.

Photograph taken in 1962 when I was in primary five.

Our primary school teachers used to take us for school trips to nearby historical places. One of these places was The Fortress of Al-Ukhaidir (an ancient Abbasid palace), which lies around 50km south of my home town of Karbala. It was basically a rectangular fortress, believed to have been built around 775 AD by Isa ibn Musa, the nephew of the Abbasid Caliph. Gertrude Bell conducted excavations of this site in the early 20th Century. From the information gleaned from the excavations, it is believed Al-Ukhaidir was used as an important stop-over on regional trade routes, akin to those on the Great Silk Road.

The Fortress of Al-Ukhaidir – photograph by Brendan Choi, who has given me explicit permission to use it.

Unfortunately, the fortress has now been left to crumble, and if it continues to be neglected, it will fall into total disrepair and eventually become a heap of rubble in the coming years.

When we went on school outings, my mother would give me a packed lunch consisting of a boiled egg, boiled potatoes, some bread, and a flask of water. How nice it was sitting in the shade, in lovely surroundings, eating what, to me, was a feast in those days. I would then go and play with my friends among the ruins of whichever buildings we were visiting that day.

At the age of ten, I joined the Kashafa – the Arab equivalent of the Boys' Brigade. I loved wearing the uniform, as it meant I was dressed the same as the other boys, and I enjoyed the training that went with it. Of course, the uniform was provided free to everyone who joined the Kashafa.

In 1964, I finished primary school and had to move on to Al-Thawrah intermediate school (Al-Thawrah means 'the revolution'). Fortunately, this school was also nearby so I did not have to walk too far to get there. And I still had the same classmates, as most of them were either neighbours or people who had previously lived in the same street as us and with whom I played after school.

The new names for our schools came about after the revolution of the former Prime Minister, Abd al-Karim Qasim (21.11.14 – 09.02.63). He was a nationalist Iraqi Army brigadier who seized power in the 14 July 1958 Revolution, which caused the downfall of the Iraqi monarchy and resulted in King Faisal II being executed at the age of 23. Abd al-Karim Qasim himself was subsequently overthrown following the 1963 Ba'athist Coup in February that year. Following a very short trial, he was found shot dead a short while later.

The three years I studied in the intermediate school passed very quickly, and all too soon I had to move to a secondary school. It was around this time that the Iraqi government changed the school system to three years of study instead of the two years that my older siblings attended for.

There was only one secondary school in Karbala at that time, namely the Idadeat Karbala preparatory school. The pupils, who were clever enough, and lucky enough, to attend this school, were being prepped to go to universities and colleges after passing the Baccalaureate examinations. This school was literally just across the road from our house, and consisted of two specialised sections – one for science, the other was for education. Those who were more interested in medicine or science had to attend classes in science-related subjects, medicine, and engineering; those more interested in studying for a degree in education had to attend diverse subjects such as economy, art, sports, and languages. I opted to study science-based subjects as I really wanted to go to university to study medicine and sincerely hoped that I would succeed in achieving the high grades required.

During this time my older brother, Abu Haidar, was stationed at Al Habbaniyah, but his wife and children were still living at home with us. My brother's first name is Ali, but once a male child is born, the parents lose their own identity and instead become either 'the mother of...' or 'the father of....' So, when Ali's wife gave birth to their son, Haidar, my brother was from that day onwards respectfully called 'Abu Haidar' (the father of Haidar), and his wife, Kathiyma, was called 'Umm Haidar' (the mother of Haidar).

One day, about a year later, I overheard a private conversation between my parents about my second brother, Abd-Alhussain. He was then eighteen and my mother said she wanted to see him happily married. She hoped my father would agree to her suggestion while knowing very well that my brother, having left intermediate school, did not have a job or any prospect of work at that stage. He was seven years my senior, and as far as I was concerned, the only things he thought about then were his pigeons, which he kept in a big cage on the right-hand side of our flat roof.

He spent endless hours up there feeding his precious birds, cleaning the cage, and setting them free to watch them soar high into the sky before tumbling back to earth after somersaulting several times. I sometimes went up onto the roof to watch the pigeons flying free and was amazed at how elegant they were in flight. I found it remarkable that they could fly off for so long and travel to God knows where, but eventually they would all come back to their cage. Abd-Alhussain and his friends would make bets about which birds would fly back fastest from specific places, and he would then take the pigeons to the surrounding villages before releasing them. He must have trained those birds well, as they always returned to their nest and never stayed away for more than a day or two.

Eventually, my mother told my father, 'Our neighbour has a beautiful daughter, Fatima. She has blonde hair and looks almost Caucasian. She is only a couple of years younger than Abd-Alhussain, and I think she is very suitable, and they would be a good match.'

My father could not object. He knew that if he were to forbid this marriage, his own life would be made like hell until he finally agreed. Typically, my mother used to moan repeatedly to my father until he eventually gave her whatever she wanted, just so he could get some peace and quiet.

I dreaded the idea of my brother getting married. Our house was so crowded that there was no space for anyone else to live with us, but nobody paid attention to anything I said, especially as my mother was so intent on getting her own way. Eventually, my father conceded, and both families agreed to this proposed marriage. My brother was delighted at the prospect of being married off to such a pretty girl as Fatima.

To my annoyance, the big bedroom upstairs was partitioned into two smaller rooms just before they were married. I was really upset by all this upheaval and felt it was very inconsiderate of my parents to let both married brothers stay at home with the rest of us.

However, following his marriage, Abd-Alhussain began to turn his life around, and shortly after the birth of their first child, he commenced evening classes. He eventually finished his secondary school education and then applied to study Arabic language and theology at the Faculty of Jurisprudence at the University of Kufa. Within four years, he finished his degree and managed to secure a post as a secondary school teacher. He subsequently taught Arabic Language and theology until he had a stroke shortly before reaching the official retirement age.

With so many people living in such a small space, I found myself struggling with my studies. It was bad enough that we had problems at school due to there not being enough good secondary school teachers, but to top everything off we now had to face an even bigger problem – my mother's mental health crisis. We all realised that she had not been very well for some time, and her situation was slowly but surely getting worse.

Throughout Iraq, in the middle of June, when the exam results were finalised and the marks were due to be distributed to the pupils, it was standard practice for the Ministry of Education to announce the exam results, awards, and qualifications for every student over the local radio stations.

On the day that the announcements were due to be broadcast, I was so agitated that I could not sit still for more than thirty seconds. I had the radio turned up very high to ensure I did not miss the broadcast, and could not find anything to do to help calm me down that hot Friday afternoon. It was a crucial time for all those who had sat the sixth-year secondary school exams, as the allocation of places in the country's four universities depended on these results.

I was absolutely terrified at the thought of failure; the word did not exist in my vocabulary. I absolutely thrived on success and was always proud of my achievements. Until then, I had reached every goal I had set for myself in every aspect of my personal life.

It was a torturous wait until 4pm when the results were eventually broadcast. There was a long list of the names of the cities and all the secondary schools, starting from the north of the country: Erbil, Mosul, Sulaymaniyah (all in northern Iraq, now known as Iraqi Kurdistan), and so on down to Baghdad, and then to the southern cities of Iraq, including my city – Karbala – and then Babylon (Hilla), where many of my relatives stayed.

As soon as my name and my 75% score were announced, everyone in the house shouted congratulations. My sister began ululating and my mother shouted out to the neighbours, telling them my mark. Although it was not the high score I had anticipated, I was still glad that I had passed my exams at the first attempt. I knew the mark was not high enough to get me into medicine, but as everyone else was excited and my sister was dancing around the room, I followed suit and danced around the living room with her.

I must admit that I was extremely disappointed to get 75%, but I still hoped it would be good enough for me to secure a place in Baghdad University, perhaps in the college of engineering. Unfortunately, that did not materialise, but instead, I was offered a place in the College of Science at the University of Baghdad. I was absolutely distraught that I had not achieved the goal I had set out to accomplish. To me, it was an utter disaster, and I felt I had to do something about the situation I now found myself in.

However, I blamed my disappointing result on the education system, as we had not been provided with enough teachers for the final year in the secondary schools. We only had a substitute chemistry teacher for a few months, and after that, we used to gather in groups while one of us would act as the chemistry teacher to try to reinforce our learning. At each gathering, one student would read one chapter of our book and then he would prepare himself for a discussion and problem-solving session. Surely that should not be the case if our future was so dependent on the marks we got in the final examination for the Baccalaureate?

In those days in Iraq, you could only go for further study if your marks were good enough. Those scoring between 98 to 100% were allowed to go to Medical School. Having only scored 75%, my options were either to go to university to study science, to go and get a job, or to be drafted into the army.

*

My mother had been ill for some time and, in hindsight, I now believe she was suffering from schizophrenia. She used to imagine people coming into the house late at night and going up to the roof or even going into the bedrooms. My oldest brother, Abu Haidar, had taken her to Baghdad a few times, as that was the only town in Iraq where there were psychiatrists. But every time she returned from treatment at the psychiatric clinic there, she appeared to be in an even worse state than when she'd left. The psychiatrists were giving her electric shock therapy, which they thought was the best way to solve her problems. Unfortunately, this did not seem to work long-term, so every few months there would be yet another trip to Baghdad and more money spent on what seemed to be of no real benefit to anyone, and this treatment continued for a number of years.

When she returned from Baghdad, my mother would go into the back bedroom and sleep there for hours on end, wakening only long enough to take a little green tablet four times a day. Occasionally she would sleep in the living room, and would cover herself with her black abaya – the traditional long, black cloak which women had to wear. I could see her bony, yellow fingers poking out from the material, and she would lie on her side, her thin pale face uncovered, with a few strands of grey hair resting on her shrivelled, dry cheek. I could hear her talking in her sleep, arguing, fighting the devil in her dreams. It must have been awful for her when she was in a state like that.

Eventually, though, the sessions began to make a difference and she did improve dramatically, but these sessions were not without their own complications. Each and every one of us was affected by our mother's illness. The psychiatrists then put her on antipsychotic medication, and she became stable enough to function better, and this was a vast improvement for the whole family.

The family house, by this time, was completely overcrowded. My eldest brother, Abu Haidar, his wife, and their three children were living in one bedroom. In 1970, Abu Haidar finished his BSc degree in electrical engineering from Baghdad University and was subsequently offered the position of second lieutenant in the Iraqi Air Force, which he gratefully accepted. Due to his posting, it meant that he only came home at weekends, and sometimes he stayed away for longer periods of time while stationed at the military airfield in Al Habbaniyah – an air base in Al-Anbar Province, in central Iraq. There was a fierce battle there in 1941 during World War II. There is also a lake, Lake Habbaniyah, nearby.

My second brother, Abd-Alhussain, his wife, and their daughter were living in the second bedroom of our house. My youngest sister occupied the back bedroom, while I still occupied the small partitioned bedroom off my parents' one.

Thankfully, my oldest sister married and moved to Babylon to live with her husband's family. And my second sister had married some time previously, and was living with her husband's family not far from our home. She used to come and visit us every once in a while; by then she had three children of her own to keep her busy. Her husband, Abbas, was originally from the south of Iraq, but his family had visited Karbala many years previously and had liked it so much they decided to stay.

Abbas was a builder by trade, but he was a very simple person who was easily manipulated. He was a really good family man who respected his parents and his brothers very much. Unfortunately, he trusted them to such an extent that, when asked to sign his own house over into his father's name, he agreed without any hesitation and would not listen to anyone who tried to warn him about the dangers of doing this. At that time his house was his only asset – it was everything they had – but because he trusted his father completely, he signed over the documents giving his father the deeds to his house. We were told that his father had promised him he would leave the house, or at least a very large portion of it, in his will for my brother-in-law. However, within 24 hours of Abbas signing the deeds of the house over, things went pear-shaped. Once the documents were officially in his father's name, he announced that the house was legally his, and he wanted Abbas and his wife and family to move out!

Fortunately for Abbas and my sister and the children, one of the neighbours happened to be passing and saw them sitting on the pavement with all their belongings beside them. This kind woman, who was from a poor family, offered to help them out by allowing them to live in her spare room for a little monthly rent.

Although life had suddenly become incredibly difficult for my sister and her family, we helped them as much as we could at the time, considering our own circumstances. My brother-in-law was devastated, of course, and being blamed for ruining his family's future by signing the house over to his greedy father.

As there wasn't much building work available, Abbas's income was often not enough to support the family of five, so my sister used to come to our house when things were very desperate. She knew that at least she could get a meal for herself and her children, and be able to take a small amount of food back to her devastated husband so that he would have the strength to work if and when he could find it.

One Thursday evening, I returned from my lectures at Baghdad University to find my sister's youngest daughter, Amirah, sound asleep on the floor in my bedroom. My mother, who usually was happy to see me and would have prepared me a meal, met me looking extremely sad. Something was definitely wrong. After a few minutes, she sat on the couch with her head in her hands, staring at the tiles on the living room floor as if she was inspecting it thoroughly or had lost something so tiny but precious that it was crucial she should find it urgently.

Eventually, she told me, 'There was an accident, involving your brother-in-law.'

Immediately, my head was spinning with a number of dreadful thoughts. 'What kind of accident?' I asked.

'Abbas was working at a building site and fell from the scaffold,' she replied, her face pale, and her hands and arms trembling.

'How high was the scaffold?' I asked mother, trying to find a way to calm her nerves a little. 'He fell from the third floor,' the answer came back, and this time the tears started to trickle down her face and onto her thin chin.

'Where is he at the moment? How is he?' I enquired. I had so many questions I wanted to ask.

'He is in Karbala General Hospital on a life support machine. You should see all the wires and tubes attached to him just to keep him alive. I don't think he is going to survive that much longer,' she answered while fighting back the tears.

'It is all because of that wicked, selfish, greedy, disgusting family of his,' she went on. 'They should have treated their son better than that. He is a good, hard-working lad and he was supporting them as well as his wife and family.'

'Where is my sister now?' I asked, realising that was probably why my little niece was sound asleep in my room, wrapped up with a grey cloth and a long ribbon around her.

'Your sister is at the hospital at the moment beside her poor husband. We should let her be with him as long as she wants to be,' my mother replied. Getting up to make a cup of sweet black tea, she added, 'I don't think he is going to live that long anyway.'

A few days later, Abbas died in the hospital. Within four days, his father had come to our house and demanded to take the two older children to live with him and his family. The youngest child, Amirah, was to stay with her mother and us, as she was still being breast-fed, so my sister and her daughter stayed with us from that day forward.

I will never forget how she sobbed every single day of her life for many years. In such a short time, she had lost her beloved husband and two of her three children. She was forbidden to make contact with her son, Fadthil, and her older daughter, Bushra, and did not see them until they grew up and went to secondary school, when they managed to meet without the grandfather's knowledge.

Even many years after Abbas's death, friends and relatives tried to persuade my sister to get married again, and there were a few men who asked her directly, but she adamantly refused. She did not want to sully her husband's memory.

Chapter Two

Moving on to University

Having received a pass score of 75% in the Baccalaureate, this was to be the beginning of my rollercoaster ride into a hopeful new career. I felt a combination of fear and hope. Fear of the unknown, and of what the future might hold, but also hope that something good might still occur for me even with the fairly moderate grade I had achieved. Although I felt it was only a moderate result, it was still a success story for me. To obtain such a good mark was not easy, considering the family circumstances I had endured.

During my final year at secondary school, I had done my studying outside the house, every single night after dinner. Our home was so chaotic, with so many people living in a cramped space, that there was no way I could concentrate enough there to study. So, after helping to clear up after the meals, I would go outside to the main street and look for an area where I could find enough peace and enough light to work. Most evenings, I would just sit down on the untarred ground underneath one of the lampposts in the street and try to concentrate on my studies.

The traffic was very light at night, apart from the odd taxi and every now and again the rumble of an articulated lorry carrying stones from the outskirts of the city to the factory, which lay between Karbala and Baghdad. The noise from the traffic was not a big problem to me, but the insects were! Millions and millions of these tiny insects, including hermis (something like the midges in Scotland, but even smaller and more voracious bloodsuckers) and mosquitoes, used to dance around the light of the lamppost. They fell to the ground every now and again, and I had to be vigilant of them crawling over me and sucking the blood from my skin. Some of these bugs were really big; one in particular was really ugly and ferocious-looking. It was the size of a hand, black to dark blue in colour, shaped like a crab, and was known locally as 'nadous'. They were very similar to a mixture of the Japanese Rhinoceros Beetle (Kabutomushi) and the giant scarab beetle. I have tried to find a reference to this specific bug but have not had any success. When these bugs came hurtling down, they would make such a thud. I always assumed they were poisonous insects and did my best to avoid them at all costs, but I had to concentrate on my school work and trivialize everything else. My studies had to take priority over everything else, as I knew that this would be my one and only chance to succeed and get anywhere in life.

One night I was studying as per usual underneath a lamppost, trying not to pay any attention to the articulated lorries passing by, when suddenly I heard a woman screaming her head off. The awful sound of her screams reverberated along the streets and shattered the peaceful atmosphere. I closed my book and ran the short distance to where the noise was coming from.

When I got there, I discovered a young man lying near the pavement; he had been hit by an articulated lorry. His feet were bare and his shoes were lying on the pavement near his feet. He was lying face down on the tarmac, and it was obvious that the main injury was to his head, as his skull was bleeding profusely. Although his arms were lying parallel to his body, I could see that his hands were balled-up as if he was trying to grab the tar from the street.

A river of blood, about a metre long, had trickled from his skull and was now congealing at the edge of the pavement. Although he was wearing a jacket, it had ridden up as he fell, and I could see that he had a white shirt on underneath it.

This accident had happened on the opposite side of the road to a police station, less than fifty metres away. A few people had begun to gather around the dead man, and a policeman sauntered across to investigate what was going on. He seemed surprised that this tragic accident had happened in such close proximity to the police station.

His first question was: 'Does anyone know this man?' But none of the bystanders knew the deceased, even though Karbala was a small town. The policeman hesitated before going closer to inspect the scene in a rather amateurish manner. He put his hand inside the dead man's jacket to search for any form of identification, and retrieved both a wallet and a sheet of paper. He opened the wallet and read out the name of the deceased, but still no-one recognised his name. Then he opened the folded paper and began to read what it said. It was a letter addressed to the man's father, and on reading it out many of the bystanders began to cry:

To my father:

I do not want to marry anyone else. You know the girl I want to marry and because you are not allowing me to marry her I am going to kill myself. You and you alone are to blame for this. No matter how much you are going to cry, this is not going to replace your son. See you at judgment day and we will see what God has to say.

Now we understood what had happened between this young man, who was in his mid-twenties, and his father. These things sometimes happened in the Middle East, and perhaps in other parts of the world where the rules of the society and culture dictate the outcome of a relationship between two people. It was, and still is, pathetic and inhumane, and I believe that each and every one of us has a duty to remove this medieval practice.

When I went home that night, I told my family what had happened. Everyone was saddened by this tragic loss of life that had occurred just because a love match was forbidden.

*

I still cannot really recall exactly when my mother's mental health problem really began. It must have been around 1967, when we were still living in our previous house while we were building our new one. Initially my father had decided to buy a plot of land that consisted of an area of around 400 square metres in total, which was situated about one-and-a-half kilometres away from the city centre. Having bought the land, he decided to divide the plot in half and build two houses there – one for us, and the other for my second oldest brother, Abu Zoher (born Abd-Alhussain), his wife and their family; by then they had five children.

My brother Abd-Alhussain (Abu Zoher) (01-07-1945 - 30-12-2018) [photo taken in 1975]

As far back as I remember, my father worked in the building trade. He used to buy plots of land, get engineers to draw up the building plans, and then he would organise everything else himself, from the building material to the labourers. He would work as a bricklayer himself a lot of the time, and I worked with him during the summer holidays whenever I could.

Although my Baccalaureate examination grade was just not good enough to secure the university place I wanted in Medical School, it was high enough for the Government to agree that I could study in one of the other three areas still open to me – the College of Science; the College of Agriculture; or the College of Education. If I was willing to travel further north to the Kurdistan region, I could secure a place in the College of Engineering at the University of Sulaymaniyah. After much discussion with my family, I successfully applied for a place at the College of Science at the University of Baghdad, starting in September 1970.

Getting into this university was totally unexpected, given the sheer volume of people who had applied for a placement there; Iraq at that time had few universities and colleges.

Strangely enough, first year students were not entitled to student accommodation; rather, they were left to fend for themselves, which was not easy. Many of the students had travelled to a city they had never been to before – me included, even though it was very close to Karbala. Although there is only about 100 kilometres between the two places, very few people travelled just for the sake of going to another city to discover its delights; especially Baghdad, as it was thought to be too expensive for travel, food, and drink, or to stay there overnight.

Shortly before the 1st of September, I met two very close friends – Salah, who had been given an offer to study English Language at the University of Baghdad, and Adnan, who had been offered a place in the College of Management and Economy at the University of Baghdad, because he had obtained the highest mark out of all the students in the municipality of Karbala. He was undoubtedly very clever.

We discussed the idea of sharing an apartment together in Baghdad so that we could spend more time studying and less time travelling backwards and forwards from home – for the first year at least.

As Salah had scored a very high mark in the Baccalaureate, he had been offered first choice from all the options on the admissions list and decided to study English Language and Literature. His family were of Iranian origin, but somehow his parents had managed to acquire the proper identity documents (jinsea) after many years of living in Iraq, and were eventually recognised as Iraqi citizens. His father used to have a small shop in the heart of the city centre, making and selling celebration trophies to be sold to the football teams, as well as a variety of metallic trinkets that Iranian visitors on pilgrimages to the holy city of Karbala would buy to take back home as souvenirs.

Salah told me that his mother had suffered a lot before she died. She had been diagnosed with cervical cancer, for which there was no cure then, and the only medication they could give her to relieve her pain was morphine.

'The more they gave her, the more she needed, and the shorter her life became,' he told me. He explained to me that just before her death, she was so bloated and incapacitated and in such pain that the actual cause of death on her death certificate was a morphine overdose. We met his father on numerous occasions, and my impression was of an elderly, thin, bald, short but very pleasant man with a very gentle demeanour.

Adnan, Salah and I travelled to Baghdad together that first Saturday after being informed of our university places, and spent the first few days in a hotel in the city centre. We soon realised that this was too expensive for us, but we did not have friends or relatives to help us or to give us advice on how to go about getting more affordable accommodation.

Straight away, we started our hunt for any accommodation that would suit our budget as well as our educational requirements, i.e. not too far to travel to and from the university to the accommodation. After speaking to many students, university staff, and the hotel employees and other locals, we obtained the addresses of two places that might be cheap and adequate enough for our needs.

The first place we went to view was a dingy, ancient dwelling, perhaps from the eighteenth century. We were absolutely gobsmacked to see such a dilapidated building. It was damp and dark, there were wide arches everywhere, and there was only one small musty-smelling room for rent. How on earth could anyone live there in that dump? It reminded me of a cave, and must have been thrown up in a hurry.

No matter how poor we were, this was definitely not a place any half-decent human being could live in. Thankfully, Adnan and Salah felt the same way and we left without making any promises.

The second property we went to view was in a much better condition. It consisted of one large room, and there was a toilet and shower room in the small garden at the front. The large room would have to be used as a living room, bedroom, and kitchen. It may have resembled a studio flat, but there was no kitchen, no cooking facilities whatsoever, no bed, and no settees; basically, it was a large empty room. However, we decided to take it as it was in a relatively modern building, even though there were no cooking facilities and no furniture whatsoever.

Another trip home to our respective families in Karbala had to be made. This time, we came back to Baghdad with food, kitchen utensils, crockery, and other essentials, including the traditional doshek – a bed-length piece of hard sponge that is covered with cloth, and which Arab families use as a temporary bed when visitors arrive and stay overnight. I also brought a paraffin heater. Although its main purpose was to heat the room during the bitterly cold winter, it could also be used as a portable cooker.

*

That first year passed so quickly, and we soon found ourselves in the second year of our studies, which brought with it a different set of challenges. We had to choose one main subject to study for this year, and I chose chemistry in general rather than the other science-related subjects. Also, we were given access to the university's student accommodation, where one room was allocated for every five or six students. The rooms were cramped and uncomfortable and there was not an ounce of privacy, to say the least, but we mostly coped okay and were lucky that we got on well with the other room-mates.

We used to arrange day trips to nearby places, such as the historic Tāq Kisrā (also known as the Archway of Ctesiphon), which was the remains of a Sasanian Persian monument, near to what is now the modern town of Salman Pak. Even then, I loved visiting this archway to stand and admire the brickwork; it consisted of a single-span arch of bricks that was not reinforced but somehow managed to stand the test of time.

A photograph of some of my friends (I am circled) taken in front of the Tāq Kisrā in 1970, whilst on a trip with other first year students from the College of Science, University of Baghdad.

Occasionally, we organised a trip to the beach – time permitting – and we would have our dinner there when we could afford it. The customary and most famous dish to eat on a trip to the beach is masgouf, which is barbecued fish. Masgouf is usually baked beside the River Tigris, especially along the Abu Nuwas area, where there are many cafes and restaurants spread over several kilometres beside the river advertising that you can choose the fish you want cooked for you from live fish swimming in bath tubs. The chosen fish would then be prepared in front of you and served up with salad, bread, and whatever condiments were available on the day.

My undergraduate years passed by very quickly and, having graduated in June 1975, we all had one month's leave at home before being conscripted into the national service that July for eighteen months.

Graduation day 1975 (BSc in Chemistry, College of Science, Baghdad University)

November 2010. Meeting my best friend, Professor Dr Jaafar Hussein Ali, outside the University of Karbala, Iraq. I did not know then that this would be the last time I would ever see my learned friend.

My best friend, Jaafar, finished his MSc and PhD in Quantum Chemistry, and we later met up again and worked together at the Chemistry Department, Sallahadeen University, Erbil in Kurdistan, in the north of Iraq. He later moved to Karbala University to take up the seat of Professor of Chemistry.

Unfortunately, Jaafar died suddenly in 2017 from kidney failure. I had spoken to him on the telephone only two days before he passed away, and we had been talking about him seeking new treatments for his illness.

1970: Happy days. On the far left was my friend and colleague, Jaafar Ali. On my left is another friend and colleague, Ibrahim, and I am on the right.

Chapter 3

My life as a conscript in the Iraqi Army (July 1975 until July 1977): Part One

After finishing my university degree, like thousands of other able-bodied male students I was automatically conscripted into the army for a minimum period of 18 months. Life there was both enjoyable and miserable at the same time.

At the beginning of July 1975, all the male graduates with a BSc degree in Chemistry had to travel to the army base at Camp Taji. This military installation was in the Al Taji area – a rural region around 27 km north of Baghdad – and later became known as Camp Cooke by the coalition forces after the invasion of Iraq in 2003.

We arrived on an incredibly hot day, made almost unbearable because we had to stand in the full heat of the sun in an area paved with concrete slabs. I estimate that the temperature was in the region of 45-50°C, with no breeze or humidity whatsoever. The Commander appeared with his comrades and, after a short, sharp welcome briefing, we were all ordered to go and get our hair shaved very short by the unit barber, then collect our army uniforms.

Training started in earnest, with the Sergeant Major screaming at us at exactly six o'clock the next morning to get up and be ready in half an hour for the morning parade and inspection of the troops. We hurriedly washed, shaved, and donned our army uniforms for the very first time, pausing only to look at each other and laugh at how we had been transformed from civilians with a full head of hair to being near bald and dressed in khaki uniform.

The heavy black boots we were given to wear did not help, as we had to wear thick woollen socks which were extremely uncomfortable in that searing heat. When the morning parade and the physical exercise had finished, we were told to queue up for our breakfast which, unfortunately, was the same thing every day – a plate of porridge and a type of bread roll that we call 'samoon' (a stone-baked yeast roll, commonly eaten in Iraq), that tasted like a pizza base.

After a short break, there was another training session which lasted until lunchtime. Lunch itself was usually quite good, and was normally a meat-based murgha (an aromatic curry containing pulses such as lentils or chick-peas and tomato puree, rather than a spicy curry), a bowl of rice, and some more samoon. After two hours, the afternoon training would commence, and was either physical training or learning to dismantle and rebuild military equipment and weapons, and target training.

By five o'clock in the evening, we would make our way to the mess room to have our dinner. This was usually the leftovers from lunchtime, and some more samoon. Due to such a restrictive diet, we could often be found at the shop on the base, looking for something tasty to eat. Around an hour after finishing dinner, we would always be called out for another parade and a head count, just in case someone had left the camp without permission.

The training, which was really harsh most of the time, continued for three months, until one day we were all called to muster in the middle of the camp. The Platoon Major wanted to deliver an important announcement to everyone, so we were warned to be prompt. Once on the parade ground, the Platoon Major announced that he had received a document from the Ministry of Defence, and he had to abide by the contents of that document.

He shouted, 'I am going to read some names, and those who hear their names should move to this side of the parade ground.' He indicated to his right.

We did not know what was going to happen to those whose names were called, nor to the remainder of the recruits. As the names were read out, the soldiers obediently moved to where they were told to. I heard my name being called and I moved over to the right side beside the other selected recruits.

When he finished reading the names, he added, 'Those whose names I have just read out are going to have a different type of training for the next six months, and those who pass that part of the course will be promoted to Second Lieutenant as reserved officers.'

Once segregated, our style of training immediately changed. But the best thing about the change of training was the vast improvement in the food that we were served up on a daily basis. From breakfast to dinner, we were given what I considered to be first-class food. For the following six months, we had to attend many lectures, undergo lots of night exercises and more day training, and then finally take both a written and a practical examination. A few days after the exams, the results were announced. Those who passed were then told where they were being sent to, and whether or not they were to be promoted to the rank of Second Lieutenant.

We were bussed out to another camp, where we had to march around the area a few times until the Prime Minister arrived. We were wearing our new uniforms (without any rank) which were tailored for our own bodies.

To our huge surprise, the Vice President who at that time was Saddam Hussein, had come to our graduation ceremony. And that was the first, and only, time that I saw Saddam Hussein face-to-face and in close proximity.

Having graduated from what was called The College of Reserved Officers, we were given permission to add our stars (our new ranks) to the epaulettes on our shoulders, which felt rather good at the time, and were then called Second Lieutenants. Following our graduation ceremony, we all returned to our original army base.

The following day, our names were written on slips of paper and placed in a box. As the Sergeant Major called out our names one by one, we were told where we were to be stationed. However, we were also informed that we could swap our new positions at this stage, if anyone was willing to swap with us.

I was told that I was to be stationed in Sulymaniyah, in the north of Iraq. As I did not want to be stationed so far away, I asked if anyone would be willing to swap with me and, fortunately, one of the other new Second Lieutenants said he would prefer to go there as it was nearer his home. So, I took his place at the 6th Armoured Battalion in Baquba, Diyala Governate, instead. This placement was so much better for me, as it was much nearer to my home town, being only 50km northeast of Baghdad and one-and-a-half hours away from Karbala.

Life in the 6th Armoured Battalion was a real eye-opener and a huge learning curve for me. Our Commander was an obese, extremely unfit person, with the rank of Major. I was one of two newcomers under his authority, and there were two more senior officers above us already serving in his company, both of whom were from the south of the country. Within a few days I began to understand the way they lived during the week in that army base. Almost every evening, apart from when we had night exercises, our Commander ordered the cook to 'prepare the table', meaning that the cook had to set up the table with alcohol and some plates of mezes for the officers.

I had never realised that this kind of practice was allowed in any army in Iraq, because we were all Muslims, but then again, I was still new to this and was not *au fait* with the do's and don'ts in the army. I was amazed at how they all managed to wake up early in the mornings to perform their daily duties as if they had not had a heavy drinking session the previous night and without showing the signs of suffering from severe hangovers.

One day, our Commander informed us that he was calling an urgent meeting and we had to convene in the dining room as soon as possible. Once everyone was there, he announced that he had received orders from his superiors that we should get ready to be moved to the border between Iraq and Jordan. We were to be stationed in a specific place but were not told where at that stage. No specific time was given either, but we were informed that we had to prepare ourselves for a war situation. We later found out that the war was supposed to be with Israel. The Iraqi government was waiting for permission from the Jordanian government for the troops to travel through Jordan and to amass at the Israeli border in preparation for an incursion to fight the 'enemy' on their own soil.

Moving everyone was an enormous task, and preparations had to start promptly. Now, instead of training the soldiers, we were expected to command them and get everything packed up that was deemed necessary for the proposed war. Panic and fear spread in the camp, but this is what the soldiers were supposed to be trained for, so we just had to buckle up and get on with it.

Within 48 hours, another emergency meeting was called, and this time our superior informed us that we would be moving out the following morning at 03.00 hours. 'Just go and make sure you get yourselves ready,' was his last order. We started packing up at 23.00 hours that evening, ready for our deployment a few hours later. This meant making sure everything was in order, checking and packing the specialised vehicles, weapons, beds, and mobile cooking equipment, to name but a few things.

We all received individual orders, and I was ordered to take charge of getting together all the ammunition. I was given a list of what was required and which depot I should collect the various items from.

At 03.00 hours prompt, the Commander stood in front of us and handed out more orders, dividing up all the duties for us officers. I was to be in command of the tail-end of the long queue of vehicles, meaning that if any vehicle should require repairs or petrol, or if the driver became unwell and a replacement was required, I had to deal with it myself.

Soon the convoy started to move off, leaving the base and the town of Baquba behind us, and heading towards Baghdad. Nearly two hours passed, and we were just about to leave the boundary of Baghdad Governate when one of the vehicles broke down. I had to stay with the driver and the vehicle until it was repaired, which took a good few hours, and then we were finally on the move again, heading toward Fallujah, Al Anbar province, located roughly 69 kilometres west of Baghdad on the River Euphrates. Fallujah is an ancient city that dates back to Babylonian times, and for centuries was host to many important Jewish academies. To us Iraqis, Fallujah was historically thought of as the 'city of mosques', because there were more than 200 mosques in the city and the surrounding villages.

After refuelling in Fallujah, we were on the move again – this time, heading toward Ramadi, the capital of Al Anbar Governate. The city extends along the Euphrates and was originally founded by the Ottoman Empire in 1879, as it occupied a highly strategic location on the river and on the road west into Syria and Jordan. The roads were busy on both sides, as goods were coming in from both Syria and Jordan, and huge oil tankers were carrying their cargo in the opposite direction.

I was still following the orders I had initially received about collecting the stocks of ammunition, and we found the first ammunition depot situated on the outskirts of Fallujah. It did not take too long to upload all the boxes of ammunition and explosive materials, as they had already been stockpiled ready for us to load up into our old ZiL. ZiL was a Russian car manufacturing company that produced armoured vehicles for most of the Soviet leaders, as well as buses and armoured fighting vehicles.

It was not until that stage that it became an incredibly frightening experience for me. Here I was, sitting in an old Russian car loaded with boxes of rockets, bullets, hand grenades, and other explosive materials. If we were going to be involved in a crash or to go over a large pothole, there was the possibility that the explosives could detonate. And if that happened, the explosion would be capable of demolishing several vehicles, not just the one I was being driven in. In fact, were that to happen, both the driver and I would be blown to smithereens and not a trace of us would be left amongst the wreckage.

Slowly but surely, we continued our journey during the hot afternoon and early evening, with only a short break to get something to eat and a short nap to refresh the driver. We journeyed onwards towards the city of Ramadi, then further, towards the border between Iraq and Jordan. By the middle of the night, we were still only halfway to our destination, so I told my driver to pull over to the side of the road to take a break, as it was obvious we were both too tired to concentrate on the road ahead. For both our sakes, we had to take turns to get some sleep, so I suggested he should stretch his legs and then try to take a nap. After two hours, I would wake him up, and then I would try to get some sleep. With all the ammunition in the back of the vehicle, we would take it in turns to nap until sunrise, when we would continue on our way.

Although it was a perilous time, we were both so tired that we did manage to stagger our sleep/wake cycle until sunrise, when it was time to get moving once more. That early in the morning, the sun was just above the horizon – a pure orange-red ball rising over a vast empty desert as far as the eye could see. It looked like an absolutely beautiful morning and I hoped it would lead to a splendid day. We had to stop a couple of times for refuelling and then for a brief wash and a quick breakfast, then one more time *en route* for lunch.

The camp had been set up around 40km away from the border with Jordan, and it was late afternoon by the time we arrived. The Commander was sitting there with some other officers, drinking tea and smoking his cigarette. 'What kept you so long?' were his opening words to us. 'And why haven't you shaved your beards?'

I had to explain to him that our vehicle had broken down and been taken to a garage for a makeshift repair, as it was an ancient ZiL. We couldn't have taken any risks driving it too fast to catch up with the rest of the convoy. He appeared to accept my explanation and turned to resume his chat with the other officers, totally ignoring our presence.

'How bloody arrogant you are,' I muttered under my breath, then turned to go in search of my tent, which had been erected for me beside the other officers and not too far away from the Commander's tent. The boss and his companions kept up their normal habit of drinking every night in spite of (or perhaps because of) the imminent military operation and the horrendous struggles with the living conditions in the desert.

Every night I slept with my full army uniform and boots on. There were so many poisonous spiders and scorpions around! One day I saw a scorpion crawling up the inside of my tent, and I had to kill it rather than take any chances. Although only 25% of scorpions can kill a healthy human being, the neurotoxins in their sting can still cause convulsions and lead to shortness of breath.

One night, being too tired to think, I removed my boots and left them at the side of the bed before falling fast asleep. When I woke up in the morning, I turned my boots upside down, knocked them against the floor, and found a scorpion hiding inside one of them. From then on, I decided it definitely was safer to sleep with my boots on.

One evening, it was approaching midnight and the sky was only lit by a waning half-moon. The Commander and his drinking partners finally left the tent they had been drinking inside, and went to their own tents to sleep it off. It was incredibly quiet in that vast desert, and still stiflingly hot with only a gentle breeze blowing every now and then. The Commander decided to pull his camp bed, which was only a few inches above the ground, outside the tent so that he could sleep off the drink and enjoy the intermittent breeze.

We were all falling asleep when an almighty scream came from the far end of the long row of tents where the soldiers were sleeping. I immediately jumped from my bed, grabbing my Kalashnikov rifle, and ran to investigate the cause of the commotion.

One young soldier was screaming, 'My arm! My arm!' He was running and jumping over a few other soldiers who were also sleeping outside their tents. He continued running and was now heading towards the Commander's bed, as he could not see anything in his blind panic. He jumped over the Commander's bed and kept on running and shouting until we finally caught hold of him to investigate what was going on.

By this time, everyone in the camp was awake and on full alert, including the Commander, who – in his drunken stupor – was unsure whether he was having a bad dream or whether the enemy was attacking us.

The soldier was brought back to the Commander for questioning. 'What on earth is the matter with you?' he shouted, rubbing his eyes with both fists.

The poor soldier was trembling and, holding his arm to his chest, he replied, 'I had a horrific dream. I dreamt that my arm was chopped off as a result of enemy fire, and I was experiencing excruciating phantom pain because of it.'

Now that we knew the cause of his theatrics, a soldier jumping over sleeping comrades – especially our fat commander – in the middle of the night, was absolutely hilarious. Even now, after all these years, when I remember the chaos and the screaming and shouting, I laugh to myself until the tears start to run down my cheeks.

It was not at all funny, though, being camped out there in the desert. There was fierce heat during the day, freezing cold very late at night, and then there were the sandstorms. When they blew, we would be covered in sand, which got into every single crevice in our bodies, underneath our clothing, in our food, our beds, and even in our equipment and weapons.

The effects on the soldiers of having to live like this varied. Some thrived on it, but others could not tolerate the harsh life in that desolate location and really suffered at being trapped there with no way out. Unfortunately, some felt that their only means of escaping the dire situation was to take their own lives.

Committing suicide in the army is an extremely messy business for all concerned, not just for the man's family and friends, but also his army comrades and the troop commander.

One very hot afternoon while we were sitting drinking tea, we heard a gun being fired. It was totally unexpected because there were no exercises planned for that afternoon. After some time, we heard the dreaded news that a soldier had taken his own life by leaning on his Kalashnikov and allowing the nozzle of his weapon to rest on his stomach before pulling the trigger. It is so sad to hear about the loss of any life, but to learn that someone has actually ended their own life, no matter how they did it, is absolutely devastating for all concerned.

We were all affected so badly when the horrible news reached us and felt completely helpless. Nobody had known that this soldier had reached the end of his tether, or we would have intervened. But then again, what could we have done to prevent this? I felt as though I wanted to cry, to get rid of the sad emotions that seemed to be drowning me, but there was no way I could show such weakness in front of the other soldiers or they would no longer obey any commands I gave them. I would never want to be labelled as weak by anyone.

Although the deceased was not from our platoon, nevertheless he was a human being and should have had a long life in front of him. Who knew what had been going on in his mind or what drove him to end his life in such a senseless manner?

'It is an utter shame, but life must go on,' our Commander muttered softly. Meanwhile, we all sat there in silence, staring at the blue sky overhead and contemplating what was going to happen next.

Chapter 4

My Life in the Iraqi Army (July 1975 until July 1977): Part Two

We had been stationed in the desert for approximately six months and were beginning to feel that we were living like the Bedouin (nomadic desert dwellers), when the Iraqi government decided that all the soldiers should be recalled back from the border with Jordan. We were not given any specific reasons as to why we were being brought back to our home bases, but we all assumed that the Jordanian government had eventually refused the Iraqi army the necessary permission to travel through their country to amass at the Israeli border!

We were elated when the orders came through, and we hurriedly packed up all our kit and got the vehicles ready to return to our bases.

It only took us a few days to get back to our base in Baqubah. However, we had barely settled back into our billets and our normal daily routine, when another order came through – this time from the local command office. We were to get ready for yet another exercise. Thankfully, we learned that we would be based not too far from our army base, and were to be camped up in close proximity to some date palm farms and near a small river.

One very sunny morning, our platoon had assembled and started moving on the main road towards the area where we had been told the exercises were to be held. I was in an army jeep with my driver – a very experienced soldier who was driving very competently near the front of the convoy. We were perhaps an hour into the journey when the convoy stopped.

Suddenly, a huge commotion came from the back of the convoy, so I told the driver to turn the jeep around and head to the back of the line so we could investigate what was happening. The driver swung the jeep around and sped as fast as he could towards the rear of the convoy, and as we neared there we could hear people screaming.

I will never forget the horrific sight we came across. There were three lifeless bodies lying on the pavement, all of them covered in blood that was seeping from various parts of their mangled bodies. One was a middle-aged man, who still had one leg attached – the other severed leg was lying near the body. One of our captains was standing a few feet away from the scene, vomiting copiously. Obviously the sight of this horrific accident was too much for him to bear and he couldn't take it all in.

In the middle of the road there was a mangled minibus, which had crashed into one of our Russian-made ZiLs, and it had also sustained fairly severe damage. I looked around for the driver of our vehicle and found him on the other side of the road, sitting on a fallen tree trunk with his hands covering his pale face. He was sobbing like a child who had lost his precious toy.

'What on earth happened?' I asked the shaken driver.

He replied hesitantly, 'I was just driving as normal when my vehicle, which is very heavy to steer, became separated from the other vehicles in the convoy. I was trying to overtake the car in front and managed to get parallel to it, but the driver just would not slow down to let me pass. Meanwhile, the driver of an oncoming car misjudged the distance and the speed he was going at. I began to brake, but it was just too late and there was a horrific head-on collision. It wasn't my fault; he should have slowed down, as this stretch of road is very narrow.'

On reporting back to the Commander, he ordered us all back to base – an order we readily complied with – and our exercises were delayed for a few days until all the official paperwork of the accident had been sorted out. Until then, for the protection of the army driver involved in the accident, he was put temporarily in the base prison until he would be summoned to court for trial. We had to protect him to ensure that the families of the deceased did not try to exert revenge, because according to local custom, it is an eye for an eye. So, if someone kills another – even by accident – then the deceased's family can reciprocate in the same manner. If anything had happened to our soldier, all of us on the army base would have been in deep trouble with our superiors, because everyone and everything on the base had to be secure at all times.

A lengthy report on the accident was written and hurriedly submitted to the authorities, following which the driver was officially handed over to the police and incarcerated in a civilian prison to await judgement.

At around the same time, we had another incident that I had to deal with personally. One of the soldiers in my platoon had been AWOL for two days, and I had to report him as missing. However, on the third morning after his initial disappearance, he arrived back at camp, driving his own small pick-up truck. He came straight over to me with a package, wrapped in newspaper, under his arm, and demanded to be taken to the commanding officer. He was very calm, but at the same time looked very despondent, and he asked for my assistance.

I asked him where he had been and what he thought he had been doing by disappearing like that without speaking to me first to get permission to leave the camp. I then took him to the commanding officer, and the soldier gave him the package wrapped in newspaper.

The commanding officer demanded to know what it was and why the soldier thought he could go AWOL and then return with a bribe, as he presumed that was what the package was. But when the soldier was told to open the package so that everyone could see what was inside, he immediately refused. He then announced, 'I have killed my sister, and I have brought her arm to you as proof!'

He explained to the shocked commanding officer that he had been informed that his unmarried sister was pregnant – something that had brought great shame on the family. So, as the eldest brother, he had taken it upon himself to kill her and restore the family's honour.

We were all totally shocked at this act of violence by a soldier who had, until he went AWOL, been an exemplary trouper. A report was duly filed, and I had to escort this soldier to the prison on the base. As it was a civilian matter, a report was sent to the police, and the following day the soldier was collected by civilian policemen from the nearest town and incarcerated in the town's prison to await trial.

We were not informed of the results of the trial, but I never saw that soldier ever again. So it is possible that the Muslim rule of law of an eye for an eye meant that this person was executed for his deed.

We were soon on the road again to carry out the exercises which had previously been abandoned. The chosen site looked really nice, surrounded by date palm trees, and we pitched our tents beside a river. It was now getting late in the year, and as winter was fast approaching, we had some difficulties with the clay soil when it rained. Even the smallest amount of water changed the soil into heavy, sticky clumps of material that clung to everyone's army boots, making walking so horribly difficult. There were also lots of insects – scorpions and all kinds of creepy crawlies – crawling around our camp, especially at night. And it was a regular occurrence for the soldiers to be stung or bitten as most of them were sleeping on blankets on the ground; only the officers had beds to sleep on.

One morning, I got up and hurriedly pulled my army uniform on before heading out to do my first tasks of the day. Immediately, I felt something crawling inside my shirt and stood as still as I could until the insect made its way up near the collar of the shirt. I waited for what seemed like hours, but was only a few minutes, until a scorpion became visible then I flicked it away gently with my hand. Thankfully, it fell to the ground without stinging me.

I know that, as a good Muslim, you are not supposed to kill anything, but I stood on that scorpion and ground my foot into the clay until it stopped moving. It was a small scorpion, yellowish in colour, but if it had stung me I would certainly have suffered painfully from its venomous sting.

Photo taken in 1976 with my cousin Saadiq (on the left). I am in the middle, and a colleague who was also a second lieutenant is on the right. The photo was taken outside the Officer's Mess of the 6th Armoured Division in Baquba.

The above photo was taken when I was a second lieutenant in the Iraqi Army. My cousin, Saadiq Abd Alamir Saeed Al-Kalash, was also a second lieutenant, although he was wearing civilian clothes when the photo was taken. He was eventually promoted to captain, and still held that rank when, after the fall of Saddam Hussein, he was assassinated in front of his own house because he was a Shi'a Muslim who lived with his wife and children in a Sunni Muslim area of Baghdad.

After Saddam's death, the country became unruly and there were many sectarian slaughters of Shi'a Muslims, especially those who were living in mainly Sunni areas of Iraq. During Saddam Hussein's reign, these activities never occurred because he ruled the country with such an iron fist. People had always been too scared to commit these atrocities, because the government would immediately hang the perpetrators.

There were also many people who were informers during Saddam's reign, as this was seen as a lucrative means of living because they were inevitably promoted to higher positions in the Ba'ath party.

Chapter 5

Studying Abroad

Having finished my national service in Iraq in the summer of 1977, during Saddam's regime, I had long entertained the idea of going abroad to study for my postgraduate degree. Unfortunately, my family's finances at that time were not that great. My dad was quite old by then, and he was finding fewer jobs in the housebuilding sector in the city. However, I had managed to save some money during my national service, and had deposited it in Karbala's only post office during that time, so that it was easily accessible whenever I required it.

I had discussed my idea of studying abroad with my good friend, Salah, and he had given me the names and details of a few universities which I seriously thought about applying to. These universities were mainly in the UK, but there were others in the former Yugoslavia, Bulgaria, and in Austria. Salah, by then an English language teacher, kindly and patiently helped me to put together a number of sentences in really good English, advised me what to write, and then proofread my application letters.

After a few months of correspondence with various universities – mostly rejection letters from English universities – I finally received an offer from the Chemistry Department at the University of Dundee. I was ecstatic when I received their offer, and my next step was to apply for a visa to study in the UK.

Just twenty-four hours after receiving the official offer letter from Dundee, I took a minibus from the main bus garage in Karbala city at around 3am to travel to the British Embassy in Baghdad. At 5am, I joined the queue of people outside the British Embassy, carrying with me all the required documents and the lengthy form which I had filled in beforehand.

I already had an Iraqi passport which would allow me to travel to the UK and any other country in the world... except Bulgaria! There must have been some kind of bad relationship between Iraq and Bulgaria at the time when my passport was processed, although I cannot for the love of me remember what had happened or when.

Eventually, I got to the front of the queue around lunchtime and was interviewed by one of the British Embassy officers. She thoroughly scrutinised all my documents before stamping my passport with a one-year student visa for entry to the UK, and informed me that this student visa could be renewed every year – one year at a time – for the duration of my studies in the UK.

I was over the moon. It felt like such a gigantic step forward towards going to live and study in the United Kingdom, and eventually obtaining a post-graduate degree!

Me, taken in late November 1977, a month before embarking on my journey to Britain.

Although my family were extremely apprehensive, they were nevertheless supportive of my intention to study abroad. They encouraged me, to some extent, to leave behind the messy situation that my home country was in by then due to the ongoing hostilities between Iraq and Iran.

At that time, travellers had to purchase return travel, rather than just a one-way ticket. The usual arrangement in those days was that one could return the unused portion of the ticket to the travel agent when you reached your destination, and be given a refund on the unused ticket, minus taxes and the usual commission. It seemed illogical to me. Why could I not just purchase a one-way ticket, save myself some money, and eliminate all the hassle? But those were the rules and regulations, and I had to abide by them!

My flight was eventually booked on the Iraqi Airways Airline for the 7th of December, 1977, leaving Baghdad International Airport at 12 noon. My oldest brother, Abu Haidar, drove me to the airport in his car, accompanied by my cousin, Abu Kareem. I am not entirely sure why he decided to come with us to the airport, but maybe it just seemed like a big adventure for him.

The distance from Karbala to Baghdad is only approximately 100km, and normally took between one and one-and-a-half hours, depending on both the traffic and how busy the many checkpoints along the main route from Karbala to Baghdad airport were. So, we left the house very early in the morning, and arrived at the airport before 9am.

The flight bound for London Heathrow was on time, and the journey lasted around five hours. When I got off the plane at Heathrow, it was already dark, and it was raining and very cold. Looking around, I felt frightened but excited at the same time. Everything was so different, from the foreign language being spoken to the environment.

I was lucky to find some Arabic-speaking people outside the airport who I asked for help in finding a bus to take me from the airport to the city centre. One of the men in the group told me that I should follow them to the bus stop, as they intended to take that same bus into London. It was so cold standing there waiting for the bus, and I was shivering by the time it eventually arrived.

When everyone got off the bus in the middle of London, I had no option but to get off, too. I did not have a clue where I was, so had no choice but to hail a taxi and hand the driver the slip of paper with an address that my oldest brother, Abu Haidar, had written down for me. Apparently, this was the address of a hotel where my brother had stayed a few years before, when he was sent to London to attend a course on something to do with his electrical engineering training for the Iraqi Air Force (he was still attending training courses although he was a colonel by that stage).

The taxi driver took me to the hotel, which was in the Bayswater area of London, and I stayed there overnight. First thing the next morning, I took a taxi to Kings Cross train station and booked a seat on the next available train to Dundee.

The train journey from London to Scotland seemed interminable; it took nearly ten hours until I arrived in Dundee late in the evening. I had not managed to sleep much on the train, as this was a whole new experience to me. There were very few trains in Iraq, and this was my first visit anywhere in the world outside my country! I had been amazed at the different scenery passing by as I looked out of the train window. There seemed to be two different climates – London and the south seemed much warmer; as the train sped northwards, the weather seemed to become greyer and colder.

When I finally got off the train and exited the station, I jumped into the first taxi I saw and asked the driver to drop me off at a hotel near the city centre. I had no idea that the train station was really close to the city centre! A few minutes later, he stopped outside one of the most expensive hotels in the city.

'This is the Angus Hotel,' the taxi driver told me, putting his hand out for the fare.

I did not have a clue where I was, but went inside and managed to explain in broken English to the hotel receptionist that I wished to have a room for one night only. To my surprise, she informed me that it was £25 for a room for the night (this was back in 1977)! It seemed like an exorbitant amount of money for one night – and that price did not even include breakfast!

In the morning, I asked the receptionist for directions to the University of Dundee, which turned out to be just one street away from the hotel, and I entered the first university building I found and asked for directions to their accommodation office.

Having been shown roughly where to go, I dragged my battered suitcase along the cobbled streets in the general direction I had been given. There, I asked a receptionist if there was any possibility of getting a room to stay in while I studied at the university. She told me to wait while she made enquiries with the person in charge of student accommodation.

Soon a bearded, middle-aged man appeared and began asking me questions that I could barely understand. I showed him my papers, and eventually he instructed the lady at the reception desk to check for any vacancies. After checking a large ledger on the desk, she stated that I was in luck as there were a few vacant rooms in the student accommodation, and I could therefore take a room in Belmont Hall.

The gentleman indicated that I should follow him to the halls of residence. I later discovered that he was actually a member of the academic staff, who was also in charge of the student accommodation at that time, and had taken pity on me. I followed him to another building and up to the third floor, where he opened the door, handed the key to me, then bade me farewell and good luck!

To me, Belmont Hall was fantastic accommodation, especially considering my days as a BSc student at the University of Baghdad. The accommodation was so clean, neat and tidy, and I soon discovered that, although it was not cheap, the cost included the electricity and hot water; it was cleaned every day, and we even had full board included in the cost of the room. The food turned out to be delicious, and the added bonus was that the halls of residence were very close to the chemistry department where I was to be studying for my MSc degree. I stayed in that accommodation for about two years before moving to other student accommodation in Airlie Place.

Airlie Place was self-catering accommodation which also belonged to the University of Dundee. Moving there added another aspect to my life, since I had to do my own shopping, cooking and cleaning, as well as meeting and socialising with a different set of people who shared the same apartment. I stayed in a four-bedroomed house, and shared a bathroom and a kitchen with the other three residents – all of whom were Iranians.

These three students were so very different from any of the Iranian people I had known back home in Iraq. My home city of Karbala was visited every year by thousands of Iranians, who came on a pilgrimage to the holy shrines of two of the most important imams in Islam – Imam Husayn and Imam Abbas. These visitors always showed nothing but respect, both for their religion and for everyone else they met during their pilgrimage.

However, the three Iranian students I was lodging with were completely different. They would party often and very hard, drinking alcohol and inviting girls to join them, and even to stay in their rooms overnight with them. I had never experienced anything like this in my life before, and found it strange that a group of Muslim men would get drunk and then sleep with these strange girls. To my mind, they had thrown all the normal moral rules of Islam out of the window and adopted the western way of life in all its forms.

After some time, one of the Iranians moved out and was replaced by a young Bangladeshi guy. This short, thin, shy student spoke very little English when he first arrived at the halls of residence. Remembering how difficult it had been when I first arrived in Dundee, I tried to help him settle into life there. I took him to the local supermarket and did my best to explain to him what to buy to help make his money last longer, how to cook things properly, and most importantly, I showed him how to use the appliances in the building including the cooker and the washing machine.

One morning a few days later, he was sitting in the dining room with a plate that contained a roll and some filling or other, but he was looking very perplexed. He gave me the impression that he wanted to ask me a question but was embarrassed. I asked him if he was okay and what was wrong.

'This beefburger is hard to eat,' he stated.

I was surprised by his statement and asked him, 'What is wrong with the beefburger? Let me see it? Have you cooked it properly or is it not fully cooked?'

He just looked at me as if I was speaking double Dutch. When he opened the roll to show me the contents, I saw that he had taken the beefburger straight from the freezer, and it was still frozen and totally raw.

I explained to him once more how to use the cooker and the grill, then removed the burger from the roll and put it under the grill for him. It made me realise that in some countries people had either never used these modern appliances before or perhaps never had to prepare meals for themselves. At the very least, some had never before been introduced to the delights of ready frozen meals and convenience foods.

Those people faced multiple complex tasks, including having to learn a new language, get used to the weather conditions in the UK, fathom out the customs of this country, and of course, understand the science and technology required for their own studies. That, of course, was back in 1979. Surely things must have changed for the better now, especially in the age of fast-developing technologies and the internet, except for people living in really remote areas of the world where new technologies have maybe still not caught up.

Me relaxing in some unexpected sunshine near the Nethergate in Dundee in 1979.

Me in Dundee, Scotland, UK in the late 1970s

I finished my Master of Science degree in Chemistry from the University of Dundee in 1980. That was the same year I met my wife, and the year that I started studying for my PhD.

I was fortunate enough to undertake my PhD studies in the same department and with the same supervisor (Dr William Horspool) as when I studied for my MSc. Dr Horspool was such a nice, intelligent person, who proved to be so helpful, not just to me but to all the other students under his supervision.

Graduation day June 1980: How proud I was when I finally got my MSc degree in Chemistry from the University of Dundee, Scotland.

Unfortunately, during the first year of my PhD studies, the war between Iraq and Iran escalated immensely. When I was summoned to the Iraqi Embassy in London, I informed my girlfriend, Carol, and my supervisor that I would be back in three days' time.

However, once I presented myself to the authorities at the Iraqi Embassy, I was informed that a number of students were being recalled to their country to help fight in the war and, as I was a reserve Second Lieutenant, I was included.

There were a large number of Iraqi students waiting in the Embassy, and later that night we were escorted in a convoy to a first-class hotel in the centre of London where we were given overnight accommodation and a lovely dinner. We were virtually under house arrest in that hotel, though, and the following morning after breakfast, we were escorted to Heathrow Airport and unceremoniously put on an Iraqi Airways plane and flown back to Baghdad Airport.

From there, we were driven to a training camp and kitted up, before being sent into battle. I was on the front line for six weeks before I was told that I was being sent back to my home city for a few days' rest and recuperation, then I would be allowed to fly back to the UK to continue my studies. The few days' rest at home in Karbala was to allow time for my air ticket back to the UK to be processed.

During this spell in Iran, I was unable to contact my supervisor, and could not even contact Carol to tell her what had happened to me – or even to inform either of them where I was. I discovered later that one night when Carol had been at the cinema with a work colleague, she'd been overcome with a feeling of total dread and thought she could hear explosions and the sound of gunfire while she was meant to be watching a comedy. She felt so unwell that she had left the cinema early.

That very same night was one of the nights when we experienced a lot of casualties on the battlefield, and I witnessed a few comrades being hit by a bomb which landed directly in front of them. Luckily, I was further behind them, and came to no harm. Carol's premonition was really accurate, even though she had no idea that I was fighting in Iran at that exact moment!

A week later, I was on a flight back to the UK. I couldn't wait to get back to finish my studies and return to what now felt like a normal life for me. Five days after I returned, I received a letter from the Iraqi Government stating that, as a thank you and in lieu of payment while in the combat situation in Iran, I was to be given a small stipend to help me during the remainder of my PhD studies.

It was around this time that Carol and I had decided to get married. We went to the Registry Office and arranged a time and date for the official ceremony, and Carol also booked a hall to have the reception in.

Unfortunately, with eight weeks left to go to the ceremony, Carol was informed that the club had closed without notice and she had lost her deposit. She started looking for other venues and we settled on a small local pub that held private functions, and the manager was happy to allow us to hold the wedding reception there. The deposit was paid, menus were arranged, and the wedding cake was ordered. We were in love, and we felt that nothing would come between us and our future together. How wrong could we be!

Everything seemed to be going so well until about three weeks before the registry office ceremony was due to take place when I was recalled to the Iraqi Embassy in London. There was no way I could disobey any command to attend a meeting at the Iraqi Embassy, as that would have been seen as dissidence and someone would have been sent to pick me up from Dundee and forcibly transport me to London. When I told Carol, my supervisor, and my friends about my latest recall to the Iraqi Embassy, they all advised me not to go. But I just had to go there, or face God only knows what repercussions!

The same scenario played out, and I soon found myself back in Iraq. Within 24 hours of my arrival on Iraqi soil, I was with a platoon of soldiers deployed along the Iraq/Iran border, with orders to march forward inside

Iranian territory. I must admit that it was one of the worst periods of time that I have ever been through.

Once we managed to get just inside the Iranian border, we were positioned very close to a hurriedly constructed medical and casualty evacuation centre, and I saw hundreds of dead and dying people within a short space of time. I tried to think of the dead bodies as if they were people in a long deep sleep so that it would not affect me too much. But those poor souls who were close to death were in a totally different category. It was dreadful to see army personnel suffering so badly because of their lost limbs or the pain they were suffering from shrapnel wounds; it was horrific to hear them screaming and to watch them writhing in agony. Those images are etched on my mind for ever more.

One hot afternoon, I was doing my daily ablutions near the river where we had camped. There was a very narrow bridge nearby which was only wide enough for one vehicle at a time to cross over it. Suddenly, an ambulance from the nearby medical base came flying along the road, heading straight towards the bridge on some unknown mission of mercy. Close to the start of the bridge, without warning another car came at high speed from the other side. The ambulance driver swerved to the right, trying to avoid the smaller, faster car which by that time was more than halfway across the bridge. Unfortunately, by swerving, the ambulance took out the right side of the bridge, causing most of the structure to collapse into the river along with both the ambulance and the car. I saw the whole accident unravel in front of me in slow motion.

Several nearby soldiers jumped into the muddy river and managed to wrench open the doors of the ambulance, but they were unable to open the doors of the other vehicle. They rescued the ambulance driver who, it turned out, was not the usual ambulance driver but the unit's medical doctor. He had sustained a deep gash in his forehead.

The proper ambulance driver, who was a front seat passenger at the time of the crash, had a huge cut in his thigh, and a mixture of water and blood was pouring down his leg from the wound as he kept screaming about the pain in his leg. More soldiers ran over and jumped into the water to try to rescue the people still trapped inside the submerged car. Eventually they managed to prise open the car doors and pulled out the occupants one by one, then dragged them up to the bank of the river and started to perform mouth-to-mouth resuscitation. Unfortunately, all their efforts were in vain, and the four men were pronounced dead at the scene. The medic and the ambulance driver were fortunate to escape with their lives, but I hoped and prayed that I would never witness such a horrible scene ever again.

My comrades and I during one of our incursions over the Iranian border. Thankfully, we managed to get a short respite under this bridge during a lull in the fighting.

Our platoon spent almost two months in that hellhole just inside the Iranian border, until we finally received the orders to retreat and return to our army base. Soon after our return, we were given permission to leave Iraq and go back to our studies abroad. This, of course, meant a lot more form-filling and visa applications had to be completed again. But we were told that our return tickets would be validated, so at least that meant we would not have so much expenses to fork out this time. A few days later, with the paperwork complete, we all flew out from Baghdad International Airport (or Saddam International as it was still called then) and I was thrilled to be going back to the UK and my postgraduate studies.

The first thing I did on arrival in Dundee was to take a taxi to Carol's mum's house, as she was still living at home. She was so relieved and happy to see me alive and kicking, but then I got hell from her as she had only just received a pile of letters the evening before that I had written to her. I had asked a friend of mine to get them to her, and although he had arrived in Dundee a week earlier, he had only contacted her two days before my arrival to ask her to come and see him. As she did not know this student, she asked her sister to go with her to his student accommodation.

She had been really upset on reading the letters and finding out that I had once more been on the battlefront. And of course, she was annoyed that she had had to cancel the wedding ceremony at the registry office and the reception at the local pub. Naturally, she was furious at the amount of money that she had lost because I had been called up again.

With all that had happened, Carol was wary about trusting me and unsure whether she still wanted anything to do with me. She was convinced that I could have got word about my whereabouts back to her one way or another, and even suggested that perhaps I had a wife back home in Iraq and the story of being on the front line was just that – a story!

It took a while for Carol to believe me and settle back down into a normal routine again. She was always fearful that I would 'disappear' again, and when I asked her to book another slot at the registry office, she was very hesitant. Eventually, she agreed to give it one more try, but insisted that she would not book any venue for a wedding reception because she did not believe it would actually happen.

We did get a new slot at the Registry Office and, on 7th September, 1981, we finally became man and wife. Carol's mother and her siblings and their spouses were there to witness the ceremony, and we all then went to a posh Indian restaurant for lunch. On the following Saturday we held a reception for family and friends, but instead of hiring a hall, we had the party in Carol's sister's house.

Happily back at university, I worked really hard over the next year to make up for my lost time and to try to finish my PhD degree on schedule. I worked so hard that my supervisor, Dr Horspool, made a request to the University of Dundee Senate to exempt me from having to pay the third-year fees.

By the end of the second year, however, it was agreed that I had completed enough experiments and my results were so good that I was advised to stop doing any further research and start writing up my PhD thesis for examination by the external examiner. After I sat my PhD viva, I was informed that I had passed at the first attempt. What a fantastic result that was!

By the time I graduated with my PhD in Chemistry, I was already married and had two children. My greatest priority therefore was to get a job so that I could support my wife and family.

I am in the second row, at the right, standing behind the seated academics in this photo, which was taken in 1982 in front of the Chemistry Department, University of Dundee.

My wife and I on our wedding Day: Dundee September 1981

My PhD graduation day in June 1983. Sitting in our front garden with our daughter, Layla, and our son, Ramsay, in my arms.

Although I applied for hundreds of jobs, I was unable to get a permanent position anywhere in the UK. In the meantime, I began working voluntarily with my former supervisor as an honorary research fellow, in the hope that I would soon get a position somewhere. But after several months, I knew that I had to get a job to support my family and, above all, to have some self-respect. I did not want to have to rely on social security or any other form of hand-out from the British Government.

Another big complication which had started to rear its ugly head was that I had borrowed money from some relatives to help me pay my way initially through university, and now that my family knew I had graduated, they all wanted me to repay them every penny that I had borrowed from them.

Due to the repeated phone calls and messages from my relatives insisting that I repay my debt, and because there were no prospects of any paid job in sight, my wife and I made the momentous decision to sell up everything we had in the UK and go back to Iraq. Despite the horrible conditions the country was in, due to the continuing war between Iran and Iraq, I knew I was needed in my country and I would easily get a job.

The relative I had borrowed most from was one of my brothers-in-law, Setaar, my youngest sister's husband (God rest his soul). As well as being my brother–in-law, Setaar was also my cousin. But I owed him a debt, and he now expected me to pay that debt back immediately!

*

Towards the end of Saddam's reign of terror in Iraq (around 2002), Setaar was taken under arrest by the Iraqi intelligence officers (the Amin) and quickly removed to an undisclosed location. He was never seen alive again!

Quite some time after the liberation of Iraq by the American soldiers and their allies in 2003, many mass graves (said to be around 250 of them) were discovered at various locations inside the country. The authorities tried to identify as many of the bodies as possible, mostly from the remnants of items of clothing, jewellery, or identity documents found on or near them. At one of these mass graves, the remains of Setaar were unearthed. He had been killed by a single bullet to the back of his head, and been buried with all his clothes on, including the shoes he was wearing and whatever else he had on his body at the time of execution. His identity papers were still in the remains of his shirt pocket.

The people who excavated the sites and removed the remains announced the identities of a number of the deceased from the ID cards found on or near their bodies. My sister's oldest son travelled from his home in Babylon (also called Hilla) to the site of the mass grave, collected his father's remains and placed them in a small coffin, which he then brought back to Najaf (another holy city) so that my brother-in-law could have a proper burial.

My younger sister had always hoped and prayed that her husband would eventually return home to her and their children. The discovery of his body left her broken-hearted; she was officially a widow, left to bring up her two young daughters and three sons on her own. Her eldest son left school to work in his late father's bicycle repair shop, so that he could help his mother feed his siblings, but life has been hard for them ever since.

Chapter 6

Going Back to Iraq

We were running low on finances and I could not pay my family back the money I had borrowed from them. Their demands were escalating, but my wife had only just returned to work after being on maternity leave while I stayed home looking after the children with my mother-in-law's help. Money was tight, and there did not seem to be any way out of the situation.

Not long after Carol returned to work, there was an announcement that the factory she was working in was looking for redundancies. We thought this was a fantastic opportunity, so she applied for her redundancy and the money was used to purchase the cheapest possible tickets for us to travel to Iraq. We bought the cheapest one-way tickets for flights from Heathrow Airport to Copenhagen, then after a very short stop-over, a flight from there to Saddam International Airport in Baghdad.

Leaving Britain was not an easy decision, especially with two very young children. Our daughter, Layla, was less than two years old, and Ramsay was only six months old. We informed the local housing authority that we were going to be leaving the council house we were living in, then began sorting through all our possessions. Some were packed into large tea chests to be shipped by sea to Iraq, and the remainder were either distributed to my wife's family or uplifted by various charities.

Travelling with two young children was going to be difficult, so to make things a little bit easier, we decided to fly directly from Dundee Airport to

Heathrow, rather than take the train or a bus which would have added at least another twelve hours to our trip.

When we left Dundee, it was on a very cold morning in early November 1983. We'd deliberately chosen this time of year, because the climate in wintertime in Iraq would be closer in temperature to a fairly warm summer's day in the UK. We also felt it would be better to go at that time of year because it was not too close to Christmas, so it would not upset the children or Carol's mother and the rest of the family quite as much.

The plane we took from Dundee Airport was very small, less than a 20-seater. So, when we hit a pocket of turbulence halfway between Dundee and London, it felt as if the whole plane was shaking about like a baby's rattle in a giant's hand. Within minutes of hitting this turbulence, both children were violently sick all over their mother, who was holding onto them both at that stage.

When we finally landed in London, the first thing we had to do was take the children to the toilet to get them cleaned up and a change of clothes. And poor Carol had to change out of her soiled clothes and clean herself up as much as possible for the next stage of our journey.

*****

Carol's story:

Not for the first time, I asked myself what on earth I had done! Here we were, flying in an absolutely tiny plane, on the very first leg of what would be an epic journey. Me; someone who had never even been in a plane before in my life, never mind having visited a foreign country on holiday. But here we were – all four of us – on the first leg of a journey that I would never have dreamed off making before. I would be flying in not just one, but three aeroplanes in less than 24 hours, to Iraq – not a simple holiday destination for a week or two of sun, sea, and sand! Certainly, there would be sun, sea, and sand, but probably too much of it – and not just for a two-week visit!

How did it all start, and how did I get to be here at that minute in time? It is a long story, and it all started at the Barracuda Night Club in Dundee, where I would go almost every Friday with my sister, Kathleen. We would dance the night away then walk the long journey home, going through the city centre and up the Hilltown – a steep incline. Then, almost halfway home, we would stop off at Rough and Frasers Bakery and buy warm, fresh baked rolls that would still be lovely and soft at breakfast time a few hours later.

More often than not, I would dance most of the night with this gorgeous man with lovely curly hair and the darkest, deepest brown eyes I had ever seen. To me, he was gorgeous, and he had such a lovely smile that made his eyes crinkle at the corners. I would dance and dance with him every time he was there, but before the nightclub closed I would always make an excuse that I was popping off to the toilet, or going to check my make-up, or that I had just spotted someone I knew and was only going over to say hello. I would then go to the cloakroom and wait on my sister coming in, then we would sneak out alone.

I really liked that chap, but I was so scared of getting involved with an Arab. For all I knew, he was probably married and had a couple of kids back home. Still, week after week I would meet him there, and I would run out and away from him at the end of the night.

During this time, I often went with my mother to the Wellgate Shopping Centre, which was almost in the middle of Dundee City Centre. It was a popular place to go shopping since its opening in 1978, and there was a Tesco supermarket there where we liked to buy our groceries. Inside the centre, on the top floor, there was an iconic clock, which fascinated everyone. Every hour, one of the doors opened, animated figures moved, and a nursery rhyme chimed. Just before noon, there would always be crowds of people with children standing waiting for twelve o'clock to chime, as that was when all the doors opened one by one to reveal nursery rhyme scenes, then the doors would slowly close after all twelve doors had opened.

I often stood there watching the clock, and on a number of occasions I bumped into Abed accompanied by different children. I could not believe that he had so many children yet could still find time to go out dancing on Friday nights. What was his wife thinking? However, he soon explained to me that he was actually a single man. A lot of the other students were married and had brought their wives and children with them when they came to study in Dundee. But as he was single and did not have any children, he had plenty of time to study, so he often took his friends' children out for a couple of hours to give them time to study or just to be with their wives. Wow! If that was true, then he really was someone special, I thought to myself. However, I was still very wary of having anything to do with an Arab, as there were so many stories and anecdotes about them being cut-throats and not treating women nicely.

My dancing with him and then disappearing went on for about six months, until it was nearing Christmas. Eventually, one night after we had danced together all evening, I told him to wait for me while I got my coat. He said he would see me the following week, but I told him to stay put as he was going to be taking me home that night. I don't think he believed me, but I rushed out of the hall to get my coat and came hurrying back in just as he was about to leave with his friends. He was very surprised to see me standing in front of him with my coat over my arms, and his gorgeous smile grew even wider when I linked my arm through his and said my sister had just left so he and I were leaving together.

We took a taxi to my house where, as usual, my mother was sitting up waiting for my sister and I to come home. We sat with her and had a cup of tea, and after about thirty minutes, my mother announced that it was time for my friend to go as she was going to her bed and I had to go to mine as I was working in the morning. So I phoned a taxi for Abed to go back to his student accommodation, and we arranged to meet at the Barracuda the following Friday.

That was the start of our whirlwind romance. But because Abed was called up twice to fight in the Iraqi army, there were a few stops and starts in our relationship. Eventually, though, we were married and settled down to life as a married couple. After our daughter was born, I went back to work because my new husband was still a student, and my mother looked after her. Then when Ramsay was born, she again helped us by looking after both of the children while I went to work. My mother was really good with the children and she worried about our financial situation. Unfortunately, being a widow, she was unable to help us financially.

However, my mother put the fear of God into me when she heard that Abed had decided he had to go back to Iraq to pay off his debts. At that time, there were a lot of programmes on television about men stealing their children from their partners and taking them home to their own countries. Each time she watched one of these programmes, my mum spoke to me about her fears. So that was another reason why I decided to up sticks and go with my husband to live in Iraq – not only because I loved him to death and he was a fantastic father, but just in case he decided to try to take the children from me. The rest is history!

*****

After a few hours' wait at Heathrow Airport, it was finally time for us to go through security to the boarding gate. When I handed over my passport to the security officer, he looked up at me and asked me a very important question: 'Are you *really* sure you want to leave Britain? Because if you pass through this section, you will not be able to return to the UK unless you reapply for an entry visa to this country! I can see that you have a stamp on your passport which shows that you have 'leave to remain' in this country, but once you pass through this gate you will *not* be allowed to come back. Not unless you manage to obtain a valid visa to enter the UK again.'

At that point, I turned and looked at my wife as if I was questioning her, asking her what we should do at that critical point. But her response was simple. 'Since we now have no house, no jobs, and no furniture, and because some of our stuff is in boxes and has been shipped to Iraq already, we have to go,' she said.

I was incredibly hesitant at that point, not knowing what was best for us as a family. If we stayed in Britain, I faced the prospect of long-term unemployment and more demands for repayment from my family. Or we could travel to a country that had been at war for so many years and was governed by a dictator who had no mercy on his own relatives, his own people, or the people in neighbouring countries.

I had to make an instant decision, but we were at the point of no return. We crossed the barrier together as a family. Then we boarded the plane taking us to Copenhagen on the second leg of our journey towards a war-torn country and the unknown, but with definite employment prospects.

Having settled on board the massive plane, the stewardess brought a pack containing a colouring book, pencils, a rubber, and a small comic for our daughter, to keep her amused on the journey. We had lunch on this flight and as we were ravenous we ate everything, although I cannot recall what was served.

When we finally arrived in Copenhagen, there was barely enough time for us to catch our connection to Baghdad. However, the staff at the airport had already thought of that. As we hurried off the plane, we discovered that there was a small electric buggy waiting to ferry us from one terminal to the other for our onward connection. We were then rushed through the terminals in that smooth, nippy buggy, with me sitting at the front beside the driver, and my wife and the children in the back alongside Ramsay's carrycot.

Our third flight was on another Scandinavian Airline Airways (SAS) plane. As we waited to board, a stewardess asked Carol if she was Mrs Khalaf. When my wife nodded apprehensively, the stewardess handed her a carrier bag that contained a pack of four disposable baby nappies as well as another colouring book and coloured crayons for the children. My wife was amazed at the kindness of the stewardess and explained to me that she had happened to mention to the stewardess on the last plane that our son had a tummy upset and she just hoped that she had enough nappies to get to Baghdad.

This plane, which was travelling directly to Baghdad, had few passengers on board. It was now very late in the day, and I clearly remember that we were served some kind of meal of fish and boiled vegetables.

By the time the plane touched down at Saddam Airport, it was nearly midnight and I was not only shattered by then, but I was also absolutely terrified. I am sure Carol felt the same, but she was too tired to even speak. After finishing the necessary paperwork for the entry procedures, we proceeded to walk through the airport, but Carol said she needed the toilet, so I showed her where the ladies were.

A few minutes later, she came running out and the look of disgust on her face was almost comical. She announced that the place was absolutely stinking, that the toilet was actually a hole in the ground, and that there was no toilet roll – only a filthy plastic jug filled with water! I did not have the heart to tell her that it was like that in most of the public toilets in Iraq.

In the arrivals lounge, we were met by my oldest brother Abu Haidar, who had been waiting for us with his wife since late that evening. He quickly led us through the airport doors towards the car park. At that time he was driving a Toyota Super, which was in excellent condition and was obviously fairly new. He explained that the car had been presented to him by Saddam Hussein's government because he was now a highly esteemed colonel in the Iraqi Air Force and specialised in electrical engineering for aircrafts. To think that he had only finished his BSc degree in electrical engineering from Baghdad University just before joining the Air Force, and now he was a specialist!

As we were being driven from the airport towards Karbala, Carol commented on the horrific rotten egg smell that wafted in from the countryside we were passing through. I explained to her that the smell was sulphur and was coming from the salt marshes from either side of the motorway. These salt marshes were abundant in that region of Iraq.

We arrived at my brother's house in Karbala in the early hours of the morning, and were both shattered. Carol was clearly feeling extremely apprehensive, as everything seemed so very different from what she was used to back in Scotland.

The first thing my sister-in-law did was to prepare a pot of very strong tea. Then she cut a raw onion in half and told us we should both eat it immediately, as onions would kill any new bacteria that our bodies were not used to. We both refused to eat onion at that time of the morning, but instead opted for a cup of very strong tea before going to bed. We were then shown to our room on the second floor of the house. It was a big room, and in the centre of it there was an enormous double bed, which we would have to share with Layla while Ramsay slept in the carrycot we had brought with us from the UK.

Sleeping in a strange environment was pretty difficult even though we were both exhausted. Trying to get comfortable was pretty much impossible, because that old double bed creaked and groaned every single time we moved, and there seemed to be a couple of springs sticking up through the mattress. I decided I would have a proper look at the bed after breakfast.

In the morning, I discovered that the bed frame only had three metal legs; where the fourth leg should have been, my brother had put a piece of wood in place to support the weight of the bed. So that was why it made such a horrible noise, and it was also uncomfortable because there were a number of rusty and broken springs. To make matters worse, my sister-in-law hinted that we had been making such a noise making love all night long! Obviously, she did not realise how bad the bed was, or else she just did not care and was only trying to annoy us!

Life in Iraq became more and more challenging every day. First and foremost, there was the issue of finding a job. And secondly, because I was still technically an army reservist, there was a high possibility that I would be called up again to fight against the Iranians because the Iraq/Iran war was still ongoing. If that were to happen, I dreaded to think about what would happen to Carol and the children while I was away.

After being in Iraq for three weeks, I realised that I had to take Carol and the children to the police station to register that they were now living in the country. When we got there, we were told that we should go to the Maktab al Eqama (the Eqama) [the Foreign Residence Office, part of the Secret Service at that time] to register her as being an alien in this country.

So, the next day, we took the bus into the desert where the Eqama offices were. Eventually we were informed that Carol should have registered within seven days of arriving in the country, and because she had not done so we were fined 300 Iraqi Dinars (the equivalent of £600 at that time) with a maximum of seven days to pay the fine. We did not have that kind of money, so we asked my brother to give us a loan to pay it. Unfortunately, he said that he did not have any money so we would have to get it elsewhere.

One of my brother's neighbours was a medical doctor, and we had already made friends with him and his wife. They heard about our problem and offered us a loan, saying that we could pay him back whenever we could afford it and not to worry about it. The next day, we took the bus back to the Eqama and were eventually escorted back to the officer who had interviewed us the previous day. He took the money without issuing us with a receipt, then informed us that Carol would have to get certificates to prove that she was free of any illnesses such as TB, cholera, and HIV, and return in two weeks' time with the requisite paperwork.

My niece, Iman, worked in a clinic and also in a hospital lab, and she agreed to take the necessary blood samples and run the tests for us. Because she was my niece, she used completely new needles to draw the bloods – normally they reused needles which had been haphazardly 'sterilised'. Iman also arranged for the x-ray to be taken and said Carol would need to get at least half a dozen photos taken to be handed over for her files at the Eqama.

Having got all the test results, we subsequently returned to the Eqama, but this time I left Carol to go in by herself while I waited outside with our children in the desert sand. Like everyone in Iraq, I was scared of the bureaucracy and the officers housed in that building. It felt like hours before Carol came out and told me she had to report there every four weeks as long as she lived in Iraq.

A few weeks later, a member of the Amin came to the door and told us that Carol had to attend the Eqama a week earlier than usual. When she went there to report to the officer in charge of her case, he said he had a 'gift' for her, and returned the 300 Iraqi dinars fine! The first thing we did when we got back to my brother's house was to go to the medical doctor and repay our loan in full! That was a happy day for both of us.

At that time in Iraq, scholars who had obtained a PhD in a foreign country and subsequently returned home to work in universities were officially granted a one-off licence to import a brand-new car without having to pay any import taxes. Having received the necessary paperwork to allow me to buy a new car, I did not have the funds to actually purchase one.

Fortunately for me, Abu Haidar knew a car dealer who would be prepared to buy my import permit. I went to visit the dealer in his salesroom in Baghdad and he was more than happy to take my paperwork to Kuwait and buy a brand-new car, drive it back to Iraq, then sell it in his garage. So I left the saleroom with a sum of 8000 Iraqi dinars, which was more than enough to pay my debts to the family and still have enough left over to be self-sufficient for a month or two. Of course, I knew that the car was worth more than triple that amount, but I was so grateful because I would never have been able to afford to buy it myself and at least the money would settle all my debts.

Once the deal was sealed, I took my money in cash, put it in an ordinary carrier bag, and then took the minibus from the bus depot in Baghdad back to Karbala. That incident was a daring operation to me, because there were many police checkpoints between Baghdad and Karbala, and all cars and buses were routinely searched at these checkpoints. If at any stage the police did a very thorough search and found the money, I could have been arrested and taken to the Iraqi Intelligence Office for interrogation by the Amin, and the money would most certainly have disappeared.

As luck would have it, I got through all the checkpoints with no problems. As a precaution, though, I had left Carol and the children at my brother's house so that they would not be involved if we were stopped *en route* and anything untoward occurred.

The following day, I travelled to Babylon to visit my brother-in-law, Setaar, who had lent me a large sum of money years before when I left Iraq to study in the UK. He had phoned me repeatedly over the last year or so, especially after learning that I had graduated with my PhD. He had made it clear that he wanted the loan repaid as soon as possible, saying that he desperately needed the money as it was a loan and not a gift! If he had not been so insistent, I would definitely not have come back to Iraq with my wife and children.

Anyway, I repaid the money I borrowed from him, and gave him an additional amount of money as a 'reward' for his generosity and assistance to me in my time of need. This extra money was given to him as a bonus, especially as there is no interest given on money in banks in Muslim countries, so this money would have been the equivalent of interest to him.

In my mother's house with Carol and Layla. I had tried on my old army uniform before going to the army base the next day, and although it had been in storage for a long time, it was still a good fit. (January 1984)

Another photo of me taken early in the morning before setting off for the army base on my one year's service as a reserve officer.

Photo taken in the officers' mess after my promotion to first lieutenant in 1984.

As I had also borrowed some money from Abu Haidar when I left to study in the UK, I also repaid him his money. But instead of thanking me for repaying the loan, he actually demanded that I pay back twice the amount I had originally borrowed because it had taken me so long to repay him! As soon as he was given the lump sum, he went out and bought an absolutely enormous TV which he set up in the lounge. Obviously he had not really needed the money and could easily have allowed me to return just the original loan.

Carol was upset at this turn of events, because we were desperately in need of cash to get accommodation, and to pay for furniture and food for the four of us.

Having been enlisted back into the army for a whole year following my return to Iraq, I again had to undergo intensive training in a camp. It meant I only managed to get home on Thursday nights, and had to travel back to camp either late on Friday nights or early Saturday mornings, leaving Carol and the children with my sister-in-law.

Every week when my brother came home on a Thursday evening, he would order one of his sons to bring the scales down from the top of the wardrobe and he insisted that Carol was weighed. Every week the scales would show that she had lost some more weight, and Abu Haidar would complain to his wife that she could not have been feeding Carol properly. At that time, Iraqi men preferred their wives to be plump. Carol was actually told it was better for a woman to be 'a pillow for her husband', instead of being too thin.

So, my brother started bringing home extra high calorific food from the air base to try to fatten Carol up again! But this caused arguments between Abu Haidar and his wife, who accused him of bringing home special fattening foods like 'guemer' (full fat cream) for Carol yet he had never brought that home for her even though she had repeatedly asked him to get it for her as she was very thin and wanted to put on weight!

After a few weeks, Carol informed me that she could no longer stay with my brother and sister-in-law. She was being left to do all the washing and cleaning, and our children were continually being told off because they were exploring the house and gardens.

One day there had been a big argument because Ramsay had found a huge carton containing around 720 eggs on the floor of one of the storerooms. There was rationing in place, but because Abu Haidar was so high up in the Iraqi Air Force, he was able to procure large amounts of items that were unavailable for the ordinary citizens. Ramsay had found the carton of eggs and was picking them out of the box one at a time then throwing them on the ground. As they smashed on the floor, he was fascinated watching the white and yellow contents spread slowly over the marble floor.

Carol found him by the time he had smashed six eggs, which was only a tiny fraction of the number of eggs in the carton. However, this caused such a huge row with my sister-in-law, even though Carol washed the floor and cleaned the whole room until it was sparkling. My wife felt that the loss of a few eggs was not a big deal because there were so many eggs in the carton, and as they were perishable they were supposed to be used up before the 'Best Before' date. Also, Ramsay was only about ten months old by then, and was too young to understand what he was doing!

I was also told that Layla, at only two-and-a-half years old, had been left to fry fish in a huge frying pan set over a large gas ring in the back garden, and Carol had been shocked to come back from the toilet to see her doing this. What if the whole pan had fallen and the contents, including the hot oil, had scalded our precious daughter?

My oldest brother, Ali Ibrahim (Abu Haidar) [01-01-1940 to 08-09-2012], in his Iraqi Air Force Captain's uniform.

A later photo of Abu Haidar in his Iraqi Air Force Colonel uniform.

The following week when I came home on leave, Carol warned me not to eat the meal that was put down to me for my dinner that night. She explained that my sister-in-law had been heating and reheating the food then just adding more fresh meat and vegetables to the pot, instead of throwing the old food away and cooking the meal from scratch. I thought my wife was exaggerating so, when I was told the food was ready, I sat down with the family and began to eat, and encouraged the children to eat the food by alternately spooning some food into their mouths while eating mine.

Carol was furious with me, but I told her it was fine because the food was boiling hot, and surely she was mistaken. Nobody would be stupid enough to keep on reheating the same food like that.

Oh my gosh! How wrong could I be! Suffice to say that over the next twenty-four hours, I was stuck in the upstairs toilet with diarrhoea. That was bad enough, but both Layla and Ramsay were sitting in front of me and we were all suffering with the same malaise. Carol kept coming into the toilet and hosing the floor down because the mess was everywhere and the place smelled really badly. The toilets were Eastern-style, which meant they were only holes in the ground, so the contents went through a pipe and into a septic tank which was emptied only once or twice a year. Umm Haidar's children were also all unwell, and they took turns running in and out of the downstairs toilet.

That night, I decided that it was time for my family to move out of there and live with my mother, my widowed sister, and her daughter. I determined to speak to my family when I came home next weekend, and we would move in with them as soon as possible. I knew we would be a bit cramped, but we had to make the move and we still did not have enough money to rent a flat of our own.

*****

Carol's story:

While we were living at my brother-in-law's house, there were many things that happened that I could not speak to my husband about – partly because I felt he would not believe me, and partly because I did not want to stir up trouble as we were lucky that Abu Haidar was kind enough to let us stay there rent-free. Often, Umm Haidar would shout and spit at her older children and throw cups or plates at them if they annoyed or disobeyed her, rather than trying to speak to them nicely and explain what the problem was. I would try to placate her and tell her this was not nice and that I was worried about how this behaviour would affect my children. Would they think that this was normal?

One of the worst things was that sometimes I felt like I was Umm Haidar's slave. She was not the healthiest person, and looked as if a strong wind would blow her over. I knew the normal household chores were a bit of a struggle for her at times, so did my best to help keep the house clean and tidy.

Her oldest daughter, Iman, helped with the younger children, getting them up and dressed for school and bathing them at night. However, there were so many other chores and I hated the untidiness, but the more chores I did, the more chores seemed to be left for me. I was constantly being told that it was time I started to do the cooking, but I explained that I had never cooked for such a large family before and I did not know where to start.

This food was nothing like the food I had cooked back home in Dundee! Every meal was cooked from scratch in Iraq, and it all took so long to make. One meal alone could take one hour of preparation, then the food would be cooked for up to four hours before it was declared ready to eat. There were no pressure cookers to help save time.

There were also no vacuum cleaners to clean the floors – instead, there were maknasas (brushes made from the smaller branches of the date palm trees interwoven and tied together so they can be used for sweeping up) and the floor would be washed down so that the dust did not rise and resettle again. For this reason, there were little round holes slightly above ground level in every room in the house that the water was swept out through. Even in high summer, when it was too hot, the family would throw cold water down on the ground to help cool the room. This was done when the electricity was cut off, which was a regular occurrence.

Certainly, there was a very old washing machine, but it had so many idiosyncrasies that I could not for the life of me get it to work. Everyone else knew exactly where to hit it to get it to work properly, but first you had to plug it into a slack socket that scared the life out of me because I could see sparks coming from it!

Going to the butcher's shop was an experience in itself. There would be cows' heads, with the tongues sticking out of their mouths, hanging from the ceiling. And if you wanted to buy some meat, you did not get nice cuts the way you do in the UK. If you could buy meat at all, you had to take what you were given, and you would be sold very little amount of actual meat. It was usually a big pile of bones and another pile of fat, so that there was more fat and bone (shaham wa athum is the Arabic term) than there was meat.

Still, we were grateful for all the little mercies. And I must admit that the Arab women could make a really tasty meal out of a pot full of pulses, lashings of tomato puree, some spices, and very little else. Most meals were either full of broad beans, chickpeas, lentils, split peas, or black-eyed peas, with a small amount of beef added to the pot. If you were lucky, you might be able to buy one or two chickens or some small fish, but mostly it was pulses that families survived on.

I soon learned that you had to buy vegetables when they were plentiful in summer, and leave them to dry so that you had vegetables in winter. I used to help thread okra onto string and hang it up from the hooks in the ceiling until they dried out. Once dried, the okra was wrapped up in clean paper and then bundled up in old newspaper until they were needed in winter.

Once I visited the market with Umm Amirah and we bought two live chickens. I was given the task of carrying them onto the bus, having been told to hold them upside down with their claws interlinked in my fingers. Everything went well until this man in a pristine white suit sat next to me and the chickens flapped their wings and managed to do the toilet on the man's trouser legs! He shouted his head off at me and I was mortified.

*****

With Carol and the children settled into the front bedroom of my parents' house, I felt a little bit easier. My wife got on really well with my sister, Umm Amirah, and my sister-in-law, Umm Zoher, who lived in the extension that my father had built onto the end of our family's house. Carol was now being given more freedom, and accompanied my sister to the market and to the mosques on a daily basis, so she seemed a lot happier there and her Arabic was improving greatly.

One Thursday evening when I came home, Carol told me that she had suffered from an upset tummy for four days. My sister, Umm Amirah, took her to the GP, but as Carol did not yet have the correct documents, Umm Amirah told the GP that she was the one who had the symptoms Carol was complaining of. The GP took bloods from Umm Amirah and pronounced her healthy, but gave her a course of medication just in case.

When they got back to the house, Umm Amirah was so upset that she went straight to her bed for the rest of that day. Carol had had no idea that my sister was petrified of needles, and having blood taken had been enough to make her physically unwell!

One day while out walking into the town with my sister and the children, Carol had her first experience of being caught in the middle of a sandstorm.

She told me afterwards how difficult it had been to get their bearings and that even Umm Amirah had struggled to find the nearest mosque where they could shelter to wait out the tempest that was blowing outside.

I was informed that it was a scary but amazing experience and one that she was glad to have witnessed. But she was also glad when they managed to get shelter in the mosque when it was most needed. In the end, they had to stay in the mosque for around three hours until the wind quietened down and they were able to go about their normal business.

By the time they went back outside, Carol had been amazed to see everything covered in a thin layer of red sand. And of course, there was a lot of cleaning to do when they got home, because the miniscule grains of sand had infiltrated every nook and cranny and the red dust was everywhere. The children had to be stripped and bathed immediately, as their clothes were tinged red and covered in tiny specks of sand.

After that first experience, Carol found that she could smell a sandstorm coming before it happened, so she would shut all the windows and doors and put papers or rags into all the cracks she could cover. She was never wrong once, and my mother came to appreciate Carol's ability because she was asthmatic, and the fewer grains of sand getting into the house and covering everything meant that she was not so badly affected.

Due to the effects of the sandstorms, Carol decided that one of the broken windows would need to be replaced. She measured the window and asked her sister-in-law where she could find a glazier to replace the broken window. She was told there was a place in the souk where you could buy glass, but nobody was able to replace it. However, Carol replied that all she needed was a pane of glass and she would replace it herself.

At that time in Iraq, it was totally unheard of for a woman to be able to do a repair like that – it was a man's job, but there were no men present to carry out this task. Carol insisted on paying the glazier a visit, and the following morning they went to the shop and bought the pane of glass cut to the measurements she had provided. She also bought enough 'mahjoon' (putty) to replace the old stuff.

Within hours of arriving back at the house, the old putty and the broken glass had been removed and the new pane of glass installed. Carol admitted the putty was difficult to work with as it was so greasy, but she did her best to smooth it out and ensure there was enough to cover the small gaps around the windowpane.

My mother told her the glass would fall out in thirty minutes, but Carol told her to have faith. Everyone in the house then went out to inspect Carol's work, and all agreed it would fall out by that time the next day. Suffice to say, the pane of glass was still *in situ* many years later, although the same could not be said for the other panes of glass in that window! And certainly, my mother was glad to see that the glass was still in place months later when the next sandstorm hit the area.

After a while, Carol felt that she was familiar enough with the layout of the souks and markets in Karbala to be able to go out on her own with the children. She loved to visit the 'Alaawi' – the bazaar in the centre of the town where women would sit in the middle of the street selling their wares, including home-baked bread, cheese, fruit and vegetables from their own small farms.

Carol would often go out looking for a shop selling fresh eggs, but because of the war embargo, she would not be able to find any eggs. However, she did find someone selling the familiar small sardines that we call 'hirish', and which my mother loved.

Once, she went out to try to buy chickens, but instead brought home two baby chicks that she asked Umm Amirah to help her to rear. Unfortunately, they were too small, so they did not survive more than five days. However, Carol persisted in going out looking for provisions on a daily basis and would bring back whatever she could find on sale and be grateful for it. Whatever she managed to buy was a great boon for the rest of the family, and they looked forward to seeing what she had managed to procure that day.

On one occasion, she even managed to find a butcher selling frozen New Zealand mince in two-kilogram poly bags. When she got back to the house, they scraped off the defrosted mince and made kebabs for dinner that night. And the mince that was still frozen was put into the freezer to be used another day.

As Carol went out walking around the streets every day, she often managed to find foods that were in very short supply. She would tell me how she would argue with shopkeepers over the fact they were over-pricing the stock on offer, even going so far as to tell them that she would report them to the government officials!

*****

Carol's story:

Although I was a lot happier staying at my mother-in-law's house, it was not totally uneventful. Abed hadn't warned me that his mother had mental health problems, but I soon found this out myself.

There was a water tap in the front garden to enable them to water the plants, the pomegranate and orange trees, and the grape vines. However, Ramsay always managed to open the tap to let the water run, and he delighted in playing in the mud that resulted when he left the water running. I got fed up always stripping him off and washing his clothes so I ended up tying the tap with a length of material so that he could no longer open it.

One day, though, Granny wanted to water her plants and could not untie the material to open the tap. She became really angry and was shouting at Ramsay and chasing him around the garden, threatening to cut his ear off. I knew she had no intention of doing that, but she made such a racket that got on my nerves. Harsh words were said, and she spat at me. I grabbed my two children and took them into the house to put their jackets on to take them away from the house.

Umm Amirah realised I was really upset and didn't want me to leave the house. So, when I got Ramsay dressed and into his buggy then turned around to get Layla dressed, my sister-in-law took Ramsay out of the buggy and removed his coat. I told her I was leaving, and I was not coming back, and would she please just let me get the children out of the house. But she was so upset by then that she called on Umm Zoher to come and help her to calm me down and settle the children down.

We had a stand-off for twenty minutes, and eventually I said I was just going to take the children for a walk and would come back later once we had all cooled down. I went to the Alawi and paid a visit to Abed's friend, Salah – the English language teacher who also owned a menswear shop. I sat in his shop with the children for a few hours before going back to the house.

One day, I was cleaning our bedroom and I bent to pick up what I thought was a large piece of dirty rope. It was actually a snake and, remarkably, it did not feel slimy the way I thought it would. The snake got more of a fright than I did, and as soon as I dropped it, it slithered away under a tea chest that was sitting in a corner of the room. I had screamed with fright and Abed's nephew came running into the room to see what was wrong. After my garbled explanation, he moved the full tea chest and saw the snake. He ran out of the room and came back immediately with a thick stick and again searched for the snake. When he found it, still coiled under the tea chest, he struck it a number of times with the stick until it no longer moved. Once he ascertained it was dead, he picked it up with the stick and carried it outside the house, informing me that it was still poisonous even although it was dead!

One afternoon, Amirah came home from school and said that a few schoolchildren had disappeared from school. She informed us that one of the children had written something subversive about Saddam Hussein on the door of the toilet, and this had been reported to the authorities. I do not for one minute think it was a child who wrote that; rather an adult working in the school who wrote it, trying to copy a child's scrawl.

All the children were made to write a specific sentence, and those who wrote in a very similar script were questioned. Of those questioned, four or five of the children were removed from the class and never turned up at the school again!

This was at a time when many men disappeared from the streets of Iraq – either to serve in the army, or they were arrested, or who knows what happened to them because some were never seen again. One of the neighbours – a merchant who sold bolts of cloth – was arrested and imprisoned. We were told that he had been stockpiling both material and money in his house, and was overcharging the customers in his shop. The amin who arrested him confiscated holdalls full of money.

The man eventually returned home some eight months later, looking a much lesser person than he was when arrested. He had been beaten and tortured on a regular basis, but would not tell anyone what else had happened to him. His shop was sold and he never worked again, hardly even leaving his house.

One of the meals that Abed's family loved was called 'Pacha', which consisted of the head and the hooves of sheep. This meal was always prepared over the gas ring that they would bring out into the back garden so that the smell would not permeate the house. Umm Amirah would first burn all the hair off the sheep's lower legs, head, and ears, after which they would put it into a huge pot, adding the cleaned, chopped stomach, and everything would be boiled with onions, dried limes, turmeric, and some spices.

After boiling this concoction for a number of hours until the meat was so soft that it fell apart, they would serve it to all the family. From the minute they started to prepare the food until the minute it was cooked, the smell, to me, was disgusting. I could not stand it. When dished up, it just looked like a greasy mush to me and I would not even try a spoonful.

After the very first time they cooked that meal, I asked them to warn me in advance so that I could go out with the children and stay away for the whole day. Even though it was cooked outside, I could still smell it throughout the house!

At one stage, Abed's mother had a go at me because we only had the two children. She told me that a good wife should always be ready with a bowl of hot water when her husband came home from work. The minute he entered the house, she should get down on her hands and knees and wash his feet, then give him a really good meal. Following this meal, she should jump into bed with him and make more children.

To her, I was not a good wife because I did not run to fill a bowl with water; I did not cook really good food for him (his sister, Umm Amirah did the cooking although she was teaching me how to cook good Arab food); and we only had two children! She said there was a really lovely girl living with her family at the bottom of the street, and she would give a good man like Abed many, many children! I told her I was not a baby factory and had no intention of making more children just to please her!

Abed heard this argument, but instead of standing up for me, he sided with his mother and agreed with everything she said. I was so upset at this that I walked out of the house and got on a bus to the town. I knew that there was a relative, Haji Ruthah, who stayed beside the mosque in the centre of the town, so I made my way there and sat with him and his wife for a good few hours.

Very late that night, the door went and I heard Abed's voice asking Haji Ruthah if his wife was there. Although I had asked them not to let him know that I was there, they eventually let him in and explained that I had been very upset when I arrived, and they understood that there had been a big argument. They suggested I stayed where I was that night, but Abed insisted on speaking to me. He said that Ramsay would not eat or sleep and was crying for me.

I refused to go back to that house until both he and his mother apologised to me, because I was not a 'bint al-sharie' (a street girl) a term his mother had called me! As I missed my children, I reluctantly agreed to go back with him, but warned that I would not tolerate his mother speaking to me like that. I made it clear that he had to stick up for me or I would return to the UK, taking our children with me. I was still furious that he was acting like a wimp.

*****

Carol travelled back to Dundee on several occasions, especially when her mother was hospitalised. However, whenever we were together, we often travelled to the nearby cities so that we could explore different towns and villages in the regions of Iraq that were still safe to visit. There were many areas that were out of bounds due to pockets of resistance against the Iraqi government.

We often went to visit the ruins of the ancient city of Babylon in Hilla. My wife loved visiting that area, especially the Ishtar Gate and being able to walk along the remains of the Processional Way. She was gobsmacked at how thick the walls were and the amount of work it must have taken to build them, and stood in awe at the Bas-Relief carvings of the bulls that lined the walls. The children also seemed to enjoy going there, and loved to play around the statue of the Lion of Babylon.

Of course, no trip to Hilla was complete unless we visited the remains of the Hanging Gardens of Babylon. In spite of its well-known name around the globe, and having once been regarded as one of the seven wonders of the world, it had been very badly neglected over the years and was now no more than a small hill covered with grass, with a few trees scattered around it. Obviously, the resources of the country were being directed towards the war machines and away from the heritage and history of Iraq.

Layla and Ramsay sitting on a small wall near the hanging garden of Babylon.

On one trip, we all went to visit El Hurr – a village where one of the holy men was buried. We were accompanied by my sister, Umm Amirah, who bought a necklace made of dried wild seeds and some seeds of a plant we call 'Harmal', which was used as a type of incense. When we returned home, Umm Amirah lit a small fire in the garden and added some of the Harmal seeds to the fire, then told Carol to walk over the now fragrant smelling smoke. Iraqis believed that walking over the fire would ward off any evil. My sister then gently swung both Layla and Ramsay through the smoke of the fire, so that they too would be protected!

On one of our visits to the Imam Abbas mosque, it was very busy with many people at prayer. There had been an escalation in the fighting in the Iraq/ Iran war, and subsequently there had been many deaths on the battlefields in the previous few days. One of the religious customs was for people to bring their newly dead relatives to the mosque, then carry the coffin anti-clockwise seven times around the tomb of the Imam buried there.

We had entered the mosque immediately behind a crowd of mourners carrying the coffins of the Shaheed (martyrs), who had very recently died on the battlefield. As one of the coffins was being carried up the step to go into the mosque, Carol shuddered as blood started to flow out of the coffin and onto the back of one of the pallbearers.

Less than an hour later, Carol asked me what was going on as there was another sight she had never seen before. A coffin had just been brought in, and directly behind the coffin there was a young lady wearing a beautiful white wedding dress and carrying a very tall candle. The people behind her in the procession were also carrying candles. I explained that this meant the deceased had been betrothed to be married in the next few weeks, and the lady behind the coffin was the wife-to-be. She was wearing her wedding dress and carrying her wedding candle as a mark of respect for her fiancé.

Not long after this, we went on a trip to Baghdad and visited the Telephone Exchange building as Carol wanted to phone home to speak to her mother. We had been in Baghdad less than an hour, and were walking towards the building when there was the sound of a most enormous explosion, followed seconds later by another explosion. We immediately began to run in the direction of the noise to see if there was anything we could do to help, but within minutes the surrounding roads were blocked by trucks full of soldiers who jumped down straight away and refused to allow anyone to get closer.

We were later to discover that an Iranian Earth to Earth missile had made a direct hit on civilian houses, and many people had been killed. We turned back the way we had come and continued to the Telephone Exchange and Carol phoned her mother, who told her that she was worried sick because she had heard on the news about what was happening in Iraq. As everyone knew that all the phone lines were bugged, Carol told her mother that what she had heard was all lies and propaganda and that she wished her mother could come and visit to see what a beautiful country Iraq was and how peaceful it was.

All the time Carol was carrying out this conversation, she was shaking like a leaf because we could still hear more explosions going off in the streets behind us. We were so glad to get back to the safety of Karbala that afternoon, because it was a holy city which was also important to the Iranians, and they would never bomb such a holy place! Throughout the Iraq-Iran war, Karbala was not hit once by the Iranians; however, it was eventually hit by Saddam's forces when there was a Shi'a rebellion against the Iraqi regime!

Layla (on the left) and Ramsay at the ruins of Babylon 1985, with the statue of the lion of Babylon behind us.

Carol (wearing her abaya) with Layla (on the left) and Ramsay (on the right), sitting at the top of the hanging gardens of Babylon in 1984.

The four of us on a day out at the Madinat Al Abb (city of toys). Behind us is the River Tigris.

Me at the top of the remains of the hanging gardens of Babylon in 1984

At my parents' house in Karbala, Iraq 1984.

A photo of Layla and me in the city centre of Karbala, Iraq, 1984: In the background is the golden dome and minaret of the Imam Husayn shrine.

Ramsay outside my parents' house in 1984. As there was nothing interesting to play with, he decided to bite the hosepipe!

Ramsay and Layla in the street outside my parents' house (the street was neglected just like everything else during the eight years' war with Iran). Karbala, Iraq, 1984.

This photograph was taken in the city centre of Karbala, Iraq, in 1984 (Ramsay is in the buggy and Layla is standing). The golden dome of the Imam Hussain mosque can be seen in the background, but the children were only interested in their lollipops.

A photo of the whole family, taken in a photography studio in Karbala in 1984.

Chapter 7

Life in Erbil...

During my time as an army reservist, I had been in constant contact with my best friend, Jaafar, who was a lecturer at the Chemistry Department of the College of Education at the University of Salahaddin. As the last six weeks of my army service was fast approaching, Dr Jaafar informed me that there was a vacancy for a lectureship in his department. He said the post would suit an organic chemist, so I applied for it and had an interview with the Dean of the Faculty and the Head of the Department. I was offered the post, to start immediately after I had finished my term in the army reserves.

Six weeks later, I started my first day as a lecturer and shared an office with an old friend from the past, Dr Ahmed A. H. Al-Kadhimi. He had graduated from the College of Science, University of Baghdad, at the same time as me.

From the very first day in post I started looking for accommodation for my family, because Erbil was practically at the opposite end of Iraq from Karbala. Within a month, I had managed to find a newly-built flat above a shop in Erbil. The flat was directly opposite a bakery, a small shop selling meat (when meat was available), a shop selling kitchen appliances, and less than 100 metres from the main bus garage.

There was only one bedroom, but there was a fairly big hall and a large sitting room. There was running water, but the water pressure was low so it did not always reach the flat. There was a small toilet and a wet room, but no bath. There was a double bed, but no other furniture whatsoever. However, as it meant we could be together as a family, we were not at first worried by the fact that there was only one bedroom or the other little idiosyncrasies. We knew we would look for more suitable accommodation in due course.

We quickly got into a routine of sorts. I taught general chemistry to first year students and organic chemistry to second- and fourth-year students, as well as teaching specific courses to postgraduate students. I brought a sopa (a heater run on gas canisters) from my mother's house in Karbala, and we used that for cooking on for the first few weeks, until I appropriated a spare gas ring from the department which we could use until we managed to buy a proper cooker.

As I was working in the university and my degree was from a foreign country, I was given a document which allowed me to buy a fridge and a cooker if any were to become available on the market. We lived across the road from a shop selling kitchen appliances, and when the owner found out I was teaching his sons, he promised me he would reserve both a fridge and a cooker for us as soon as they became available. Iraq was still suffering from the war embargo at that time, so all kinds of goods were either rationed or very hard to come by.

We had not registered for ration books because Carol was a 'foreigner', so we found it difficult to buy ordinary provisions. However, we found a very religious old shopkeeper who agreed to sell us a small amount of goods, such as lentils, rice, washing powder, and soap. As he was so religious, he told us he could not let us starve, but he could only sell us enough to survive and only what was surplus to his regular customers' needs.

When Carol paid him for the goods he would not let her touch his hands; instead, she had to drop the money from a height into his cloth-covered hand. He would then return the change by dropping it into her upturned hand. Every time he served her, he would say that Iraq was hot and sometimes unbearably so, and if he was not a good religious man he might go to Hell and he could not imagine how he could cope with the heat there! Carol just thought that he was a sweet little man.

For the rest of our provisions, we would make a monthly trip to Karbala and bring back the few provisions my family had put aside for us. Carol would also go out searching the shops in the streets of Erbil, to see if there were any things for sale that would help supplement the food we had. She would regularly buy home-grown items from the fruit market, and carry home huge melons or watermelons or whatever fruit and vegetables were available and in season.

*****

Carol's story:

As soon as I moved up to Erbil with my husband, I did my best to settle into normal family life for the sake of our two children. As a family we explored the town and found out where we could buy the foods that had become part of our staple diet.

Abed started work at seven-thirty in the morning and didn't come home until four or five in the afternoon, so that meant I was on my own with the children for long hours, which was difficult because we were now living in Kurdistan and very few of the people spoke either English or Arabic. The government had tried to force everyone to speak Arabic, of course, and the lessons in schools and universities were in Arabic, but the Kurdish people rebelled against that and would only speak their own dialect as much as possible.

Also, because we did not have a ration book, there were lots of foods we could not buy. There was one sweet old shopkeeper who would sell me a small amount of some of the staples, but that was never enough to feed all of us for a few days, never mind a week. We did get provisions from Abed's family, but I always felt guilty in case we were depriving them! Admittedly, there were items we were able to buy in Erbil that the family could not buy in Karbala, so taking these things, such as razor blades, toiletries, etc, to them, did help make things a bit more even.

We lived in a flat above a shop, and although it was fairly big and quiet, the one big problem was that we could not get enough water to the flat because the water pressure was not strong enough. So we only got a trickle of water. Due to this, I would have to carry a huge container of water up to the flat every morning from the standpipe in the street. Although I am calling it a huge container, to help you visualise it I would say that it was actually big enough to sit a child in it to wash them, and I would also stand in it to give myself a rudimentary shower every day. I have never seen a container in the UK that was even similar in size as that one, as it came up to my waist, but it was a very common container in Iraq and I was informed that it was called a 'tushet.'

I soon discovered that there were a lot of problems in the north of Iraq because the people had long demanded, and been promised, that they were to be given autonomy. But unfortunately, they never received their independence, so there was a band of freedom fighters attacking the Iraqi soldiers or other Iraqi officials on a regular basis. It was not unusual to hear a gun shot and see a dead soldier lying in the streets.

The first time I heard gunshot it did sound really loud, but what surprised me more was the strong smell of the gunpowder which seemed to linger in the air for a long time after the gunman had left the area. Sometimes people would carry the body away, and occasionally the body would be taken away in a car or taxi. I never saw an ambulance in Erbil.

*****

A few weeks after moving into our new accommodation, we heard new neighbours moving into the adjoining flat and I was surprised that it was my old friend Dr Ahmad from work. Like our flat, there was only one bed and no other furnishings, so his wife and daughter did not move in with him immediately.

The following evening, we invited Dr Ahmad through to share a big pot of pasta with the four of us. Ramsay was so excited to have a visitor and, unfortunately, Dr Ahmad picked up the pot of pasta to help himself just as Ramsay rushed forward to greet him. The pot of pasta went up in the air and landed all over the wall and floor as well as all over Dr Ahmad himself. We had to make another pot of pasta while Carol cleaned up the mess and Dr Ahmad went home to change.

Some days later, I was surprised to see the shopkeeper across the road beckon me over to his shop when I arrived home from work. He had exciting news for me as he had received a consignment of cookers and fridge-freezers from the government warehouse that day. The goods were purportedly for the families of shaheeds (martyrs from the war effort) but he wanted to offer us the first chance to buy the appliances, saying that all these families had stayed in the area for years and none were in need of the new appliances. By the end of that week, I had bought both items and the shopkeeper helped me carry them up the stairs to the flat. He also sold us a canister of gas so that we could use the cooker almost immediately.

By the end of that week, Dr Ahmad's wife and daughter had arrived from their home town of Kirkuk and were busy moving into the flat next door. Carol immediately invited them to use half the space in the fridge freezer and the full use of the cooker whenever they wanted it. Dr Ahmad's wife had brought cooked food from her parents' house, so she was very happy with this arrangement.

A few weeks later, it was the start of Ramadan – the time when Muslims fast between sunrise and sunset. Early every morning, drummers would walk through the streets of the town, banging hard on the drums to alert everyone that it would soon be sunrise. On hearing the drummer, the people would get up immediately to have a quick shower and an even quicker breakfast, before performing their morning prayers. They were not allowed to eat or even drink a sip of water from then until sunset. When the sun set, the families would visit each other and take freshly prepared food to each other's houses.

Dr Ahmad's wife was amazed when we visited them to end the fast in the late evenings, taking with us a variety of foods that Carol had cooked. In fact, she was so surprised that she said she felt ashamed that she could not cook and always brought home food from her mother's house, especially when she realised that Carol had cooked everything herself.

The two young boys who worked in the shop below the flat had taken Carol to the town to show her where the best spice shop in the market was. I must admit the spices Carol brought back with her were even better than the spices we brought from Karbala. I remember that on one visit back to the UK, Carol took some of the spices with her and asked a restaurateur friend of her sister if his chef could try to recreate the same spices, because we missed the ones from Erbil. Unfortunately, the spices he gave her in return were not a patch on the ones she had brought with her, and we have never found any as tasty since then.

*****

Carol's story:

We had been living in the flat for around eight months when Abed came home and told me that a big meeting had been called in the University because the Iraqi Government had decreed that the war situation with Iran was not improving and could well escalate. Therefore, all the university students and teachers were to be sent for military training during the summer break. He was worried about how we would cope, as the rumours were that they would be sent to a training camp for the whole ten weeks of the summer holidays. I told him that we would cope, just like all the rest of the families in Kurdistan would have to cope. Soon enough, the day dawned when all the students and their teachers were rounded up and bussed out to Dibis for their military training. Unfortunately, in the two weeks just before the round-up, our children both came down with chickenpox. Layla had it first, and in less than a week Ramsay succumbed to it, too. Although Layla wasn't too bad, the illness really affected Ramsay and we had to take him to the hospital because he was suffering from febrile convulsions. The poor wee soul had to get daily injections in hospital for a whole week, and after the third day he would scream like mad when we drove him along the road leading to the hospital. The only way we could placate him was by promising to buy him a toy as soon as we got to the shops after his hospital visit, and then buy him a kebab for dinner.

Ramsay was still suffering when Abed left Erbil with the rest of the university staff and students, but thankfully he was able to come home for the weekend a couple of times during this period. We were so thankful when the ten weeks of training was over and life got back to normal again. When I recounted all the things that had happened during the ten weeks, Abed was amazed that I had coped so well.

The first difference was that, because Dr Ahmad was also training at Dibis, his wife decided to go back to stay with her parents, and she then decided not to return to the flat.

A few days after Dr Ahmad's family left the flat, there was a lot of noise and it was obvious that a new family were moving in next door. The couple that moved in were Kurdish, but luckily, they both spoke some Arabic and had a spattering of English. They had a very young baby and we all seemed to get on very well.

When I explained to them that my husband was a lecturer in the Chemistry Department and was currently away at a training camp, the young man (I do not remember his name as it was so long ago) said that he would protect us as if we were his own family. He offered to give me a gun and show me how to use it, but I declined as I was worried in case either of the children got hold of it and tried to use it.

They only stayed in the flat for a few weeks before they moved out without telling me they were leaving. They actually left a few days after two trucks full of Iraqi soldiers used the area outside the shop to park under the overhang under our flat to keep out of the direct sun. The soldiers were on guard every day, and had their guns trained on the streets at all times. I did wonder if there was any connection between them arriving outside the flats and the new neighbours suddenly leaving without a word to me!

*****

A few months after the training ended and we were getting back to our normal routine, Carol told me one night that she felt she was stagnating and needed a new challenge. She had previously been asked to type up a lab book for one of the technicians, and had been given special dispensation to use the typewriter. It was forbidden by the Iraqi Government for any foreigners to be given access to typewriters, in case they typed anti-government propaganda notes for distribution to the people.

The Head of the Department had heard that Carol was looking for some kind of work, and suggested that I spoke to the Manager of the Dar Al-Kuttub (the university bookstore).

I arranged for Carol to have an interview with Dr Farhad, the Manager of the Dar Al-Kuttub, and he immediately agreed to give Carol a short trial to see how she coped. He gave her the post of Manager of the Foreign Books Department, which entailed ordering journals and specialised books from various foreign countries, excluding Russia, Poland or the Ukraine, for the university academics. However, the situation was dire because the Iraqi Government had decreed that money could not be sent abroad for any reason whatsoever, without their approval. As this could take months to sort out, it meant that new orders for books or journals could not be paid for, and companies were unwilling to send anything without payment upfront.

However, within weeks, Carol had undertaken an audit of all the outstanding orders that should have been processed, and she discovered that there were already thousands of pounds sitting with various UK publishers and distributors. Apparently, a number of orders had been made for books and journals which were long out of print, but the clerical staff in the department had not understood the letters that had arrived from those companies, as they were all in English. She therefore got permission from the head of the bookstore to send telexes to a few UK companies explaining the fiscal situation and arranging for them to redistribute some of the cash they already held on account to their sister companies. This allowed these companies to release some of the unsent orders. Dr Farhad was overjoyed a few weeks later when parcels of books and journals from the UK started to arrive.

One morning, we were driving to work when there was an air raid. We quickly jumped out of the car and ran over to a big wall and flattened ourselves against it until the Iranian jets passed overhead. They were heading towards the army base, and within minutes we could hear the sounds of explosions as the bombs were dropped.

The following morning, we woke up after sleeping upstairs on the roof, and had just descended into the kitchen when the fighter jets flew overhead again. The air raid siren did not go off until the jets were above our flat, so we stayed away from the windows until the jets passed. When Carol returned after buying fresh samoon from the bakery, she informed me there was a lot of blood in the street outside. The airmen in the planes had strafed the queue of people waiting for fresh bread with the anti-aircraft guns on board.

We also heard that a busload of students had been killed on the way to the university in Erbil from one of the outlying towns. The bus had taken a direct hit and there was a huge fire with no survivors. Those students were all in their late teens.

On another occasion there had been huge explosions coming from a nearby district to the north east of our house, in an area where Carol's friend and work colleague, Nejua, lived with her husband. This couple were originally from the Sudan, and Nejua's husband was a medical doctor who was doing specialised studies at the nearby hospital. Carol insisted that we go there immediately as Nejua was seven months pregnant.

When we were finally allowed to enter the district by the security forces, the streets outside their flat were full of debris from cars that had been hit by the explosions. We rushed up the stairs to find a scene of devastation. There was glass everywhere as the windows had been blown in and the glass table and the television had shattered into small pieces. The fridge door had been blown off its hinges, and Carol felt faint when she saw all the red blood across the kitchen walls.

Nejua came rushing into the kitchen to welcome us and apologise for the mess. She had been praying when the bombs struck, and she did not have a single scratch on her; her husband was also okay. When Carol pointed to the blood on the walls, she was told that what we could see was the result of bottles of raspberry juice that had burst into pieces with the force of the blasts! We were so happy to see that they were both okay and, having helped them clean up a bit, we left to go to our work.

Nejua subsequently returned home to the Sudan and gave birth to a little boy. Carol confided in me that, because Nejua was from a very old-fashioned family, she had been the victim of female genital mutilation. This meant that when she went into labour, she would require an operation on her genitals to open her enough for the baby to be born, and after having the baby she would need to be sewn back up again!

Nejua's husband had pleaded with his wife – and also begged Carol to speak to her – not to have everything sewn up again after having the baby. As a medical doctor, he knew how dangerous this was for his wife. Unfortunately, Nejua told Carol that her family, and her tribe, would disown her because she would be 'unclean' without this procedure. No matter how much both Carol and Nejua's husband pleaded, she said she would have to comply because she needed her family, her tribe, and all their traditions!

Due to the increase in air strikes by the Iranian fighter bombers, we were informed that the starting time at the university had been moved back from 7am to 8am, as the all-clear had normally sounded by then.

One morning a few days later, I arrived in my office to find my secretary was already there and had made a big pot of tea for us. I was very surprised to see her in so early, as she was usually late to work and always made excuses. I asked if everything was okay and she said she could not sleep so had decided to come into work to make an early start.

The following morning when she got into work at her usual late time, she told me about her lucky escape the day before when she had come in early. When she arrived back at her house in the afternoon, she discovered that an unexploded bomb had fallen through the roof of her house and landed smack bang in the middle of her bed! She realised how lucky she had been that she could not sleep the previous morning!

As we had moved to Erbil, Carol now only had to go back down to Karbala every three months to sign in with the Intelligence Officers in the Eqama. She still hated having to go there, because she felt worried and unsafe at every visit. As she had been attending there for so long, she had got to know the staff members there, and as a result she was aware of them following us when we walked through the streets of Karbala when we stayed with my family.

On one occasion, she told Dr Farhad that she had to go to Karbala to sign at the Eqama and used the expression 'Lazim a'roha' (I must go there!), only to be told that there was no such thing as 'Lazim' (must) and that they could not force her to go. Obviously, he did not want her to take time off to go there, but she insisted. She explained to him about being fined 300 Iraqi dinars on her arrival in Karbala, because she had not registered in time with them. She also explained to him that, because of various events that had occurred or things that she had witnessed while at the Eqama, she was petrified to do anything which might cause complications not only for her but also for me and the rest of my family. She was then allowed to take the time off to go back to Karbala for a few days.

One Friday morning, Carol telephoned the family in Dundee and was informed that her mother was seriously ill in hospital. The following day, we travelled down to Karbala and she went to the Eqama to see her case officer. Carol explained that her mother was at death's door and insisted on getting an exit visa for herself and the children before it was too late. She wanted to spend some time with her mother prior to her passing away.

At first, she was refused an exit visa until she explained nicely that even in Iraq all the families sat at their relatives' death beds and stayed with them until they passed away, due to their religious beliefs. And to not do so was haram (against God)! Eventually they informed her that the only way she could leave Iraq with the children was if we got divorced and if I agreed that the children could go to the UK with her.

When I heard this later, I assured Carol that it would be okay and we would get things sorted out. We went straight to the Mullah (the holy man) who had an office in Karbala. He listened to us intently but refused to grant us a divorce because he had seen us walking in the streets of Karbala many times and we had always seemed happy. So, he said he could not agree to this sacrilege. If we really wanted a divorce, we would have to go to Baghdad to the High Court and petition for a divorce there.

The following day, we went to the High Court in Baghdad and met with the Judge. We were informed we had to return a week later if we still wanted a divorce, and then we would be granted one. The following week we went back to the High Court and stood in front of the Judge. In his presence, I told Carol, 'I divorce you! I divorce you! I divorce you.' Then I agreed that she could take control of our two children and everything else that she owned. After that, I had to get a clerk to type up the divorce papers for me. This document cost me a mere thirty Iraqi Dinars (approximately £60); a trifling amount of money.

Carol then had to return to the Eqama with the divorce declaration, and once that was photocopied and documented, she was granted an exit visa. Two weeks later, she took the children and headed back to Dundee to see her mother, who was still in hospital. Thankfully, she was able to spend some time at her mother's bedside before she passed away in the early hours of the following morning. I felt awful at not being able to be there to support my wife and her family, especially when I heard that Carol had collapsed at her mother's funeral because she was so overcome with grief, and her cousin had to support her at the graveside.

One month after her mother's funeral, Carol arrived back in Iraq with our two children. She took a taxi from the airport in Baghdad straight to my mother's house in Karbala, because there had been a mix-up with the dates the neighbour gave my family for her return to Iraq and I was not at the airport to meet them, believing that she would not arrive back until the following week.

As the family would not open the door so late at night in case it was the Amin trying to arrest the men of the house, Carol had to go across to our neighbour, Abu Ziad. He opened the door to let Carol and the children stay there overnight. It just so happened that he was the neighbour whose son had taken Carol's phone call in the first place!

Within two days of arriving back in Karbala, Carol travelled once more to the Eqama to register as an alien again. She was informed that she was in the country illegally because she was no longer married to an Iraqi citizen, and we would have to remarry within seven days or she would be deported back to the UK. Of course, although we were officially divorced in the eyes of the Iraqi Government, to both Carol and I we had never really been divorced. It had simply been forced on us to allow her to get an exit visa.

As soon as Carol met me outside the building, she explained everything that had been said in the office. I still would not go inside the Eqama, as no Iraqi ever trusted what went on in that building. We went straight to the Mullah's office in Karbala and asked him if he would remarry us. When we explained everything to him, he regrettably said he could not marry us as we had been divorced by a Judge at the High Court. To officially get married again, we would have to go to the High Court in Karbala and ask the Presiding Judge there to marry us.

Undaunted, we made an appointment with the Judge, and the first question we were asked was if we were in love and if we really wanted to get married. We explained why we had had to 'divorce', and explained that in our eyes we were never divorced because we did not want one. He then asked how much of a dowry I was going to pay for my wife. I told him I had no intention of paying a dowry and that Carol did not want one – I was not buying her.

However, the Judge and some other people in the room began to shout at me when they heard this. They all insisted that I pay a dowry to marry such a beautiful woman, even though we explained we were already married and had two children. In the end, the Judge insisted that I pay Carol 3000 Iraqi Dinars, so I signed an official document agreeing that I would pay her this amount of money. Ten minutes later, we were legally married again! This 'dowry' ended up becoming a big joke between us.

However, my mother was not happy when we returned to her house that evening and told her that we had got married that day. We had slept together in the same bed in her house the night before, even though we knew we were not married in the eyes of the law when we did so!

We returned to Erbil and tried to carry on as normal a life as possible in the circumstances. We were very happy together, but the situation in Kurdistan was becoming more precarious day by day. We were also finding it more difficult to procure food, and it got to the stage where, if we managed to buy any kind of meat at all, Carol would carefully prepare it and cook meals with just enough meat in it to feed the children while we ate the rest of the meal without any meat. That way, we made sure that Layla and Ramsay got enough protein and vitamins. Carol and I often just had bread with tomatoes and fried onions, but as long as the children were healthy, we were happy. That was all that really mattered to us.

Things continued to get worse, and there were dead bodies lying in the street near our house on a regular basis. As well as the Iranian jets bombing the streets of Erbil, in the evening we had the Peshmerga freedom fighters fighting in the streets using Kalashnikovs. The government decreed a curfew, so everyone had to be home by 8pm every evening. We would sit at night listening to the fighting in the streets, and in the morning we would see all the blood and occasionally dead bodies littering the streets.

One day, Carol visited her friend who lived in a house in Zanko, a university housing compound. Carol asked her friend what on earth the noise was, and what these round black balls she could see flying over from the nearby mountain were. She was horrified to be told that they were cannonballs fired by the Peshmerga freedom fighters! She was then taken upstairs to the loft of the house and shown the bullets lying on the floor, having penetrated the thin walls of the building.

That evening, there was a banging at our front gate just before the curfew. One of my friends, a Yazidi, had suffered a heart attack and his wife pleaded with me to take him to the hospital. That drive to the hospital was horrific, as I was petrified that we would be either stopped or shot at because we were not obeying the curfew. Suffice to say, we got him to the hospital where he was successfully treated and recovered enough to return home to his wife and family two weeks later.

Carol decided it was becoming too dangerous to stay in Iraq. As the children were starting to get bigger, she felt that she could no longer wash them both from the standpipes in the street (she'd had to do this on many occasions because there was no water in the flat). Layla was reaching the age where she should be registered in school, and we knew how the children were treated at schools in Iraq. Before they were allowed to go into their classes each day, they had to sing a song extolling the praises of Saddam Hussein, then they had to parade up and down the school playground singing the Iraqi national anthem.

The last straw for Carol was when one of the neighbours pulled Ramsay inside the air raid shelter as bombs rained down outside our house. We had no idea that he had managed to get out of the house, and were told later that he had been standing looking up at the sky as the bombs were falling. We were so lucky that no harm had befallen him.

When Carol went onto the flat roof to pull the washing in later that morning, she found a piece of shrapnel that had landed in the middle of the roof. She decided there and then that enough was enough, and told me in no uncertain terms: 'If I am going to die, I would rather die in my own country than in this God-forsaken hole!'

The next day, we went back to the Eqama and Carol was given her exit visa. Less than two weeks later, we were at the airport in Baghdad saying our fond farewells.

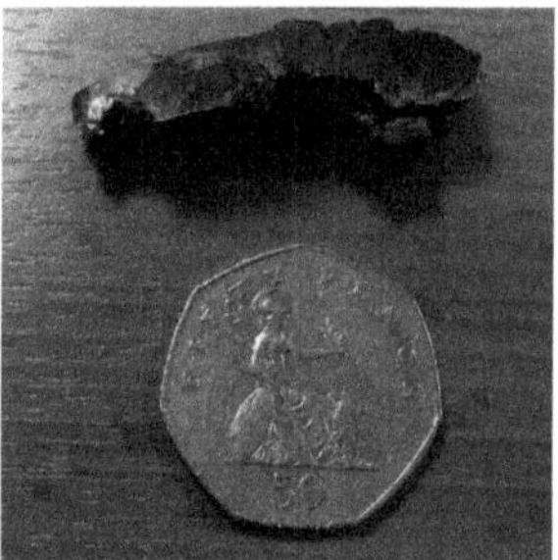

The piece of shrapnel that landed on the flat roof of the house.

We were both heartbroken, but Carol felt that there was no other solution. She was at the end of her tether, and definitely did not want the children to be brainwashed at any of the schools in Iraq. She felt it was far better for them to have a proper education in a British school, and I really had to agree with her on this matter. I promised her that somehow I would find a way to leave Iraq and return to the UK to be with her and our children.

Chapter 8

Preparations for My Perilous Journey

The earth's spinning slowed down dramatically. Objects of all sorts, shapes, and sizes were flying toward the sky – animals, debris, human beings, there were no exceptions. I found myself flying aimlessly with nothing to hold onto, nothing to grab, and nothing to help stabilize myself with. I was screaming, and my limbs were flailing everywhere just like a drowning animal. It was a totally hopeless situation as no sound was coming from my throat so nobody could help me, and it felt as though we were all in the same predicament – being sucked up by this gigantic tornado. I screamed again and again, but still no sound came from my parched throat. Death could not come fast enough to end this horrible catastrophe for me. I kicked with my legs and thrashed my arms in the hope of grabbing hold of something to slow me down or, better still, to bring me back to earth, but to no avail.

I opened my eyes and realised that I had had a horrific nightmare and I was still in my bed and I was shaking like a leaf. I had dug my fingers so deep into the palms of my hands that I had created grooves in the skin, and I was perspiring so heavily that moisture was running down my body. My legs were in spasms and felt very heavy and tired from all that kicking, my mouth was parched from all the shouting and screaming, and my heart was beating at an incredible speed.

Calm down. Calm down and take a deep breath, I said to myself. *Just thank Allah that it was only a dream and you are still alive.* But it seemed to take ages for my body to go back to normal and for the spasms in my legs to ease. Today of all days, I really needed to feel okay and for my legs to be strong enough to help me to carry out all the tasks that I had planned for the momentous day to come.

Now that I had woken up, albeit very early in the morning after such a restless night and the horrific nightmare, I jumped out of bed and crossed the room to draw the curtains back a little and survey the panorama in front of the house. Looking at my watch, I realised it was only 5.30am, but already the sun was streaming in through the partly-opened curtains, assuring me that another day had dawned and I was still alive to tell the tale. Everything was so peaceful and quiet, and the only sounds to be heard were the muted squawks and chirrups of sparrows in the front garden.

It was still a bit too early for most of the neighbours to be outdoors. Those who were already awake would be up carrying out their ablutions and readying themselves for morning prayers. Pretty soon the streets surrounding the house would be transformed into another world, the tranquil silence shattered by the cacophony of sounds that herald the normal morning hustle and bustle. Soon workers would be slamming their car doors shut, or clomping their way along the narrow streets and alleyways toward the bus depots, ready to jump onto the buses before they got too crowded. Those who didn't work would be getting ready to go to the market to buy their daily rations for the family and to look for goods to either barter or bargain for, to make their mundane lives a little more exciting. It was always better to go shopping as early in the morning as possible, before it got too hot, as the food would quickly perish and would soon be covered in flies.

I shouted to my friend, Mudhaffar, to hurry up and get out of his bed. The previous night, I had stayed at his house to allow us to make an early start at first light. He did not immediately rouse from his slumber, so I went into his room and gently pleaded with him to get up. I reminded him that we had a very long and stressful day ahead of us.

After putting the kettle on to boil, we both had a quick wash before sitting down at the table for our final breakfast here in the town of Erbil, which is also known as Howlair, as it is the capital city of the Kurdistan region of Iraq. Erbil is approximately 350 kilometres north of Baghdad. The University there meant a lot to me and I had many friends living at Zanko Campus, but I was so glad that, with a lot of luck and prayers, I would soon be leaving for good. We ate our breakfast of feta cheese, honey, and samoon bread, and a pot of very strong, sweet, black tea. As we ate, we again went over the numerous arrangements that had been made, and completed a checklist of things that we still had to do to ensure not only our own safety but also that of our friends and accomplices.

Mudhaffar told me he still had some photos that he had to burn to ensure they didn't fall into the wrong hands. We knew we had plenty of enemies, even amongst those whom we thought were our trustworthy friends and colleagues. He retrieved some photos from a drawer in the cabinet and proceeded to burn them in the sink.

'Would you like to do anything else before we leave?' I asked him. Without replying, he went into the bedroom, returning a few minutes later with a bundle of clothes in his arms.

'I thought you had already packed enough clothing for our journey? Remember, we must travel light so as not to arouse suspicion,' I said to him.

'I have packed just enough,' he replied. 'I am only going to hang these things on the washing line in the front garden. If anybody comes looking for me, they will see my 'washing' outside and think that I will be coming back later on to take them in.'

I realised that this was a very good idea. He was only protecting himself; something that I knew he was really good at. In fact, he was so good at looking after himself that, when he accidentally discovered the covert plans I had made to flee from Iraq, he had cajoled me into including him in my arrangements. He was so scared of the recent events that had occurred in Erbil and other nearby cities that he pleaded with me to use my influence to help him to escape over the border and into Iran with me.

These recent incidents included some close friends disappearing. For example, the Head of the Chemistry Department of the College of Science disappeared, and we discovered that he had been captured and killed by a group of people, and his body was found floating in a river. Many other academic staff had disappeared in mysterious circumstances.

As soon as Mudhaffar finished pinning the clothes onto the washing line, we left the house, carrying only a very small amount of luggage. We could not afford to arouse the suspicions of any of his neighbours or anyone else, as people had started reporting various things to government officials. We began walking towards the entrance of Zanko Campus – a routine journey that he made six days a week from Saturday to Thursday. Friday was the only day that Muslims did not have to go to work at that time, as it was the one day they were expected to spend time with their families, and because Fridays were the day of prayers throughout the Muslim world. Today was the first day of July 1988, the first day of our momentous journey, and the first day of the rest of my life.

As he did most days, Mudhaffar hailed one of the small taxis that sat at the entrance to the Campus and asked the driver to take us to the University's

College of Science. Before we left the taxi, we agreed to meet up again at my house at eleven o'clock sharp that morning. By doing this, we hoped to mislead the security officers who were on the prowl, assisted by the Dean of the Faculty of Education and a number of the academic staff who would be standing around counting and recording the names of all the students and staff alike.

When we arrived at the College of Science building, most of the other university staff and students had already congregated outside it. Apprehension probably doesn't adequately describe the state we were in, but we tried to pretend as if there was nothing else on our minds except the military training we had been ordered to undertake. Perhaps we could have been described as actors on that particular day. We were smiling and chatting to our other colleagues as if nothing extraordinary was going to happen, while deep inside we were both absolutely terrified. Our plans could easily be exposed, and if that happened, we would end up in prison and without doubt would both be sentenced to death for treason.

The College of Education building was originally a mosque, but was subsequently converted to an educational establishment. A few weeks previously, all the university's staff and students had been informed that they must, by Governmental Law, undertake basic army training to help in the war effort against Iran. We were told that we would be given more details nearer the time. This was the second time we had all been called up to take part in the training campaign.

The first time, we had been sent to a training camp for ten weeks. The training then had been fairly basic, and it was undertaken during the normal summer holidays. My wife and children had been left behind in our flat in Erbil at a time when both children were just getting over the chicken pox. Somehow, Carol had managed on her own with the children while I was away, but when I sometimes managed to get home on Thursday nights, she had many stories to tell. At one stage while I was away, she had been ill with sunstroke, and had been forced to descend the stairs from the roof on her backside as she could not stand without feeling dizzy. She'd had to get the children downstairs quickly because there was an air raid going on and an Iranian fighter jet had flown directly over the roof of the flat. It was not until the fighter jet passed that the air raid siren sounded its warning!

On another occasion she informed me that our next-door neighbour had offered to teach her how to use a gun, and said he would give her one to keep while I was away. She was mortified at the thought of that and declined his kind offer, which had come about because there had been a shooting of an Iraqi soldier in the street right outside our flat. Two days after that incident, she was wakened by a lot of noise in the street downstairs. When she went outside to collect water from the standpipe in the street, she discovered that two Iraqi army lorries were parked directly below the flat and surmised this was because of the shooting and other incidents in the vicinity recently, including shootings at the nearby bus garage. On the following three days, the army lorries returned and were again parked directly below the flats, and she then discovered that our next-door neighbour and his family had suddenly moved out of the flat without informing her they were leaving. That upset Carol, as she had thought that they had all become good friends!

However, back to the second stint of army training now! The Iraqi Government decreed that the appointed day when all of Salahaddin University's staff and students had to go on the training course and do their stint to help the war effort was to be Friday, the 1st of July, 1988. Every male member of staff, along with all of the male students from the entire university, had been ordered to rendezvous outside the College of Science building. A number of buses had been commandeered from the bus depot, and it was arranged that we would be transported to the Popular Army's summer training camp at Dibis, an area around 20 kilometres north-west of Erbil.

The reasoning behind using that particular rendezvous point was primarily to allay any suspicions. If anyone from the Amin (the Iraqi Government Intelligence Agency) was monitoring the roll call of people who turned up and our names were not ticked off, then they would have started searching for us immediately. If, on the other hand, nobody was checking the names off there, but did so at the disembarkation point instead and it was realised we weren't there, it would cause some confusion as our friends could vouch for us. They would genuinely remember speaking to both of us outside the College of Science while we were all waiting to board the buses. Our friends would then assume that something had happened to us, either while waiting to board the buses or while *en route*. Rumours would then abound that we had joined the 'disappeared', as there were thousands of men who went missing – it was a common occurrence in Iraq at that time.

Slowly but surely, all the buses started to fill up with the university's staff and students. I held back as long as possible and, once some of the buses had started to move off, I slowly edged away from the crowd, hoping to be able to sneak off to my own house without being noticed by anyone.

Just when I thought I had succeeded in creeping away, a good friend of mine, Abu Whisham, approached me from behind and leaned forward over my shoulder to speak to me quietly, asking me where I was off to.

'Are you going back to your house?' he whispered.

'Yes, I am going back to my house,' I replied truthfully.

Abu Whisham was a very good friend who had come to me in the past seeking my help when a relative of his had got into trouble with the Government. Fortunately, I had been able to help him out at that time. We had known each other for a long time, and he had sensed that there was something going on. Without hesitation, he told me to jump into his car and he would take me home. I was worried about this, but he told me he had made arrangements to travel to Dibis in his own car at the tail end of the line of buses.

Instinctively, I knew that I could trust Abu Whisham. As I mentioned, he had approached me for help when members of his family had suffered at the hands of Saddam's brutal regime. His cousin had been imprisoned in the past, and a huge amount of his family's money and land had been 'requisitioned' by the Government. When he had approached me for help, it was because his cousin's life had been under threat. The Amin were searching for him and there was a price on his head. I had contacts who helped his cousin to disappear, and he reappeared safe and sound a few months later in Iran!

Once I was safely ensconced in the back of Abu Whisham's car, I confided a little bit about what was happening, only giving him the bare minimum information I could without jeopardising any of the preparations. I told him that I had been planning this day for such a long time and I was about to embark on this daring escapade in the same manner that was used when I had helped his cousin to escape. I was finally going to leave this wretched country and make a bid for freedom, because I was desperate to get back to the UK to be with my wife and children.

I informed him that plans had been made to smuggle me out of Iraq that very day. I did not tell him about Mudhaffar, because he did not need to know about him and the less Abu Whisham knew, the better for his own safety – and mine. I was, however, scared in case he would tell his wife or slip up and tell another friend or colleague, then the story would spread like wildfire.

When we arrived at my house, Abu Whisham helped me double check that I had disposed of any incriminating evidence which would give the Amin any clues as to what was going on. Before he left my house that morning, I gave him my radio and a few bits and pieces which were surplus to my needs, then we hugged each other as a final goodbye. I never saw my good friend ever again after that.

After he left, I sat alone in my rented house, waiting for Mudhaffar to arrive. I wondered if he had succeeded in getting away and, if not, what was going to happen next.

As the minutes slowly ticked by, it started to get much hotter and by a quarter to eleven the heat was stifling. Mudhaffar finally arrived at my house with less than five minutes to spare before our agreed departure time. We hailed a taxi at the end of my street and asked the driver to take us to a street that was quite near to the outskirts of Erbil, where there were a row of cafés and coffee houses. One of these cafés was the pre-arranged meeting place, where we would find my friend and student, Kaka Farhad (to the Kurdish 'Kaka' is a term of endearment, and the nearest translation would be 'brother').

When we got to the café, Farhad was already sitting at one of the small tables with a cup of coffee. He sat with us for only a few minutes before leaving the café to go and meet up with his cousin who was a taxi driver. By that time, I was so nervous that I felt I was going to have a heart attack. I was extremely anxious to clear the next hurdle on our journey. To me, it would be our biggest obstacle – to get safely away from the Governate of Erbil, the town where I had lived for the past five years and where I had become a respected member of the University staff and a friend to almost everyone in the district.

Farhad eventually returned with his cousin, and they immediately loaded our scant belongings into the boot of the taxi. His cousin drove us northwards towards the very small Kurdish village of Harir. On the way there, Farhad suggested that we should stop in one of the small villages along the way to buy a present for the family who had agreed to allow us to use their home as a 'safe-house' for a couple of hours. We had to use a safe-house, as it would have been too conspicuous for two strangers to be standing in the middle of a small village where everybody knew everyone else's business, and we did not want to draw anyone's suspicions.

We realised that this family was taking a huge risk by going against Governmental Law and taking strangers into their house. We also knew that a whole village had recently been bulldozed to the ground because the Amin had received reports of a 'rebel' hiding out in one of the houses there.

Farhad suggested we go to the cattle market and buy a goat, so we agreed. Subsequently, we purchased the goat and it was put into the boot of the taxi before we carried on with the journey. Within 30 minutes, we had left most of the small villages far behind us. Farhad's cousin warned us to hide our passports and whatever money we were carrying, just in case there was any trouble during the rest of the journey.

It was lunchtime when Farhad's cousin (we never did discover his name) announced that we were close to Harir. Eventually, he stopped the car and we slowly alighted. We were taken quickly to the safe-house, and as soon as we got there the house owner took the goat from us and tied it to a tree in the middle of the courtyard. His wife smiled shyly at our kind gesture and spoke in Kurdish.

I thought she was welcoming us, but she had turned her face toward Kaka Farhad and his cousin, and then hurriedly left the room to go and prepare something for us to eat. She arranged for two chickens from her garden to be slaughtered, then she personally cleaned and skinned them and set about cooking them for us. That meal of roast chicken, rice and okra, was very tasty, but unfortunately we did not do it justice because we were so nervous. If only we had known that it was to be the last substantial meal we would receive for a number of days, perhaps we would have been able to force ourselves to eat more.

After eating what little food we could manage, we were told to go and rest for a while. Later that afternoon, two Kurdish rebels arrived at the door with a mule and a donkey. Farhad introduced us and told us that Mohammed and his friend would take us as far as the border with Iran. I looked at these two men and noticed that they both had bloodshot red eyes, and it was obvious that they were both extremely tired.

I spoke to them in Arabic, but neither of them understood a single word of what I had said. It suddenly dawned on me that once Farhad and his cousin left, we had no proper means of communicating with any of these people. Although I spoke a little Kurdish, their dialects were difficult for me to comprehend, and they spoke too rapidly for me to understand a single word.

Oh my gosh, I thought, *how on earth will we be able to communicate with these people and how can we be certain that this is not a trap?* I turned to Farhad with a serious look in my eyes and relayed my worries to him. However, Farhad gave me his assurances that we would not be left to die on the mountaintop, because I was his friend and his teacher and he knew that I had helped quite a few of the Kurdish students and his friends in the past. Because of this, he said, the Kurdish people would repay this debt as they felt they now owed me.

He told me that Mohammed had sworn to him that he would protect us as best he could within reason. He had said to Farhad, 'I guarantee that they will arrive at the border safely... but I will not be held responsible if one of them falls off the mountain or if one of them gets bitten by a snake.'

Although we were both well-educated men, neither Mudhaffar nor I had thought about the actual process they would use to smuggle us over the mountains into Iran, and we all laughed at the idea that we would be stupid enough to fall off our mounts or from a mountain, or that we would be bitten by a poisonous snake. These words had broken the tension of the situation and we all managed to relax slightly.

Mohammed turned towards us and spoke in his own language, and Farhad translated that he wanted one thousand dinars from each of us (that was equivalent to £2000 each). We handed over the money as requested and, without further prompting, we gave the family who had sheltered us for a few hours a further two hundred dinars. We also gave Farhad's cousin two hundred dinars in appreciation of the risk he had taken in driving us up to Harir.

By now it was approaching 3pm, and Kaka Mohammed gestured for us to give him our luggage. He placed the cases in waterproof bags and put them on the backs of the mule and the donkey as if they were saddles. We were told that the mule, the donkey, and the two guides would travel ahead and meet us at the forest; we would go in Farhad's cousin's taxi to the edge of the forest.

'The time has come,' Farhad's cousin told us.

We went back out with him to his taxi and he drove toward the forest which we discovered was on the northern outskirts of Harir. The area was eerily deserted, and it looked as if a tornado had hit it. Farhad explained that the destruction we had observed had been ordered by the dictator, Saddam Hussein, who wanted to destroy the Kurdish people and the whole community who lived in that area.

Farhad asked his cousin to drive us as close to the edge of the forest as possible. As we got nearer there, Farhad turned to me and said, 'We must say farewell quickly before someone sees us, but before you go please send me a letter to let me know that you are safely across the border.' We hugged each other, said a quick prayer, then said our final farewells.

1988: With three of my final year students at the end of the academic year. We are standing in front of the College, and both Farhad and the girl on his right are wearing typical Kurdish clothing.

June 1988: My friend and student, Farhad, the day he received his BSc degree in Chemistry from Salahaddin University. We heard that he had died, but we are not sure how or when.

1988: I am standing, second from the left (third row), with my final year chemistry students at the end of the academic year at the College of Education, Salahaddin University, Erbil, Iraq. This was the last group of students I taught before leaving Iraq.

Chapter 9

The Forest

We entered the forest, which was more like an overgrown orchard as it was full of trees bearing a variety of fruits, such as small apples, pears, and apricots. As it was just after 3.15pm, the sun was burning down over the canopy of trees, there was not even the smallest hint of a breeze, and the humidity was extremely high. Sitting under the trees looking at each other and contemplating our fate, we did not know what to say or think! In fact, there was nothing that we could do except wait, and we were simply too scared to even whisper, never mind speak loudly, in case somebody might hear us. If anyone happened to be walking past, they would have thought that we were a strange sight sitting stock-still in amongst all those fruit trees. Actually, the word 'strange' was too mild an adjective to describe us, especially as we were wearing so many items of clothes in that searing heat. I was wearing the full Kurdish outfit, including the rank (exceptionally wide trousers), a choga (a jacket that goes inside the top of the trousers so that it looks as though the wearer is wearing a one-piece outfit), and a thick cummerbund; Mudhaffar was wearing baggy grey trousers and a thick grey shirt.

After sitting in this orchard for around 30 minutes, I took a quick glance at my watch and realised that we should have performed our customary Asur Salat (afternoon prayers). I told Mudhaffar that, no matter how we felt and how scared we were, we should somehow undertake our ablutions and prepare to do our prayers. Luckily, there was a small, clear stream nearby, so we managed to perform the traditional Wuḍū (ablutions consisting of washing the face, hands, feet, and arms prior to performing our prayers). We then proceeded to pray, beseeching Allah to stay with us and help us on the perilous journey ahead.

Shortly after finishing our prayers, there was a rustling sound and we heard footsteps coming towards us, so we decided to take refuge behind some slightly larger trees, just in case of trouble. Thankfully, the noise was made by the two smugglers returning to pick us up. They had brought with them the mule and the donkey, which were to be our only means of travel over the next leg of our journey.

'Hey, we are okay! It is them. They have come, just as they promised,' Mudhaffar whispered to me.

Along with our bags, they had brought several containers of sugar and tea, and there were some other items that were obviously black-market goods. Everything was piled up high on the backs of the animals. We were so overjoyed when we realised that it was our smugglers that we both tried to speak to them simultaneously, momentarily forgetting that their Arabic left a lot to be desired. In very basic, broken Arabic (and with a smattering of Kurdish), Kaka Mohammed told us that we would have to stay there amongst the trees until nightfall before it would be safe enough for us to resume our journey.

'Dema xwarinê,' (dinner time) Kaka Hussein said, before delving into one of the saddles and retrieving a couple of cucumbers, some bread, and some tomatoes. He went to one of the fields nearby and returned with some stalks of celery, then washed the vegetables in the same stream where we had performed our ablutions. There was a dead tree-trunk lying close beside the riverbank, so we sat there and ate our meagre rations, even though we still had little appetite for food of any kind due to the dire circumstances we were in at that moment.

Once we'd eaten, we just had to sit there and wait until we were told it was safe to continue our journey. As darkness fell, the heat started to ease a bit and we were asked, through gestures, to help put the saddles on the back of the pack animals in preparation for our travels.

We finally set of at around half past eight that evening. We had been led to understand that during this next stage of our trek, we would have to pass by many Iraqi observation posts. As we passed these buildings, we would have to pretend that we were a group of smugglers who had travelled back and forwards through this area on a regular basis. In actual fact, there are huge numbers of smugglers who go over these routes on a regular basis, bringing in goods to and from Iran to sell on the black market in Iraq, and *vice versa*.

These black-market goods were relatively easy to find and, more often than not, were of a far superior quality than the goods legally on sale in Iraq. Even when my wife and children were still living with me in Erbil, we often went to the Souk Al Ketchek (Black Market Bazaar) to buy clothes for the children or material to make curtains for our huge wall-to-wall windows. My wife loved the chenille ready-made curtains, as it saved her a lot of time cutting and sewing material, and she also liked the patterns.

Although it was relatively easy to buy goods on the black market, you had to be very careful because the intelligence officers would often pose as normal customers pretending to be looking for things to buy, then they would suddenly produce guns and round up both the traders selling the goods and the customers who were buying the items. Also, if you were unlucky enough to be travelling through a checkpoint and were searched and found to be carrying black market goods, whatever you were carrying would be confiscated from you. If you were lucky, you would only get a telling-off, as they could not prove that you bought the items or whether you had been given the items as a gift. Many people were 'unknowingly' given black market gifts when visiting their friends or relatives!

We walked for what seemed like hours on end, up through hills and down through valleys, struggling to make our way through the tall, dry grasses, shrubs, and bushes until our legs bled from the tiny cuts inflicted by the plants. Eventually, after what seemed like an eternity to us, we were told that we could sit on top of the two animals.

Our arduous journey continued in this manner during the pitch-black night until we suddenly came close to walking right into one of the Peshmerga patrol units (the military soldiers who held themselves responsible for security in the so-called autonomous region of Kurdistan) that combed that area. Kaka Mohammed gestured for us to dismount and hide in the bushes while they negotiated a deal with the Peshmerga. When the conversation finally ended, the Peshmerga moved off and our two guides started walking in the opposite direction from where we had been told to hide.

Petrified, we ran towards the direction that we thought they were heading in, because although we could not see them in the darkness, we could hear the now-familiar sounds of the donkey and the mule slowly plodding along further and further away from us.

When we finally caught up with the two men, they both laughed at us as if to say that we must have been mad to think they would really have left us. But from then on, we were more on our guard than ever. To our relief, we only travelled a short distance after that until we found some shelter.

Having rested at this shelter for a short while, we were told we had to start moving again. By midnight, we were again mounted; I was astride the mule, and Mudhaffar was on the donkey. If it had not been so dangerous, it would have been absolutely hilarious, because he is such a tall person and there he was, riding a beast that was about half the size of a horse. As we travelled onwards, Mudhaffar's legs were being dragged along through the tall, dry blades of grass. Each time he brushed past a prickly gorse bush, a thorn scratched him and he cursed and swore.

We continued along in this manner until about 2.30am, when we were unfortunate enough to bump into another group of Peshmerga patrolling the area.

However, this time the Peshmerga seemed to be quite happy to see Kaka Mohammed and his comrade Kaka Hussein. Our guides quickly explained the situation we were in to this group of men and, thankfully, they were more than happy to allow us to continue our journey.

Eventually we arrived at the mouth of a cave, which we learned was one of the hideouts often used by the Peshmerga; in fact, there were already some men ensconced in the cave when we arrived. It soon became apparent that this was their hideout, and they had been sheltering there for quite some time.

An authoritative, although somewhat muffled, voice told us to dismount. 'Come down here! You are staying here tonight!' It was our guide who spoke to us, and we realised that he spoke abruptly because he was trying to show off in front of the Peshmerga, and also because of his lack of Arabic.

We stayed there with this small band of men for the remainder of that night. Although they might have been cut-throats for all we knew, we were so exhausted that we actually slept for a few hours, although we both looked and felt absolutely exhausted when we woke up. No matter what we had been through, though, we both vowed that we would help each other as much as possible to ensure we both survived our trials and tribulations and would live to tell the tale of our travels once we reached safety.

While we sat there talking to each other the following morning, one of the men started cooking a breakfast of spring onions and corned beef mixed with tomato puree, and of course, the customary thin, round, dry Kurdish bread (similar to lavash). *What a mixture,* I thought to myself. However, as we were both starving, we tucked into this meal and our guides thanked the group and agreed that it was absolutely delicious. Again, we were told that we would have to stay in the mouth of the cave until much later that evening when the sun had gone down.

While we were camped out there in the cave, a small troupe of men were bidding farewell to the others before going away to do whatever duties they had been allocated. As they said their farewells, I sat watching one of the younger men. At first, I could not fathom why he had caught my attention; there was something different about him, but I could not put my finger on it at first.

Eventually the penny dropped, and I realised what was different about him - one of his sleeves seemed to look very baggy and was just swinging about. It turned out that he had a limb reduction, possibly from a birth defect, that left him with a very short arm, but he still had a fully functioning hand. Amazingly (to me at least), he was able to operate the Kalashnikov rifle that was slung over his shoulder. Kalashnikovs were standard issue for the Peshmerga, as they were for many freedom-fighters worldwide, and it was a regular part of their uniform. I realised then what a courageous fighter and an extraordinary person he must have been!

Shortly after that group of men left, our guide came into the cave with one of the Peshmerga who spoke Arabic. This freedom-fighter warned us that as darkness had fallen, we had to ensure we were fully prepared in case any complications might arise. We had to tie the belts of the saddles around the animals and ensure that all the black-market goods were well and truly secured. By this time, the other guide, Kaka Hussein, had disappeared and we were left with only Kaka Mohammed to guide us through to the next stage of our journey. We left the mouth of the cave soon after.

We walked for many hours during that evening and eventually reached a field full of vegetables, including more cucumbers and tomatoes. Kaka Mohammed gestured that we were to rest up there for a while. We later discovered that the main reason we were to stay put for some time in that field was so that we could meet up with yet another guide who was far more familiar with the area we were to travel through next.

When the next guide finally arrived, he at least was able to speak slightly more Arabic than the guide he had replaced. Speaking to us in halting Arabic, he explained that he had once been reluctantly conscripted into the Iraqi Army and had served in Southern Iraq for a short period of time during his national service.

When he finished talking to us, he set about making a small fire so that he could cook some food. He went into a field and picked some tomatoes and onions, which he chopped up and placed in an old, fire-blackened pot. A short while later, he told us the food was ready. It was bad enough that we were only eating par-boiled vegetables, but I couldn't believe my eyes when I saw the bread that he proffered us. I know I might sound ungrateful, but it really was something that I would not even throw out to the birds. It was so old that it was dry and crumbly, and mould was starting to form around the edges. At the very least it made me realise how lucky we had been until then, and how we normally took all the little luxuries in life for granted.

I thought back to when we lived in Erbil, and either my wife or I (usually Carol) would stand in a queue at the baker's shop and buy fresh samoon and Kurdish bread straight from the hot oven. As it was so hot, we would carry a clean piece of cloth to wrap the bread in so that we could carry it in our arms across the road to our house without burning ourselves. There were many times when one of us was in the queue when the air siren would sound, and within minutes we would see Iranian fighter jets flying overhead. As the sirens were a common occurrence then, we did not make a big deal of it; instead, everyone went about our normal daily lives.

Now, however, I pondered over the plight of the people throughout the world who were starving and realised that they would probably be so grateful for this bread and the vegetables we were about to eat. Still, I did not want to eat this sad bread offering, even though I felt so hungry I could have eaten a scabby horse.

I was scared that the bread would give me an upset stomach, thus causing problems for us during the rest of the journey ahead. As we were travelling out in the wilds, there was no proper means of cleaning ourselves after going to the toilet. Instead, we would have to use whatever paper we had, and when that was finished, we would have to use the leaves or long grass to try to clean ourselves. I wondered if this was the normal standard of life for all the resistance fighters and rebels who hid out in the hills and valleys of Kurdistan. Surely they couldn't survive eating this kind of food day in and day out, especially when we were always taught that an army fought on its stomach. I also wondered how they managed to keep themselves clean when trekking through the mountains!

We had barely finished the meal, with the customary istikan (a small glass cup) of strong black tea, when we were told we had to get up and continue our long trek through the Kurdish countryside. After travelling for five hours we felt as though we could no longer continue. We were both so very tired by then, as we were still not used to travelling at night. During that stage of the journey, we had passed several rivers and thick forests in pitch-black darkness, as the moon had been hidden by the thick clouds that seemed to hang oppressively low in the sky. We only knew there were rivers because of the sound the water made; the forests looked like black depths, so we could not tell whether they were big or not.

Eventually, we arrived at an area that was obviously a familiar landmark to our guides. 'Wait here!' one guide commanded, before the two of them disappeared into the all-pervasive darkness that stretched its fingers around the trees and snaked right into the depths of the forest. Shortly thereafter, we heard the sounds of dogs barking in the distance, but they did not come any nearer to us, and eventually, we could no longer hear them.

The minutes slowly ticked by into what seemed like hours as we stood alone, in silence, in that dark, God-forbidden hole. After what felt like an eternity, we heard noises coming from the edge of the forest. The sounds were those of galloping horses, and they seemed to be coming straight towards us. We both froze, unsure whether it was our two guides or if we had been reported to a band of Peshmerga or, worse, the Iraqi Amin!

The clouds decided to part slightly for us at that very moment, and a small sliver of moon gleamed down on the scene. *Oh, thank heavens!* I thought.

'At last, the wanderers return,' we both said in unison.

For all it was only a small sliver of moon, it still managed to spread an eerie glow over the valley, revealing mountain-tops towering high above us. 'At least we will now be able to see where we are going,' I said to Mudhaffar.

In what now seemed to be the normal pattern, only one of the original guides returned, and he had a new companion with him. The guide never mentioned anything about where he had been, nor did he introduce his new companion to us.

Once again the journey resumed, and after an arduous struggle onwards and upwards, we found ourselves standing at the top of a mountain. I looked at my watch, but the moon had disappeared behind a cloud again and I could not make out what time it was. The animals were sweating by now, and because there were no reins to restrain them, it was becoming more difficult to control them.

We had never been mountain climbing in our lives before and were therefore both complete novices, but it was obvious even to us that the forthcoming descent down that mountain was going to be an absolute nightmare for us. Fortunately, both guides were familiar with all the perils that this feat entailed, and they motioned for us both to dismount. We then spent the next couple of hours sliding and slithering ever downwards towards the base at the other side of the mountain.

For all this leg of the journey was undertaken during the night and we were at quite a high altitude, we were not in the least bit cold. On the contrary, we were both dripping with perspiration, and even if the moon had been high in a totally cloudless sky, we still would not have been able to see anything due to the amount of perspiration running down our faces, into our eyes, and down the back of our necks.

When we eventually reached the floor of the valley, after a number of scary episodes, we were finally told that we could mount the animals again. The clouds had eventually parted and the moon was now directly overhead, so I could easily read the time on my watch. It was only 3.30am!

An hour later, Kaka Mohammed told us to dismount again and gestured that we should get some sleep by using the age-old sign of cradling his head in his hands. I was surprised by this, because we were now out in the open with no visible sign of shelter of any kind, apart from a few rocks and the long grass. Our guide yawned and gestured that he was going to sleep whether we liked it or not.

We sat on the ground with our backs against a rock, thinking that at the very least we could rest for a little while. Imagine my surprise when, less than five minutes later, I heard the sound of loud snoring coming from all three of my companions. I could not possibly sleep; instead, I slid down onto the bare ground to lie flat on my back, looked up at the stars, and imagined that the moon was a lantern in the heart of the sky. I hoped my wife and children were all safe and sound asleep at that moment. I had been so busy concentrating on myself that I had hardly had the chance to think about them!

I looked around at the lush vegetation around me and silently sent up a prayer, asking Allah to help us in the middle of our precarious situation. Two hours passed before the newer guide woke up and roused the others. Without having anything to eat, we started to move once more.

Chapter 10

The Next Mountain

By the time dawn had broken over the horizon, we had arrived at a small village. One of the guides went up to the door of a dilapidated house and spoke to the owner in their own language about our arrival. The family seemed to be very kind people; at least, they were very kind to us as they welcomed us into their home. Shortly after we arrived, the wife went into the kitchen and prepared a breakfast of fairly thin yoghurt, bread, and strong black tea for all of us. This was the kind of breakfast my family would prepare for us at home in Karbala, except that we would have had either double cream or soft cheese instead of yoghurt. Following breakfast, the husband told us we could lie down and relax for a little while in the small room to the rear of the house.

Each room was almost identical to all the others, and most of the outside walls had gaps for windows but they were all unglazed. I was desperate to use the toilet, so I asked one of the children who were running in and out of the room and staring at us every now and again, if he could tell me where the toilet was.

To my astonishment, the reply was, 'We don't have one.' Luckily, another child jumped up to help. 'If you want to use the toilet, I can take you to the mosque where you would be allowed to use the toilet there,' he replied.

The mosque was just a short distance away from the house and there were no questions asked when the child informed the imam that I needed to use the toilet. The child waited until I was finished and then he led me back to the house and straight into the bedroom, and shortly afterwards I fell asleep.

When we woke up a few hours later, the family were in the middle of lunch preparations and once it was ready we sat and shared a simple lentil stew and fresh bread which the wife had made over a simple ring in the kitchen. Considering the food we had eaten recently, we ate heartily and enjoyed what felt like a meal fit for a king.

After lunch one of the younger men in the house said, 'I have already arranged for a Land Rover to take you to Khanaqin.' Khanaqin, although still in Iraq, sits near the Iranian border on the Alwand tributary of the Diyala River.

Hearing this made us realise that, although we had been travelling for some three days, we were still inside Iraqi territory and were not as close to the Iraq/Iran border as we had hoped to be. Instead, it seemed that we had been going around and around in circles, circumnavigating the Kurdish mountains in the most northerly part of Iraq. This news was very disappointing and worrying for us, because we had hoped to be close to crossing the border!

After lunch, we went back to the bedroom and lay down on the dosheks and fell fast asleep, because we were still exhausted. After two hours, we were shaken awake and told it was time to leave. The sun was still very high in the sky, so thankfully we didn't have far to walk to reach a car, which was parked at the side of the verge. Although we were apprehensive, it appeared that the car was actually waiting for us, and we were delighted at this form of transport after so many miles of walking or sitting on the back of the mule or the horse.

Kaka Mohammed walked us over to the car and put his head in through the window. He gave the driver some money, then he just abandoned us – without a further word or even a backward glance.

Once we were seated in the car with our bags secured in the boot, the driver drove us through long, winding, dirt tracks that passed for roads. Obviously, he knew which roads to take to avoid the Iraqi checkpoints that were still scattered along the way. Eventually, he informed us in broken Arabic that we were now in Khanaqin, and that we would have to stay with one of his friends for a little while.

The driver went up to the first house but, unfortunately, there was no answer to the knock on the door. 'No worry!' he said. 'I have other friend.' And he promptly walked further down the road with us following him, dragging our cases behind us.

He stopped at a house further down the street, where a woman answered the door, but she seemed to inform the driver that her husband was not at home. However, he persuaded her to let us all in and, most importantly, he stayed with us until her husband came back from what we later discovered was a 'shopping trip'. As was the custom for people living in these regions, this man had bought as much material as he could to transport over the mountains and across the border into Iran.

From the discussion the two men had (which lasted for around two hours), it became obvious that the owner of the house, Kaka Murad, was leaving that night to smuggle black-market goods, including the material, into Iran.

Kaka Murad's wife prepared us a simple dinner and then we were informed that we would be leaving at one o'clock in the morning, so should try to get some sleep. We were told that we would have to travel all night long and it would not be safe for us to stop anywhere at all *en route* for a rest. We tried to follow this advice and get some shut-eye, but we were both too fraught with worry to sleep after everything we had been through. Instead, we just lay down on the floor and rested our tired, aching limbs. We both lay there with our eyes closed, but neither of us managed to sleep for more than thirty minutes.

We must have eventually dozed off, though, as some time later Kaka Murad came into the room and told us both to get up. 'The time came. We must now go!' he said. Within five minutes we were back outside, but unfortunately, the Land Rover was nowhere in sight and we would be riding animals again. This time, instead of a horse and a mule, we were both given mules to ride on.

We started to move off very slowly so as to make as little noise as possible. The roads were absolutely empty and the whole village appeared to be dead, apart from a couple of stray dogs barking at each other.

We had not been travelling for very long when we arrived at the foothills of a huge mountain with a sharp cliff-face and ragged edges. *Oh, my gosh!* I thought. *We are not going up there, surely. These animals will never be able to climb such a high, steep mountain as that, will they?*

The two mules were laden with makeshift saddles full of black-market goods and they were also carrying us! And this guy was expecting them to be able to ascend this steep incline to boot? No way! Sure enough, after about ten minutes of slipping and sliding, the animals just could not cope with climbing that mountain while carrying all that weight. We must have been like the proverbial straw that broke the camel's back and it was all too much for them. The two men managed to convey to us that we should get off the animals and start climbing ourselves, as it was far too dangerous to struggle on the way we were. We had no choice but to start climbing up that monstrosity of a mountain, which was so high that we couldn't even see the summit!

We had been climbing slowly but surely for a number of hours when Mudhaffar suddenly started shouting and gesticulating. 'Look! Look! We can't go on any further. That snake is blocking our path. We were warned about these snakes!'

The guide started throwing stones at it and eventually it slithered away. We were told to be quiet and to resume climbing. Time passed by and we were still climbing up, higher and higher, but seemingly making no progress whatsoever.

My attention was suddenly drawn to one of the mules as it was trying to commit suicide. I had heard stories in the past about animals that would commit suicide rather than go on climbing up sheer mountainsides, but I had imagined they were just old wives' tales. I had personally never witnessed anything like that before, and I hoped I wouldn't see a scene like that again. That poor mule was carrying two full sacks of sugar, each weighing 50 kilogrammes, as well as many other items – and the rock-face was exceptionally steep.

The poor animal must have decided it just could not take the struggle any longer, and decided to jump off the cliff rather than carry on climbing under all that weight. Fortunately, it only fell around fifteen to twenty metres. So, the two guides scrambled back down the cliff after it, removed one of the sacks from the mule's back, and then pulled and cajoled the animal back up the side of the mountain to where we were waiting for them.

Our climb continued slowly but surely until dawn, when we eventually reached the top of that mountain. We found a fairly flattish area and sat there for a few minutes to get some rest. While we rested, we heard the exchange of artillery shells which were being fired from both sides of the mountain. The Iraqis were pounding the Iranians on the other side of the border, and they were returning fire just as quickly. We sat there listening to the whiz and thud of the shells exploding, although we could not see anything.

After a short respite, our guide said, 'We go now. This time it will be easy, no!' And with these words, we began our descent down the other side of the mountain that we had just climbed. Although we had taken many hours to climb up the mountain, our descent took around half that time. Once we reached the bottom, we got back on the mules and our journey continued.

After travelling for a long time, we were tired, hungry, and irritable. Eventually, we arrived at the house of a family that Kaka Murad knew well, and they seemed fairly happy to welcome us into their home and therefore he left us there to get on with his own business. This house was very crudely made and consisted of one single room that was piled high with beds and clothes. In one corner they had a small paraffin heater, with no cooker or a sink but a jerry can holding water. There was no toilet either, and I dread to think what they did if they needed to use the facilities.

Unfortunately, nobody in the family spoke a single word of Arabic, but they sent one of the children down to the village to bring back someone they could trust to explain to us in Arabic how much further we would have to travel to reach the Iranian border. They also agreed to prepare something 'very simple' for us to eat, and returned to the room with some goat's milk yoghurt, some very thin home-made bread, and a pot of sweet, black tea. Obviously, this family was very poor and struggling to make ends meet.

After a while, an old man arrived at the house and greeted us in Arabic. We explained to him why we were there, and why we had decided that we had to leave Iraq. He spoke good Arabic and translated everything we said to the Kurdish family. Their oldest son, who was in his late teens, agreed to take us to the meeting place of the Peshmerga, and we were told we would have to give him seventy dinars each in return.

By this time, both Mudhaffar and I were very upset. It seemed to us that all these so-called smugglers had done was take money from us and take us around and around in circles. We had been travelling for miles and miles, yet we had only completed a small fraction of the journey and were still no nearer to the border with Iran than we had been a few days ago! It seemed that all their promises of helping us and getting us over the border into Iran had been nothing but lies after lies.

What made us feel even worse was the fact that all of those people knew we were at their mercy. They knew we would have to keep on forking out money to all and sundry if we were to fulfil our hopes and dreams of leaving Iraq. I am sure they also knew that there was no way we could retrace our steps and go home again, even if we wanted to, so we were utterly and completely lost!

In the end, we handed over the amount of money stipulated by the youth and asked him to take us to the Peshmerga immediately. When this was translated to him, he shook his head and told the old man that he would take us later that afternoon and definitely not right now. We were therefore stuck there with his family until nearer four o'clock that afternoon, when he left the house for a short time and came back with two horses, then gestured for us to get up onto them and ride. Within forty minutes, we arrived at a very rocky and uneven track that seemed to descend from a large mountain with a wide, flat face that tapered to a very narrow path, less than a metre wide. This track seemed to be wrapped around the bottom of the mountain and looked to go on and on, going round and round and round.

We rode around this curving track for quite some time, with the youth stopping every now and then to let us catch up with him. When we finally caught up with him, we realised that the track was now curving downwards and, looking below, we saw a scene that had us both quivering with fear. The track led down to another exceptionally deep valley that was scarily narrow, with a very steep path leading down to it.

From our position on top of the horses, we had a clear view of the scenery and could hear a waterfall below us in the distance. But it was absolutely impossible to see the water that must have been cascading down the hillside, hitting the floor of the valley. If we had not been so petrified of the sight before us, we would both have admitted that it was absolutely breath-taking and such a marvellous sight. There were thousands of trees, so lush and green, and they seemed to be jutting out at right angles to the slope unfolding below us.

I felt my legs turning to jelly, and my heart was beating so fast and irregularly that I thought I was going to collapse. I looked at Mudhaffar and exclaimed, 'If either horse slipped just once, that would be the end of the rider.' It was obvious that he was just as scared as I was, and he just stared at the scene below us, with his mouth wide open, unable to utter a single word.

This is it! I thought. We had heard so many stories about people who had tried to escape from Iraq and had asked smugglers to help them on their quest. The stories were that many of these would-be escapees had been thrown over the mountains and left for dead, while the smugglers took all their belongings for themselves. Surely, if that was to be our fate, then this was the very place for them to do it.

Nervously, we began our descent, slowly, so very, very slowly. We continued warily down the valley until we arrived at a few farmsteads that seemed to be embedded in the side of the mountain. When I saw these buildings, I thought to myself, *Thank heavens! We must be in a safer area now! Surely there are no other mountains or valleys between here and Iran that are as bad as the one we have just come from.* However, we had managed it and lived to tell the tale.

It was not until we got closer to the farm buildings that we noticed there were half a dozen or so armed men sitting under the shade of some trees. Our guide completely ignored them and gestured to us to start crossing a bridge made of tree trunks and mud. Suddenly, people started shouting, but we were unsure if they were shouting at us or not. Our guide started to cross the narrow, hand-made bridge and we began to follow him. Meantime, we could hear footsteps running up behind us. The armed men were running after us and shouting at us in Kurdish.

Their first question, which I understood, was 'Who are you?' Then they continued their barrage of questions. 'Where are you coming from?' Where are you going?' 'Why are you here?' We did not answer any of their questions, but simply pointed to our guide, expecting him to reply to them. He started to mumble, stammer, and then stutter, and he simply could not give them any satisfactory answers. At that point, they gestured for us to dismount.

After we dismounted, Mudhaffar said, 'Ok! Ok! No harm done. We will now return the same way we came.' He followed this up by saying, 'We came here to see the beautiful scenery in these mountains and valleys, but obviously you do not want us to cross this bridge.'

For the first time in my life, I was convinced I was going to be killed by a firing squad at the hands of the 'Fursan' (the Knights). 'Fursan' was the name given to small bands of Kurdish people who were followers of Saddam Hussein and believed he was 'the great leader'. They were against the Peshmerga, and tried to maintain control in the north of Iraq.

I was positive that we had been stupid enough to be caught by the Fursan, and if it was them, they had the right to execute us on the spot. Failing that, they could take us to their territorial leaders who would form an army-style court and pass judgement on us within minutes. We'd be accused of being spies and we'd be tortured before being assassinated by firing squad.

We had heard so many stories about the Fursan, the worst being that they managed to creep up on people and, after garrotting them to death, they would gouge out their eyes and leave coins in the eye sockets. This was to warn people that they should not join any resistance groups or fight against Saddam, as they would be caught and given the same treatment.

Thankfully, our luck must have been in as one of the armed men, who spoke good Arabic, said to us, 'Do you not know that this area has been liberated from Saddam's forces? Do you not realise that we are Peshmerga and we are in charge of this territory?'

On hearing this news, the blood rushed back to our faces and we managed to speak without stammering or stuttering. Immediately, I explained to the men that we were fleeing from Saddam's brutal regime, and that we were trying to find a way over the border to escape to Iran.

We were escorted to the group's leader and our story recounted to him. Once he was satisfied that our story was true, and we had shown him our passports to prove our true identities, the leader shook our hands. He then wrote a short letter on our behalf and told us that we had to give the letter to his superior – a man, we were told, that we would definitely meet later at the Peshmerga headquarters, and who had the power to facilitate our journey over the border and into Iran.

We went with that small troupe of men back to their headquarters where the rest of the Peshmerga were billeted. This 'headquarters' consisted of only two tents, although one of them was actually huge. Their leader, we were to discover later, was called Kaka Ali. After welcoming us to his encampment, Kaka Ali asked us how much we had paid the guide. We told him that we had paid 70 dinars each.

Kaka Ali turned to our guide and spoke to him in Kurdish. For our sake, he translated everything he had said to the boy, explaining that he told him the going rate now was just 50 dinars so he should return 20 dinars to each of us. However, we were just so grateful to have come out of this situation alive so far, and to have accomplished yet another stage of our journey, that we told Kaka Ali to let the boy keep the money as a gift from us.

We were invited into the bigger of the two tents where a group of Peshmerga were already sitting around a big mat spread out on the floor. Until that point, we had not realised what time it was, nor had we realised how hungry we were. The freedom-fighters had just started eating a meal consisting of minced meat kebabs, roasted tomatoes, roasted onions, the thin Kurdish bread, and the customary watery yoghurt drink that we call laben. We were invited to sit with them and share their meal.

We soon discovered that a number of the men could speak Arabic, and as we all sat on the ground in that tent eating that lovely meal, we had the opportunity to discuss many things, not least the political situation in Iraq and how Saddam was ruling (and ruining) the country. It was absolutely fantastic to be able to speak in Arabic and to know that some of these men understood almost every word we said and could answer us back. All in all, we spent a very pleasant evening with these rebels, considering the state we had been in when we'd arrived there.

After breakfast the following day, we asked Kaka Ali if he could also give us a letter of recommendation to take with us, as advised by the small band of Peshmerga the night before. The smaller band of Peshmerga had explained that these letters of recommendation should be shown to the leaders of any other bands of Peshmerga patrolling the area that we might be fortunate (or unfortunate) enough to meet. However, his reply was, 'Not today, but maybe tomorrow!' So, we decided it was best to stay in their campsite amongst the mountains. At least we were getting well fed, which was a real bonus.

Around lunchtime the next day, we were told to report to Kaka Ali in the smaller of the two tents. He told us he wanted to take us to his commanding officer, who was in charge of the operations in that area. We had no option but to attend this meeting with their leader.

Their commanding officer seemed to be very well educated, and he appeared to understand our plight. We showed him photos of our wives and children, then let him see our passports and other documentary evidence, including proof of our jobs in the University of Salahaddin to show that we were also well educated and not just black marketeers who had been caught trying to smuggle items for profit. Once he was convinced that we really were trying to escape from Iraq and hoping to join our wives in Britain, he seemed to be very sympathetic and asked us to join him for lunch. It was a simple meal consisting of rice and sardines, for which he apologised. 'This is all that we can offer you under the present circumstances' he said. We thanked him profusely for his hospitality and generosity, and we thanked Allah for all that we had.

We stayed a third night in the tent, hoping that the following day would be an even better day and that we would finally get the results we hoped for. After breakfast on the fourth morning, Kaka Ali came to see us and informed us that he had arranged for two mules and a proper guide for us.

Just after lunchtime, we were introduced to our new guide when he arrived with the mules. We could not wait to mount the animals and prayed that we would finally manage to reach our goal. We said fond farewells to this small band of Peshmerga.

One young chap had offered to take us because he knew the route well, but Kaka Ali refused to allow him to take us. He explained that he had already arranged for a specific guide for us – one who was trustworthy and very brave. He also informed the volunteer that he must not, under any circumstances, go with us, because they could not afford to lose him for any length of time.

We began the next step of our journey with the knowledge that we still had a fair bit to travel, up and down more mountains and valleys that skirted the border between Iraq and Iran, before we reached our destination. We also now knew that not all people were money-grabbers who were out to fleece us. Instead, there were many people who still had goodness in their hearts and who wanted to help.

We were, at long last, starting to feel a bit more hopeful for our future.

Chapter 11

The Qandil Mountain Range

After several hours continuous travel, we arrived at our next resting place, which was really for the mules, so that they could get some feed, water, and a rest. While we were waiting for the mules to graze and recover from the journey, we met a woman with her two children who were travelling in the same direction as us. We started to pack up and leave just as she mounted her own horse and lifted one of her children up and placed him in front of her. Our guide lifted her other child up and placed him in front of Mudhaffar on his horse. While the horses travelled along at a leisurely pace, it left us ample time to drink in the marvellous scenery that slowly unfolded before us. Less than two hours into our journey, we came to a small farmhouse, which was where the woman traveller and her two children were heading, so we bade them farewell then continued on our journey.

We felt at peace with the world on that round of the journey, at least until we discovered the next obstacle in our way. We were riding along a track that gently sloped downwards into a lush valley lined by tall trees. As we went further downwards, the track curved around and the trees became denser. We continued going down and eventually the trees became sparser, so we were able to see that another huge mountain was looming ahead of us. As was typical of these mountains, this one seemed to loom higher and higher, away up into the clouds. However, unlike the other mountains that we had struggled to scale and then marvelled at the wonderful view from the top before slithering down the other side, this one appeared to be so high that the upper regions were shrouded in mist and snow and we could not see the apex.

Although this was so scary to look at, we had to get used to the idea that this was just another hurdle to overcome and we needed to pass over this one to get nearer our goal.

In a bid to get more information, and also to make polite conversation, I spurred the horse on to ride a bit faster so that I could catch up with our guide, who was now a fair bit in front of us. I asked him what the name of this particular mountain was and was disheartened by his reply. 'This is part of the Qandil – Zagros Mountain Range,' he said, and went on to explain that we had to climb that mountain in front of us, which he called the Kuhe Haji Ebrahim. With a hint of irony, he added, 'This is the highest mountain of the range and is over 3000 metres big. We climb up from Iraq but we go down from very, very near to Iran.'

Very surprisingly, this part of the mountain range was a hive of activity compared to the previous legs of our journey. There were great numbers of Kurdish convoys travelling along this route with their pack animals, most of which were heavily laden with goods. Obviously, most of these people were smuggling black-market merchandise across the borders. Undoubtedly, there were as many people coming towards us from the Iranian side of the mountain as there were travelling from Iraq and into Iran.

One of the travellers made a comment to his companion as they passed us by. I understood what he said which was, 'Iraq is far better than Iran, so why do they want to escape to Iran? They are wrong, and it is better for them to go back to their own country.'

I assume they thought we were escaping, because we were not laden down with goods like them. Also, we looked different to them in the way we dressed and the way we sat atop the horses. Neither of us uttered a word at this. For all we knew, they might have been cut-throats, prepared to kill us and take our belongings for themselves. Even if we did have the courage to reply, I do not think we would have had the words to respond to them.

We could not really blame them for their sentiments, though, as we knew that some people would think we were mad to undertake this journey in the first place. Most of these smugglers seemed to be happy with their lot in life. They were almost certainly making a hefty profit from the people who were prepared to pay vast sums of money for the goods they smuggled, and a lot of them thought more about money than they did about anything else. Yes, definitely some of those people were more than happy with their lot. If they were discovered selling black-market goods, they would just run away and set up their 'business' elsewhere, with no taxes or any rent to pay.

The vast majority of these people thought they were 'free', as very few of them had enjoyed a proper education and even fewer had lived abroad and knew what real freedom tasted like. Thankfully, they didn't have a clue about what was going on inside our minds, about the freedom that we so badly missed, and how much the two of us longed to be back at home in the UK with our wives and families. I suppose, one can never tell how good or bad life is for someone else.

We continued climbing the Kuhe Haji Ebrahim Mountain for the rest of that day until we felt we could not go on any longer and were desperate to rest for a while. The guide cajoled us into going up a bit further to a place where we could safely sit down on an overhang and take a break for a little while. Twenty minutes later, we reached the area where a bit of an overhang afforded some shelter for us.

Unbelievably, the snow was more than two metres deep in places that high up on the mountain, even though this was in July – the hottest month of the year in Iraq. Normally, the temperature ranges between 40-50 degrees centigrade in the middle and the southern part of Iraq. On this mountain, it was well below zero; perhaps as low as minus 15 to minus 20 degrees.

Our guide began to clear the upper layers of snow and gave us a handful each to quench our thirst. We were shivering in the freezing cold, so we had to dismount and put on our heavy coats. The guide then motioned for us to continue our journey on foot, because the animals were struggling to get through the deep snowdrifts. So, we walked for some time until it became safe enough for us to remount our horses.

With the guide urging us on, we realised that being immobile on that part of the mountain for any length of time would have been tantamount to suicide, because we would have frozen to death. Thank heavens, we did not have to climb to the apex of that mountain; instead, we were able to follow a route around the side of it when we were about three-quarters of the way up. Then we started to descend slowly around the side of the mountain, and at a slight decline on this circuitous route.

It was getting very late by this time, and the snow was not quite as deep on this side. We were really thirsty and hungry, but the only thing we could see was snow and more snow, with just a little grass protruding more and more as we looked down from where we were standing.

At this point, the guide indicated that we should sit down at a small outcrop. From one of the saddle bags, he brought out an old pot and scraped away a few inches of ice from the mountain edge before scooping up some cleaner-looking snow which he put into the pot to make tea. He took some wood from the saddle bag and placed it on top of a stone that was jutting up, then managed to start a fire so that he could boil the snow. Once the contents of the pot were hot enough, he made tea for us and rummaged in another pouch to produce some stale bread and cheese. By this stage on our journey, it did not matter how stale it was; we were grateful for anything, and greedily drank the tea and ate the bread and cheese.

Having finished our rations, we looked around at our surroundings. What a beautiful panorama was spread out before our eyes – it was absolutely amazing. Against the white snow and ice, we seemed to be so close to the clouds that I felt I could reach out and touch them. We could also see the trees clinging to the rock face, and the long grass that still occasionally managed to peep out above the snow. I would not have believed it if someone had told me you would find so much snow on the mountains in northern Iraq during the middle of summer. However, here we were, sitting halfway up a mountain, drinking tea made from melted snow and eating stale food, and we both had to admit that we had been unaware of how beautiful our country could be.

If only there was peace in the Middle East, and everyone could live as one with neither threat to man nor beast! Just think of the tourism opportunities there would be; so many people would love to climb these mountains and see the panoramic view set out before them.

We stayed where we were for the rest of that night, huddled together to keep the cold at bay. The next morning, we woke early and continued our descent. Eventually, we arrived at a small place which the guide called 'Jawzah' – in Arabic, which means 'walnut'. I do not really know why this area was called by that name, but can only assume there must have been walnut trees growing nearby in the past.

There were no houses there; instead, there were a few shops and a Peshmerga base, and we soon discovered that this area was basically a rendezvous point for the smugglers crossing from both Iraq and Iran. The most amazing concept was that these smugglers were actually paying taxes to the Peshmerga for the black-market goods they were smuggling across the border.

There was a small bank (a cabin made from sheets of zinc, and attached with wood and a small flat roof) where people were freely able to exchange their money, and in any currency they wanted – Iraqi Dinars, Iranian Tomans, American Dollars, or German Marks. The people who were working there were a mixture of Iraqi Kurds and Iranian Kurds, and they all spoke the three commonest languages used there fluently – Arabic, Kurdish, and Farsi (the Iranian Language). The place was beautiful, with hills on one side, and on the other side a wide river, whose water flowed really fast as it gushed down from the tops of the hills, bringing with it a lot of mud.

As the day wore on, my friend Mudhaffar managed to change some of his Iraqi Dinars to Iranian Tomans. The Peshmerga who crowded around us were friendly people and very generous to us. They all appeared happy to speak to us – except for one man. He seemed to be really upset when he met us. I discovered later that he was suffering from mental health problems and that he continually ranted and raved at everyone, not just us. We heard him on numerous occasions shouting and swearing at God, crying out, 'He is the one who put us in this miserable situation in the first place' and other statements of a similar nature. At one point, he whispered to us that he was a communist, then he opened his jacket and pointed at his chest saying, 'See. I wear a red shirt.'

That evening, we ate a small but proper dinner, sitting on the ground amongst that friendly group of people. After the meal, we were offered the use of a tent and some tatty blankets to use as bedding, having been told that we could safely camp with them there beside the river. As I said earlier, the water flowed so fast in that river and it was unbelievably muddy as it brought all the debris in its wake as it flowed down from the tops of the mountains. These treacherous waters were carrying with them small boulders and branches from the trees that grew on the banks of the river.

We spent another night there on that small clearing in the mountain range, and the only thing heard all night was the thundering of the water as it flowed past where we were trying to sleep. I must admit, though, when we woke up in the morning, the weather was beautiful and the sun was already shining high in the sky. In fact, the weather was so nice that it felt as if Allah was looking down upon us with kindness at long last. Waking up to that clement weather certainly helped us to gain a better perspective of all that we had seen and done over the past few days.

We remained close to the tent until we heard the leader of the Peshmerga shouting and gesturing for us to come and join them for breakfast. Prior to eating, we did the same as the Peshmerga – we walked over to the river and washed ourselves the best we could in the fast-flowing water. That water was a complete shock to the system, I can tell you; it was absolutely freezing and not half as clean as we had expected water from the mountain to be. In fact, it was so muddy that I felt I was dirtier than I had been in the first place. After performing our ablutions, we went to join the rest of the men for a breakfast of stale bread, yoghurt, and cups of black tea.

After our meal, one of the Peshmerga said he was going to hire two fresh mules for us and therefore needed some of our money so he could exchange it for Iranian Tomans. I told him that I needed to exchange the Iraqi dinars I had into Tomans, and he said he would help get me a good rate of exchange. We went to one of the small huts and the Peshmerga member negotiated a really good rate for me. He insisted at that stage that I should count the money myself before he went off to organise transport for us.

I counted this strange money, and it came to almost two million Toman. I stashed the notes away in the briefcase that I had brought with me, and it felt as though it was jam-packed with money. True to his word, the Peshmerga soldier returned some two hours later and told me that everything was fixed, and fresh mules were ready and waiting for us.

We left Jawzah later that morning, with our guide leading us through deep valleys and quite high mountains until lunchtime when we arrived at our next pre-arranged meeting point, which seemed to be slap-bang in the middle of nowhere. We were very surprised to find a few shops selling simple, albeit essential, items for travellers passing through that region.

Mudhaffar bought some biscuits while our guide started collecting a few dead tree branches and dry weeds to get a fire going. He plucked an old metal teapot from his bag and filled it with some water and tea leaves that he had also been carrying with him in the bag. We sat on the grass in the bright afternoon sunshine, sipping sweet black tea and eating biscuits. Indeed, that small snack seemed very tasty, perhaps because it did not consist of hard bread and cheese, or perhaps it was the caffeine in the strong tea that did the trick and put us in a relaxed mood.

Having sated our appetite, we continued on our way atop the mules until we came to yet another steep mountain. At this point in our journey, as so many other times before, we had to dismount from the mules and start climbing, leaving the mules behind us. That climb up the mountain was one of the most arduous tasks we had faced for the past few days. Every so often, I would stop to ask the guide if we were nearly there. It felt as though we would never reach the summit, but the guide kept replying, 'Not too far now, just another few minutes'!

Eventually, after what seemed to be an eternity, he told us that this was the last mountain we would have to climb, and after this we would be riding in cars instead of on animals. We didn't dare believe him at first, but a short time later, he told us to look down.

He said, 'Look. See, this is the jeep over there in that valley. See, look further and you see those people. They are Iranian border guards and that is the checkpoint.' He then indicated that we were about to start our descent down this other side of the mountain and towards that valley.

This side of the mountain was very difficult to manoeuvre. There were so many small stones and boulders jutting out, and the mountainside terrain was obviously causing difficulty for the horses. They were slipping and sliding over the ground as soon as they stepped onto the small stones.

By this time, I was experiencing many different feelings. To a great extent, I was really happy to see how close we were to the border, but at the same time I was extremely frightened as I didn't know what could possibly lie ahead. Would the border guards allow us to cross? Would we be shot as spies? Would we be taken prisoner? Only Allah knew what fate he had in store for us that evening.

The guide told us that we were coming up to the headquarters of the Peshmerga, and just a short way away from their headquarters were the Iranian border guards. We proceeded cautiously toward the first checkpoint, where we were met by a group of Peshmerga freedom fighters. Surprisingly, they welcomed us heartily and took us to a resting-place where we sat down apprehensively. As it was dinner time, the men had already started preparing their meal and we were invited to sit down with them and have some food. We were astonished to see the amount and choice of food that was being served up – mince kebabs on skewers; roasted onions, tomatoes and peppers; various fruits and yoghurt.

We ate until we felt we would burst, then tea was served. One of the leaders started a long discussion with us regarding the political situation in the north of Iraq and the fate of the Kurdish people. They talked to us as if we were delegates representing Saddam's regime and we were negotiating a settlement for the Kurdish people. Eventually, we managed to assure them that we were not politicians but that we were apolitical, and were running away to Iran for a specific reason that had nothing to do with politics.

By midnight, as everybody was starting to yawn, the discussion came to an end and the Peshmerga leaders decided to call it a day. We were shown to a tent that was only ever used for visitors. Absolutely exhausted, I put my briefcase of money under my head and tried to sleep, but suddenly noticed something rather peculiar. There were absolutely huge spiders crawling around, and bouncing up and down, as if they were on a spring. I didn't even like the smallest of spiders, but these were horrible creatures. I estimated the length of each leg to be in the region of 20 to 25 centimetres. I had never seen anything like them before and have never seen anything like them since, not even in any of the museums or university departments that I have visited since arriving back in Britain.

Our guide was with us in the tent, and he had noticed my apprehension at the sight of these spiders. He told us not to worry, that they were not poisonous and were really quite harmless. His last words to us before he dropped off were to ignore them and go to sleep. As we were utterly exhausted from our travels, we eventually did fall asleep, regardless of the presence of those horrible gigantic spiders.

We woke the next morning to golden rays of sunshine filtering in through the gaps in the tent, as well as a cold breeze coming up from underneath. Thanking God is something we ought to do every time we wake up in such a hostile environment, and we certainly gave our grateful thanks that we survived yet another night. After a very simple breakfast, one of the Peshmerga captains wrote a letter for us indicating our present circumstances, in the belief that nobody would cause us any further problems especially as we were preparing to enter Iran.

That captain was extremely nice to us and declared, 'I am going to personally take you in my own car across the border.' It was an old jeep, but to us it was a luxurious mode of transport and definitely a thousand times better than the donkey, the mule, and the horse combined. We were informed that, as we were to be driven across the border to Iran, the guards at the checkpoint would not intervene or try to stop us; they would think that we were also Peshmerga, so no questions would be asked. The captain also said that he would arrange further transport for us when we reached the first village inside Iran, and thankfully, he kept his promise.

After thanking everybody for their very kind hospitality and all their help, we got into the jeep. The Iranian checkpoint was only 20 to 30 metres away at the most, and we only saw two border guards. They looked tired and were obviously badly malnourished. Their faces were pale and drawn, and they were very thin. As for their clothes, well, you can imagine how bad they looked and smelled, as they had to sit in the heat for so many hours. The bright sunshine had bleached their clothes and fermented their bodies.

The Peshmerga captain drove us through the checkpoint and, as we'd been told, nobody stopped him. Instead, they saluted and greeted him in a friendly manner. It was obvious to me that those security guards must have known him fairly well and he must have been well-liked. He then drove us on through the Iranian border to the boundary of the first Iranian village, where someone was already waiting for us.

Chapter 12

Our first experiences inside Iran

The Peshmerga captain drove us onwards into Iran, taking us to the next rendezvous point – the boundary of the first village – where yet another guide was already waiting to take us through the next stage of our journey. We were so grateful to the captain and offered him a fairly large sum of money as a gesture of thanks, but he refused this, saying it was his pleasure and that we should just pray for him, for his family, and his beloved Kurdistan. The captain then left us and headed back towards his headquarters.

Our new guide was Kurdish and introduced himself as Kareem. He took us to the house of an Iranian family that he was friendly with, and spoke to the man of the house in what appeared to me to be fluent Farsi. Turning back to us, he explained that our sojourn here was only a temporary measure and that he would be back in a short while. When he left us with the family, we were unsure what was going to happen next, but it transpired that Kareem had only gone to a nearby kebab shop. He soon returned with freshly-cooked mince kebabs, vegetables, and bread for everyone, including the family whose house we were in. We had not realised that it was so close to lunchtime and the family did not have any food prepared; they certainly did not have enough food for us as well as themselves.

Once we had eaten our share of the food, the lady of the house brought through a pot of tea and some istikans so that we could all have a few cups of strong, hot, black tea. Because we had drank so much liquid, I had to answer the call of nature, so I asked generally where the toilet was. The couple's little daughter understood some Arabic and informed me that there were no toilets in the house, but that they used a communal toilet in the village. She gestured for me to follow her and she would show me to the toilet. I was absolutely astonished to find that it was in the middle of the street. The building consisted of a small cubicle with three brick walls and a curtain where you would normally have expected the door to be. The actual toilet itself was only a hole in the ground, with no running water anywhere and definitely no toilet paper. Before I entered the cubicle, the girl handed me a jug of water to wash myself after using the toilet, which was absolutely filthy anyway. I was so embarrassed at this lack of hygienic facilities, but then again, needs must!

After lunch, Kareem again left the house, and when he returned some time later, he brought one of his relatives with him. Kareem's relative told us that he was going to arrange for a car to take us to one of the bigger cities in Iran, but first he needed to see what we had in our suitcases, especially any photos that we may have been carrying with us. He explained that if we were stopped and searched at any point by the Iranian morality guards (the Gasht–e- Erhad), any photos of women, especially if they were not wearing veils or chadors (black clothing covering the woman's head and shoulders), would mean trouble for all of us. We had to show him all the photos we had, and upon seeing a photo of my wife without any head covering, he informed me that the photo had to be ripped up and disposed of.

I could not argue with him, because he obviously knew how strict the morality guards were, so I tore the photo into tiny pieces. He also looked through the books we were carrying. I was carrying a book containing the names of the students who had graduated under my tutelage, but because the book contained a photo of Saddam Hussein in the fly cover, he ripped that page out, also saying that it would cause trouble for us.

When night fell, Kareem told us that we should leave this house as it was far too risky for everyone, and because there was not enough room here for strangers to sleep. Perhaps it was also a matter of honour for the family as, when all was said and done, they were living in a very small village amongst tribal people.

We followed him to a small store where sacks of flour were kept. There was a storm lantern in the middle of the room which Kareem lit. His relative came in a short while later with a number of containers of soup and a pile of Iranian bread. A short while later, some more Kurdish people arrived. After we had all eaten some of this vegetable soup and bread, we were told to spread some of the empty sacks on the ground and try to make ourselves as comfortable as possible. When the other Kurdish people also took a few sacks and spread them on the ground, we realised that they would be sleeping in the room with us that night. We took a few more empty sacks to use as covers, to try to keep ourselves a bit warmer during the night, but you can imagine what we looked like when we woke up the following morning. We were covered from top to toe in the remains of the flour dust from the sacks!

Early that morning, Kareem came to the store with Reza, another friend of his. Although Reza was Kurdish, he spoke very good Arabic and informed us that he was going to take us to another town not too far away from where we were at present. He explained that this town was closer to the Iranian capital of Teheran, which is where we wanted to be. We hoped that our situation would be better and a little less precarious in this new town we were moving to.

Our journey began with a ride in an old car that seemed to generate more noise than it did speed. That said, when it was going downhill, it went very, very fast, but it was incredibly slow on the straight or even going up the slightest slope.

We passed through many checkpoints on the way from that small village to our destination, but all of the soldiers on the checkpoints just waved us through, except at one. At this particular checkpoint, there were only two guards, both of whom were wearing strips of green cloth on their foreheads with the slogan 'Ya Hussein' written on them. We recognised these slogans, as these words were often worn on the clothes of pilgrims visiting Karbala and other holy shrines, who were there praying to Imam Hussein, asking him to give them mercy and forgiveness.

These two guards stopped our car and ordered us all to get out, before thoroughly searching us and our belongings. Amongst the things we were carrying were two items they were not happy about. In one of my bags, I had a graduation photo which included some female Kurdish students of mine, who had their heads uncovered. I had also at some point bought a tin of corned beef and forgotten all about it.

We were ordered to accompany the two guards to their commanding officer. We managed to convince the commanding officer that the tin contained food, namely cooked corned beef, and that it was not a bomb or any other form of explosive. I also explained that the photo was one that I had asked to be taken for me with the last group of my students who had just graduated from the University of Salahaddin. It was something for me to remember them by, and also to prove that I had taught these students; nothing more, and nothing less than that.

The commanding officer took the can of corned beef from us and then gave us permission to go. Reza was visibly shaken by this experience, but composed himself enough to get into the car and continue to drive us towards our destination.

He drove on in silence until we came to a small town. The townsfolk here appeared to be very poor, and it was obvious that the area had been neglected for quite some time. This may have been because any governmental grants for the upkeep of the town were not filtering down to them, or due to the economic constraints caused by the massive expenditure on the huge war budget caused by the Iraq/Iran war that was still raging. Whatever the reason, it was obvious that this small town was more like a very under-developed village with almost no amenities to its name.

We asked Reza to take us to a public bath because we had not had a bath for two whole weeks, nor had we managed to change our clothes during that time. Between that and the heat, and we were still covered in flour and dust from the floor of the store, we felt that we were starting to become really rife. The flour residue had become damp due to the effects of our perspiration, and I can only imagine that we were becoming like fermented wheat left for bacteria to grow on it.

Reza agreed that we both needed to freshen up, so he took us to a public bath not far from where a friend of his stayed. I must admit the public bath was a lot better than I had envisaged, although there were no baths at all – only showers. We were so desperate to have a thorough wash and get fresh clothes on to get rid of the smell, if nothing else!

That hot shower was absolutely fantastic and so refreshing! We even shaved for the first time in a couple of weeks. Gosh, it felt fantastic to be clean again. We put on short-sleeved shirts and ties as if we were in Europe.

When we went back outside, we asked Reza if he could dispose of our dirty clothes as there were no rubbish bins in the vicinity. But he was totally taken aback. 'No!' he cried. 'There are many poor people who would be so grateful to take them; once washed, they will be as good as new, as far as they are concerned.'

Then he looked at us and not the dirty clothes we were carrying. He opened his mouth to say something, then stopped, as if he wanted to say something but was too embarrassed. He eventually plucked up the courage to warn us, 'You must take those ties off immediately! It is against the law to wear ties in Iran, as it is anti-Islamic!' He also admonished us for shaving, which was also not allowed in Iran.

When I asked him why it was wrong and anti-Islamic to wear ties, Reza responded, 'Don't you know that the tie represents the cross? And since this is an Islamic country, we should not have anything to do with Christianity, and we must not wear anything that represents it.'

We took our ties off immediately, and kept them hidden in our cases from then on.

Reza told us he would take us to a friend of his who had a better car, and would persuade his friend to take us to another, slightly bigger, town where there was a Peshmerga office. He hoped they would be able to assist us more there.

True to his word, Reza took us to his friend, whom he introduced as Jawad. After a short discussion, Jawad agreed to drive us to the next town. We told him we were very hungry and wanted to find something to eat first, so we bought some biscuits and watermelon and ate them while Jawad busied himself preparing his car for the journey. He seemed to be a very nice person, but his command of the Arabic language left a lot to be desired, so he did not talk much. Or perhaps he was very shy or embarrassed in case he made too many grammatical errors – who knows? We didn't really care as long as somebody spoke to us and explained where we were going and what we should do when we got there.

Jawad managed to explain that when we got to the next town, we should be able to arrange a meeting with one of the Peshmerga leaders. I had not realised that there were so many Peshmerga in Iran – I thought they were all based inside Iraq, or on the border between Iraq and Iran!

He said that he personally knew Kaka Ali, another Peshmerga leader, who was known to be a good man and had a reputation for helping those in need. Jawad was positive this man would help us as much as he could.

A few hours later, we arrived in the town. Unfortunately, although Jawad said he knew this Peshmerga leader personally, he did not know the man's address or where his office was. So, he stopped some people in one of the streets and asked if they knew Kaka Ali, the Peshmerga leader. Thankfully, these people all knew where he lived, and we were given the directions to his house.

When we arrived at the house, we waited while Jawad talked to Kaka Ali and explained what Reza had told him about us and our current situation. Kaka Ali told us to wait for him and he would be back out to speak to us in a few minutes. When he came back outside, he said he would take us to a hotel.

We walked a short distance from his house, and on the way Kaka Ali informed us that we were going to a hotel that was for refugees. He said he would help us as much as he could and that, for the time being, our food and accommodation at the hotel would be free. We could not believe that this stranger was being so kind to us. This meant that two different Kaka Alis were kind, generous Peshmerga leaders. Ali is a common name, so it was not in the least surprising to have two men named the same and in such important positions in the Peshmerga. This Kaka Ali was small in stature, slightly built, and had a good command of the Arabic language as well as Kurdish, his mother tongue.

When we arrived at the building, we discovered that it was actually a hostel that was built on three levels, with each level containing either five or six rooms. On the ground floor, there was a dining room and a reception area. The receptionist informed us about the mealtimes and a few ground rules before taking us to a room on the third floor. The room was sparsely furnished but it contained two single beds, one narrow wardrobe, and a set of drawers. On each floor, there was a shared bathroom with a shower.

Breakfast was at 6.30 every morning, and consisted of fried eggs and Kurdish bread. Lunch was from 12 noon to 1pm, and every day it was a typical dish of murgha and rice, with some thin bread and salad. Dinner was served from 6.30 to 7.30pm, and was usually either roast chicken or roast lamb, with boiled potatoes and massive amounts of salad. We were really grateful to be served this ample food on a daily basis, and after each meal we would thank Allah and ask him to look mercifully on unlucky refugees, the Peshmerga, and the people smugglers, who would only have some stale bread and cheese or par-boiled vegetables pulled up from the fields on their journeys.

The morning after we arrived at the hostel, we asked a few boarders we met at breakfast whether there was a telephone in the house or some other means of phoning abroad. We were informed that there was a telegram office five minutes' walk from the hostel. We followed their excellent directions, and when we got there we sent telegrams to our respective wives. We subsequently found out that my wife received her telegram but Mudhaffar's wife did not receive hers. In the telegrams, we informed our wives that we had safely reached Iran, and we asked them to get in touch with their MPs or anyone else they could think of who might be able to help us to get back safely to the UK.

On our third evening at the hostel, Kaka Ali came to visit us and brought a letter for each of us from someone in authority giving us permission to travel freely in the town for the next four weeks. This piece of paper was basically like a get-out-of-jail-free ticket if we were to be stopped by any of the security forces or the morality police. However, Kaka Ali also informed us that a meeting had been set up for us for the next morning with one of the Iranian Army leaders, and said he would pick us up after breakfast and take us to the Army Barracks.

We were totally unprepared for this piece of news, and pointed out that we could not speak Farsi, so how would we be able to communicate and understand everything that was happening? He told us not to worry, that he would stay with us during the interviews, and he would be our spokesman and translate everything on our behalf. We stayed up most of the night rehearsing what we might have to say and what kind of questions we might be asked.

Soon after breakfast the next morning, Kaka Ali came to the hotel to drive us to an Army Training Barracks. He reassured us that he would do his best to help us during the interviews. Following a short journey, we arrived at what looked more like a prison than an army barracks. The gate to the compound was absolutely enormous, and within that gate there was another, smaller one, which had a bell. Kaka Ali rang the bell and we waited for somebody to answer.

After less than five minutes, a guard opened the smaller door a fraction, just enough to see who was outside. Kaka Ali spoke to the guard in Farsi and the door was closed again, then we waited anxiously. After ten interminable minutes, the same guard returned and allowed us entry. He was a middle-aged man, who looked very tired. His eyes were sunken into his head and his long, straggly beard and unkempt moustache did not help to make him look any younger.

As we walked a short distance to the main barracks building, we could see soldiers being drilled in the yard. They were running up and down in formation, and shouting something in Farsi that I could not understand.

When the guard took us to the officer's room, the man was already standing waiting for us. He shook our hands but there was no hint of warmth in his handshake; indeed, he looked to me as if he had suffered a hard life and had become cynical about everything. He immediately launched a volley of questions, one after the other with no hesitation, about the Iraqi regime, the Iraqi army, the situation amongst the ordinary citizens of Iraq, etc. etc.

We explained that we had no interest whatsoever in politics or the political situation in Iraq, and that we had escaped from Iraq because we did not want any involvement in politics. We explained that we were just lecturers who wanted to use our degrees to educate people, and nothing else. He asked the same questions over and over again, and eventually, when he was satisfied that our stories had not changed one little bit, he brought the questioning to a close. He then asked us for photos of ourselves, which we handed over to him. Thankfully, we had been pre-warned that we may need to provide a number of photos of ourselves to various people, so we had come prepared with plenty.

When my wife Carol first arrived in Karbala, she complained about the number of photos she had to have taken for all the various forms and departments in the Maktab Al Eqama. They requested photos for so many documents, and Carol even had to go to one of the hospitals for an x-ray to prove that she did not have TB, and blood taken to check that she did not have cholera or any other infectious diseases. My niece, Iman, who worked in a medical clinic, drew the bloods for those tests. At least that way we knew the needles were new and unused, because medical equipment, like everything else in Iraq at that time, was in short supply due to the sanctions caused by the Iran-Iraq war.

The Iranian officer took the photos and then left the room, telling us to remain where we were. Fifteen minutes later, he returned to the office, sat down at his desk and opened the folder he was carrying. He brought out two documents which gave us permission to leave the town we were in, and to travel to the capital, Tehran. We thanked him profusely and left his office in a lighter mood.

Kaka Ali drove us back to the hostel and waited for us while we collected our belongings, then he dropped us off at the bus station. Even he was surprised at how quickly we had been given this travel document; he told us that it usually took weeks to be processed.

It was lunchtime by the time we got to the bus station, so we went into a small café and had a light snack, then bought one-way tickets to Tehran. We were told that we would have to wait until early evening for the next bus going east to the capital; it would travel overnight and arrive in Tehran early the following morning.

We waited patiently and, just as the sun was setting, the bus pulled into the station. Within ten minutes of its arrival, the bus departed, with us sitting in two seats slap-bang in the middle of the coach to try to blend in with the other passengers. The journey was very long and there were checkpoints in every town and village we passed through. However, we were not stopped or questioned at any of the checkpoints, because we were indistinguishable from any of the Iranians; we had not shaved since the day we were told off by Reza for being clean-shaven.

Halfway through the journey, in the middle of the night, the bus stopped at a roadside restaurant and most of the passengers got off to get something to eat, or just to have a cup of tea. As Mudhaffar and I had not eaten much that day, we decided to have a meal there. We ordered kebab, rice, and salad, followed by an istikan of tea, but had to eat the food pretty quickly so that we would not be left behind when the bus departed.

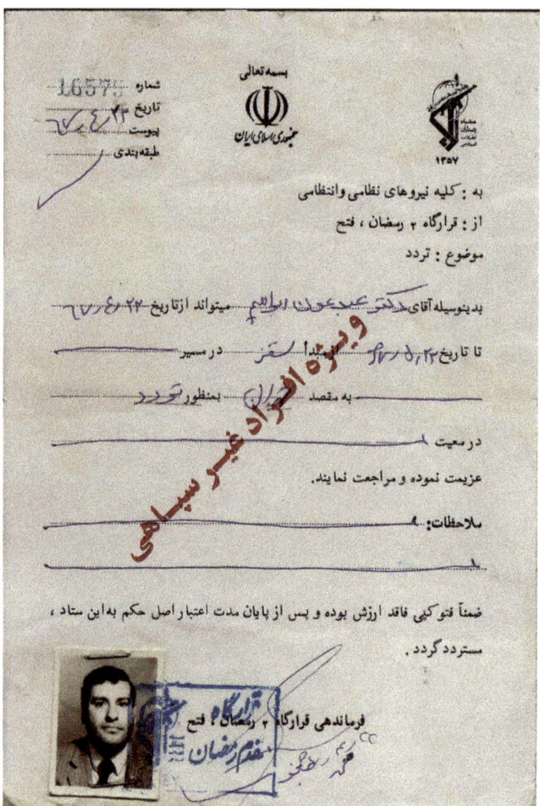

بسمه تعالی

جمهوری اسلامی ایران

۱۳۵۷

شماره 16575

تاریخ

پیوست

طبقه‌بندی

به : کلیه نیروهای نظامی وانتظامی

از : قرارگاه ۲ رمضان ، فتح

موضوع : تردد

بدینوسیله آقای .... میتواند ازتاریخ ....

تا تاریخ .... از مبدا .... در مسیر ....

به مقصد .... بمنظور ....

در معیت ....

عزیمت نموده و مراجعت نمایند.

ملاحظات: ....

ویژه افراد غیر سپاهی

ضمناً فتوکپی فاقد ارزش بوده و پس از پایان مدت اعتبار اصل حکم به‌این ستاد ، مسترد گردد .

فرماندهی قرارگاه ۲ رمضان ، فتح

قرارگاه مقدم رمضان

The document I was given by the army officer. It was issued on Wednesday, 13th July, 1988. (22/4/1367 in the Iranian Calendar). The only words I could translate roughly meant 'This document gives permission for the holder to be in Iran as long as he is unarmed'!

Chapter 13

Our Arrival in Tehran

We finally arrived in Tehran at 6am on Thursday, 14th July, 1988. This date was the anniversary of the 14 July 1958 Iraqi revolution which resulted in the Hashemite monarchy being overthrown and the Hashemite Kingdom of Iraq being renamed the Republic of Iraq. Therefore, back in Iraq, this day would have been a national holiday; however, that morning, we did not know what fate would have in store for us.

As the bus arrived in Tehran, the sun was just above the horizon and all the signs were that this would be yet another hot day. The bus depot was extremely busy even at that time of the morning, and there were people shouting loudly in all directions, trying to attract the attention of the busy travellers. The whole area was so crowded with people and their wares that we could not figure out where any of the exits were, never mind where the nearest one to us was. There were so many bodies crowded into each square metre of space!

Allah must have been on our side, though, as a young pale-faced lad, wearing a black collarless shirt and black trousers, approached us. Very dead-pan, he spoke to us rapidly in Farsi, but unfortunately I did not understand one single word of what he said. He stood looking at us expectantly, waiting on our response, but of course neither of us could reply to him.

Using the broken Farsi I had learned from my childhood friends, and hoping that he would understand what I was trying to say, I tried to ask him if he could give us directions to a hotel that was not too far from the city centre but that was not too expensive. Thankfully, he had got the gist of what I had tried to say, and led us out of the bus depot to his car. It was a small vehicle, similar to a jeep, but which we had never seen before, either in Iraq or in the UK. As soon as we were seated, he started the engine and then drove off like a maniac, very fast and with seemingly no sense whatsoever of the Highway Code. Thankfully, once we got away from the bus depot the pedestrians thinned out and the streets became quite empty as it was still too early for most people to be out and about.

After being driven around for ten minutes or so, we arrived in Tehran town centre. The driver had taken us to one of the biggest hotels in the capital and he left us sitting in the car while he went to the hotel reception to ask if they were prepared to accept any foreign visitors. A little while later, he came back to inform us that the receptionist said there were no vacancies.

He then drove us to another hotel, and the answer was the same there. Eventually, he took us to The Howayza – a five-star hotel – where he was told we could rent a room on a nightly basis. Mudhaffar and I were very happy to hear this good news, but at the same time we were very apprehensive about the cost of staying in such a posh hotel even for one night. We were not sure whether we could afford it! I whispered my trepidation to Mudhaffar, saying I was worried that we could not afford to stay there, but his reply was that only time would tell and everything was in the hands of Allah.

When we were shown to our room, we were surprised at how spacious it was; there were two single beds, a big double wardrobe, and a set of drawers. There was also a cubicle with a toilet, sink, and a shower. Although there was no television or fridge, there was what we felt was the most important feature of the room – a central cooling system that worked properly! There was a huge window and beautiful light apricot coloured curtains, which were obviously made from very expensive material, the likes of which we had never seen in Iraq. When we opened the curtains to look at the view, our window was overlooking the main street and, as our room was on the fifth floor, we could see the skyline of the whole city and further afield.

By the time we had settled ourselves into the room, it was only approaching 7am, but we had spent a fairly uncomfortable night on the bus so were both tired. We both lay down on top of our beds to get some rest, and I quickly nodded off to sleep.

Around ninety minutes later, I woke with a start and quickly went over to Mudhaffar's bed and shook him awake. 'We must hurry, I said, 'otherwise we will miss breakfast.' We had been informed by the receptionist that we were welcome to go down for breakfast that morning between 7am and 9am; after that time, the door to the restaurant would be closed, to stop people trying to get in whilst the breakfast remains were being cleared away.

Without taking the time to wash our faces, we hurried from the room and located the lift to take us to the dining room on the first floor. We could not believe how nice the dining room was as it was so lavishly decorated and extremely well furnished. When you consider that this country had been at war with Iraq for eight years, it was remarkable to see such splendour; back in Iraq, things were very different. In Iraq, we only had electricity for a few hours a day and it was difficult to buy anything at all, never mind buy nice things for the house or for the hotels.

The dining room itself was not very big; accommodating at most seven tables that each had ample room for six guests to sit around. There were quite a few people working in the restaurant and the staff were very considerate and helpful to us both. They took the time to explain to us what each dish consisted of and what the guests usually preferred to eat. As we were still unsure of the food, we both opted for fried eggs, croissants, and some Nan Barbari (thick long bread coated with sesame seeds).

After finishing our breakfast, we went to ask the receptionist how we could get to the Office of The High Commission of the Islamic Revolution in Iraq. Whilst this was an organisation that believed in spreading the faith of Islam throughout the world, I had also learnt that, due to the Iraq-Iran war, their primary aim at that time was to topple Saddam's regime, to establish Iraq once again as a 'Pillar of Islam', and to help all Iraqi refugees. We had heard all about this organisation when we were in Iraq, and had been advised that they were our best hope as they were an integral part of some of the most powerful organisations in Iran and other Islamic countries at that time. If anyone could help us to get out of Iran safely then the people in this organisation were the ones who were best placed to help us to do so legally and safely.

The receptionist tried his best to explain to us in English how to get there and he even offered to sell us bus tickets that we could use. We later found out that all the bus fares in Iran were exceptionally cheap, each one costing just a fraction of a penny. However, as we were not familiar with the town, never mind the buses, we were very unsure of travelling alone in a country where we could hardly speak the language; we did not even have a legal entry visa to be there!

The receptionist explained that the Office of The High Commission of the Islamic Revolution in Iraq was not too far from the hotel, and he drew us a map of how to get there. As we followed his directions, we found that his information was really accurate, and we passed the various landmarks on the drawing as we walked along. It was around eleven o'clock in the morning and already very hot. As we were walking fast to try to get there as soon as possible, we soon began to feel uncomfortable due to the heat.

We were desperate to get to that building as soon as possible, not only because we were afraid we would get picked up by the secret police but also because we were desperate to find out if any of the staff members there could assist us to get out of Iran as soon as possible. Unfortunately, we somehow managed to miss one of the turns we should have taken and got ourselves well and truly lost. Asking directions at any time is an embarrassment, but every minute was crucial to us.

After stopping and asking a number of people, we finally found someone who could understand our request for assistance, and we followed his directions to safely arrive at the offices we required. It was an ordinary-looking four-storey building, except for the fact that it was guarded by a uniformed armed guard. Unfortunately, that meant that we now had another dilemma on our hands. We did not know the name of anyone in this organisation, never mind anyone powerful enough to assist us.

To get around that problem, we started shouting random names that came into our heads, like Ali, Hussein, and Abbas, as they are very common Arab names and we had been informed that more Arabs than Iranians worked there. We were aiming our voices towards the windows of the second, third, and fourth floors, hoping that someone would hear us and would look out the window and speak to us.

Suddenly, one of the windows opened and a thin gentleman shouted down to us in clear Arabic, 'What do you want? Why are you making such a noise?'

'We are Iraqis and we desperately need some help,' I replied.

I asked him if he would please come down to speak to us in person so that we could explain to him our situation. Thankfully, the person who shouted down to us was a kind, trusting person. He told us to go back to the front door and wait for him to come down to speak to us. Sure enough, he appeared at the door a few minutes later and told the armed guard that we were his guests.

He escorted us up to his office on the second floor of the building. Once we were inside the office and the door was shut, he introduced himself as Sayed Hamza. There were two other occupants in the office, but he did not introduce them to us.

One was a tall, very thin, blue-eyed, ginger-haired man, who introduced himself to us as Abu Ayad. The other man in the room, who was of medium build with slicked-back, fairly long hair, did not introduce himself by name at this stage. He was very talkative, and I felt as though we could not get a word in edgeways. He talked and talked and talked, especially about politics and the political situation in Iraq.

The other two men called him 'Doctor', but I did not think he was a genuine medical doctor, rather I thought he had most probably graduated with a PhD degree. We eventually found out that he did indeed have a PhD, obtained while studying politics in France, and his thesis was on 'Middle Eastern politics and the ideology of their leaders'. A few weeks after our meeting, we heard that he had taken his own life by wrapping a tie around his neck and tying it to the ceiling fan. We both felt awful when we heard that, because he had turned out to be a nice person to talk to and there was no hint that he suffered from depression or was unhappy with his life.

From that very first meeting with Abu Ayad, he became a friend to both of us and tried his utmost to help us get out of our predicament. We discussed the problem of us being illegally smuggled into Iran as this meant we did not have the proper legal documents that we needed to get out of Iran and back to the UK. We asked him if it was possible to get assistance to obtain a *bona fide* exit visa without having a valid entry visa stamped on our Iraqi passports, and pleaded with him to help us get out of Iran legally and legitimately.

'Unfortunately,' he said, 'in a situation such as this, you need to bribe people left, right, and centre.' He explained that it was not an easy task as we would need to bribe too many people, especially those in high positions, which would be very difficult, especially if you did not know who you were dealing with. However, he personally knew one of the police captains who was in charge of processing exit visas. As a favour, he could get him to do this for both of us, he said, but the cost would be substantial! No new surprises there, then!

Although we both listened to him carefully and thoroughly considered his proposal, we had hoped that there might just be an easier or perhaps a cheaper alternative. However, before we left his office that day, Abu Ayad arranged a meeting for us with the Chief of Staff of the High Commission of the Islamic Revolution in Iraq, Sayed Mohammed, for the following morning.

The next morning, we left the hotel just before nine o'clock and headed back to the office of the High Commission of the Islamic Revolution in Iraq. Mudhaffar and I had discussed and continually rehearsed our sentences and all the possible answers to the questions that we expected to be asked. We had to try to be word-perfect by the time we reached the building.

When we finally arrived there the army guard on sentry duty searched both of us thoroughly. Once he was happy that we were not concealing anything on our persons, he called on another member of staff to escort us to a medium-sized room on the ground floor of the building, just off to the left of a long corridor.

The room was nice and quiet but there were no seats whatsoever; instead, there were long pieces of uncovered foam cushions (so not a proper doshek), just big enough for people to sit down on. There was a large window along one wall, and there was also an old table in the left-hand corner of the room with a number of copies of the Holy Quran on top. We sat cross-legged on these foam cushions, as there was nothing else to do while we were waiting to be seen.

After thirty minutes, we heard someone shouting in the corridor, 'Praise the Lord, Praise the Lord.' Immediately we understood that somebody very important and of high religious status was coming into the building. We looked out the window to see what was going on, and in the driveway there was a white Mercedes car. As a guard opened the door, a gentleman wearing a black turban, grey gown, and a black abaya was getting out of the car.

We were kept waiting in that room for an hour until Abu Ayad popped in to see us. 'I told you I would set up a meeting for you with Sayed Mohammed when we met yesterday,' he said. 'He has just arrived now, so I will explain the protocol you should use when you meet him, because he is a great holy man and he must be respected.' It transpired that this Sayed Mohammed was the man we had seen getting out of the car.

We were told that when introduced to him, the normal protocol was to shake his hand and then kiss it. We should not call him by either his first name or his family name, but instead, we had to use the term 'Sayeedna' (which translated means 'our master'). We were also informed that, if at any point his assistant flicked his hand at us, it meant that the conversation was finished and we should shake Sayed Mohammed's hand once more and then immediately leave the room without any further ado.

We were eventually taken to meet Sayed Mohammed, who was a handsome man with a long, salt and pepper coloured beard and moustache, and a little grey hair showing through his turban. He turned out to be a very pleasant person to talk to, and we hoped and prayed that he would also be helpful to us.

He opened the conversation by asking, 'How was your trip?' And before we could utter a word, he continued, 'I know it must have been very difficult, as we have met many people who managed to escape from Iraq by crossing the border into Iran; they told us all the horrible stories about the hazards and perils they encountered throughout their arduous journeys.' He then continued to ask many questions about our journey and things that came to pass during our long trek. Eventually, he came to the crux of the matter by asking us, 'How can we help you and what are you intending to do now?'

Sayed Mohammed stopped speaking and tilted his head, waiting for our responses. We explained to His Holiness that we both wanted to leave Iran as soon as possible so that we could find our way back to the UK to our wives and families. We explained that we had been smuggled into Iran and therefore did not have an entry visa stamped on our passports; we wanted to leave Iran, but to do so we both required exit visas and did not know how that could be achieved. We were therefore asking him if there was any way on earth that he could help us, or at least give us an idea of how we could get an exit visa stamped on our passports and how we could proceed from there.

On hearing this, he turned to one of the two aides with him and told him to type up letters for us to take to the Iranian Home Office asking if they could possibly issue both of us with an exit visa for as soon as possible. As we began to thank him profusely, the second aide gestured to us that it was time to leave; we had obviously taken up enough of Sayed Mohammed's time. We shook hands with Sayed Mohammed once more and hurriedly left the room.

When we exited the room, Abu Ayad was already waiting for us. He took us back to the room we had been in previously and told us to sit there while the letters were typed up for us.

We had been sitting there waiting patiently for twenty minutes or so when I thought I heard a very familiar voice, but for the life of me, I could not remember whose voice it was. Suddenly, a tall man with receding hair put his head around the door of the room to see if it was free.

'Hassan? Is that really you, Hassan?' I asked.

The man came into the room and I was so surprised to find that it was, indeed, an old friend of mine from Erbil.

'Oh my gosh!' I said. 'It is so good to see you here! I never, ever, thought I would find someone that I helped to escape from Iraq here. Why are you still here, and what are you doing with yourself?' I asked him.

Hassan was the middle child of three siblings. His older brother, Mahdy, had lived in Iran for many years, ever since he'd had to flee Iraq because of his affiliation with a political party that opposed the ruling Ba'ath Party led by Saddam Hussein at that time. Both Hassan and his younger brother, Ali, who were both veterinary surgeons, had also had to leave the country – not because of their political affiliations, nor because they were against the government, but because of their brother. The Iraqi Government had passed a death sentence *in absentia* on their brother Mahdy, and because of this, the Iraqi regime decreed that all his family should be punished as well, because they had not informed the government about his political activities.

We had known a really lovely family in Karbala whose young son went absent without leave from the Iraqi army, and because he was not caught (and shot dead as punishment), all the family were punished instead. Those of his relatives who were in employment were sacked from their jobs; the older unmarried sister was forbidden to get married; and the family lost their own business and were left almost destitute because of the way they were treated. All because they were related to the youth who had gone AWOL from the Iraqi army.

It was normal at that time for the Iraqi Government to treat all relatives of any 'dissidents' in this manner. My friend, Abu Whisham, who drove me to my house on the day I was to go to Dibis, was the cousin of these three men. He helped me that day because it was he who approached me to ask for help when the family heard about the proclamation of the death sentence on Mahdy. I, in turn, had enlisted the help of one of my students, Kaka Farhad, to negotiate with the smugglers to help Ali and Hassan to escape from Iraq.

Hassan sat with Mudhaffar and I and we talked for hours about so many things. We began by discussing his journey across the mountains when he fled from Iraq to Iran. We wanted to know if he had faced the same problems we had experienced, and whether he was passed from one smuggler to another during the different stages of his journey with his brother. Hassan comforted us by saying, 'We are all safe now, and the imam (Sayed Mohammed) is a very good person who will do all he can to facilitate your onward travel to Britain.'

Hassan informed us that he had already typed up letters for us to the Iranian Home Office Minister, asking him to look kindly on us and to issue exit visas so that we could both leave Iran legally. He said he still had to give the letters back to Sayed Mohammed for his signature, then all we had to do would be to get an appointment with the Home Office Minister and, hopefully, one of their staff members would be given permission to stamp our passports with an official exit visa.

We waited until the late afternoon before we received the signed letters, but we were both ecstatic when they were handed over. We thanked everybody concerned and thought that we were finished and that was the end of it. We were obviously so wrong!

Another official from the High Commission of the Islamic Revolution in Iraq came to the room we were sitting in and asked us politely if we would go with him for 'a little discussion' before we left the building. I thought this was rather odd, and wondered why this person wanted to discuss anything with us when we had already spoken to officials for two days running. Anyway, we dutifully followed him from that room, out of the building and into another one.

This was only a two storey-building, with balconies on the second floor, and it was hidden from view because of the main building. We were taken to a room on the second floor and the official gestured for us to enter. 'Al-salamu alaykum (peace upon you),' I said, on entering the room. The standard reply of 'wa alaykumu al-salam (and peace be upon you, too)' was uttered. A middle-aged man wearing a white turban and cloaked in a very thin abaya was sitting on an old chair. As he was wearing a white turban, we called him 'Mullah.'

He put his hand out and we both took turns to shake his hand. He politely welcomed us to his small office and asked us to sit on the carpet facing him. A young gentleman came into the room and sat down on a chair beside the Mullah, as if he was a secretary preparing to take the minutes of an important meeting. The Mullah started by asking us our names, our dates of birth, and so on and so forth, until he came to questions about the price of vegetables and meat in the Iraqi markets. Then he went on to the political questions.

'We are not politicians,' I said, 'so why all these questions?'

He answered, 'These questions are just for the record. We like to monitor the economic situation in Iraq and its impact on the people of Iraq.'

Then he asked us if we had any proof of identity on us and any documents to prove that we both had university degrees. Thankfully, we both had copies of our university degrees and other certificates, as well as our passports, so we handed them over for him to scrutinise. The young gentleman took them from us and explained that they would be photocopied and returned to us. He left the office and came back with our documents a few minutes later.

As soon as the documents were returned to us, the Mullah stood up and thanked us. He assured us that the information we had given them and the copies of our documents would be kept in a safe and secure place.

When we got out of that building, Hassan was waiting for us. He told us it was well past lunchtime and he wanted to invite us to his home for a very late lunch. However, as his house was quite far away and there would be no time to cook a proper meal, he would take us to a nearby restaurant instead. We agreed, and after walking for around fifteen minutes in the soaring heat, we arrived at a fairly big restaurant.

Hassan told us that there were two floors to this restaurant, but it was obvious that the ground floor was very busy with diners, and there did not seem to be any spare tables. He therefore led us down a set of stairs to the basement. This section of the restaurant was not quite as busy as upstairs, and not as hot either, as there were ceiling fans that were all set to the highest speed. We only had to wait five minutes until a table in the middle of the dining room was vacated by diners and we were gestured to sit down. After a further five minutes, the waiter came over to take our order.

Hassan ordered for the three of us, stating that we would all have Chelow Kebab. He explained that Chelow Kebab was simply minced lamb wrapped around a skewer and then cooked over red hot charcoal. Once cooked, the meat was buried under a bed of plain boiled rice with a side of baked tomatoes.

'That is it?' I queried. 'Is there anything else to go with it?'

Hassan replied that there would also be a jug of ice-cold water.

Once the meal was served, we quickly made short work of it. Hassan explained that this was the most famous traditional meal served throughout Iran and, I have to say, it really was delicious. We thanked him profusely when he insisted on paying.

Afterwards, Hassan walked with us back to the hotel we were staying at. He insisted that he would come to the hotel to meet us the following day so that he could take us to the Home Office. As it was quite far away, he would take us to his brother's workplace, and he assured us that his brother would be more than happy to give us a lift there.

The following morning, a Tuesday, we sat in the reception area from around eight o'clock waiting for Hassan to come and collect us. He eventually showed up at nine o'clock and said that we would have to leave immediately. He explained that Mahdy worked as an engineer in an electricity company not too far from where we were staying.

When we eventually met Mahdy outside his office, he gave us a cool welcome and told us we would have to wait until he finished what he was doing.

'I will give you a lift there but then I will have to leave you, as I have to get back to work,' he said. 'You will have to find your own way back by yourself, as I am not going to go inside the Home Office Building with you; I just do not have the time for this,' he muttered. The expression on his face made it obvious that he did not want to get involved with us and our problems.

Eventually Mahdy brought his car around and picked us up. He dropped Hassan off near to the building housing the High Commission of the Islamic Revolution in Iraq, before driving us to the Iranian Home Office a further twenty minutes away. As he approached the road leading to the building, he pointed it out and said, 'That is the Home Office up ahead. I wish you luck.' As soon as we got out of the car, he sped off, leaving us standing in bewilderment in the middle of the road.

We immediately headed toward the main entrance where a few guards were sitting in a small security cubicle just outside the entrance to the building. After giving them the usual 'Al-salamu alaykum' greeting, I asked if it was at all possible for us to see an officer who could help us with our case.

One of the guards drew us a dirty look and then said in a condescending manner, 'Tell your friend to go and wear a proper shirt!'

I looked at Mudhaffar to see what had caused offence to the guard and realised that he was wearing a shirt with short sleeves instead of full, long sleeves. I had forgotten that we had been warned that the Iranians believe wearing short-sleeved shirts is a violation of the Islamic law. There was no such ideology in Iraq, where men could wear almost anything they wanted, including wearing ties, shaving their beards and moustaches, or even shaving their heads if they were so inclined. It was only women who were not allowed to show any bare flesh when outside in the street.

However, in Iran, there were actually morality police who checked what people were wearing, and they had the power to arrest people for not being properly dressed. Of course, in reality there is no such thing in Islam where men are banned from wearing short-sleeved shirts, and I have no idea where they got this law from as there is nothing in the Koran about that.

We went looking for the nearest tailor's shop so that we could purchase a new, long-sleeved shirt for Mudhaffar to wear, and thankfully, we found a small clothing retailer just a short walk away, and Mudhaffar bought a suitable, plain, long-sleeved shirt and immediately put it on.

We returned to the Iranian Home Office and again spoke to the security guards in the small cubicle, asking if we could now see someone in charge. However, we were then ordered to bring photocopies of all our documents and identification papers. That meant another trip back in the direction we had come from, to try to find a shop with photocopying facilities. We were lucky that we managed to find a small kiosk which had a fax and a photocopier, and for a small sum of money, we managed to get photocopies of all our documents.

We went back to the Iranian Home Office for a third time. On this occasion, after a very thorough body search, the guards finally allowed us to enter the main building. When we got inside, there did not appear to be anybody in charge and things were totally chaotic. People were sitting around looking dejected, others were making their way out of the building with unhappy expressions, and others were moving slowly from one room to another.

We had a quick look into some of the rooms where the doors were ajar. In at least two offices we saw women working away behind desks while they had their babies beside them in prams. Apparently, the Iranian government had pronounced a law that allowed women to take their babies with them to their work place so that they could still do their jobs without having to arrange for childminders!

While we were wandering around trying to find the correct office, or at least find someone who could direct us to the correct office, we met a couple of Arabic-speaking men who were also trying to get exit visas approved. From the discussion we had with them, it soon became clear that they had been trying for months to get an exit visa but to no avail – even though they had the same letters of recommendation from The High Commission of the Islamic Revolution in Iraq. That made us realise that what we were doing was not going to lead us anywhere fast, so we would have to find an alternative solution to get us out of Iran as soon as humanly possible.

Chapter 14

Abu Ahmad and Abu Ayad

A few nights later, we were sitting in the hotel dining room speaking about various matters. Our conversation was mostly about what our next course of action should be if it was not feasible to get help from the chaotic Iranian Home Office. It soon became apparent to me that someone was covertly watching us and seemed to be straining hard to overhear our conversation even though we were speaking in our native Arabic language.

After about ten minutes, the man eventually approached our table and asked us – in a different Arabic dialect from ours – if he could sit down at our table and speak to us. Although we were both very wary, we moved one of the chairs so that he could sit beside us.

'Are you both of Iraqi origin?' the man asked very slowly but politely.

'Why do you want to know where we are from? Who are you?' I replied very warily, knowing that it must be obvious from our speech that we were Iraqis.

I felt that it would only be spies or Iranian government officials who would be interested in listening to our conversation, because most of the indigenous population had enough problems of their own without wanting to get involved in other people's problems.

Without further hesitation, the man stood up and introduced himself as Abu Ahmad. He said he was from Ahwaz in the south west of Iran. He seemed to be in his late twenties or early thirties at the most, was not very tall but was a bit overweight. He did not have the demeanour of an intelligence officer or anything sinister like that, but we could not be too careful, especially as we were now in the country illegally.

Abu Ahmad was very smartly dressed and wore a black shirt under a black suit that was so well cut that it was obviously very expensive. He had smooth black hair that was slicked back over to one side and was obviously looked after by a professional hairstylist rather than being cut by a family member or small local barber, which was the normal custom in both Iraq and Iran as wages were very low and money was scarce. Due to his demeanour and the cut of his clothes and hair, he had the appearance of a wealthy businessman. Both Mudhaffar and I had the impression that he was a genuine person, and not from either the Iranian or the Iraqi intelligence service. So, we decided to trust him, to a certain extent, and began to converse with him.

Following our initially stilted conversation, we spent a relaxed evening in Abu Ahmad's company. He explained that he was a successful businessman involved in the manufacture and sale of fire extinguishers. He was a very amiable person and we relaxed in his company as he regaled us with stories of his travels up and down Iran touting for business. We sat together for hours that night talking about many subjects, and eventually the topic got around to the Iraq-Iran war, its implications on the economy of both countries, and the effects it was having on the ordinary people.

After that very first meeting, we met up with Abu Ahmad in the hotel dining room every night and talked at length about everyone's exploits that day and how much progress (or rather, lack of progress) we had made that day. Every night, Abu Ahmad insisted on picking up the tab for that evening's food and drink, and every night I would ask him why he was so interested in what happened to us and why he insisted on paying for our meal each night.

Every night, he would give us the same answer: 'Thank heavens I am in a far better situation than you are in, in your present predicament. I am a very successful businessman and I thank my God that He has given me more than enough to make life easy for my family and me. I can honestly tell you that I am a millionaire and the cost of a few meals is nothing to me, but the price of that food is far more important to you. I feel that, in different circumstances, we could have been really good friends and I would do anything in my power to help my friends; so, what is the cost of a few meals amongst good friends? It is nothing to me, so please do not mention it again and do not worry about it!'

A few nights later, our new ginger-haired friend, Abu Ayad from the Office of The High Commission of the Islamic Revolution in Iraq, came to the hotel to pay us a visit.

'I have good news for you,' he said with a big smile on his face.

He must have made some progress, I thought.

'I have managed to find someone in the Foreign Office who is willing to help you. He is one of those in charge of issuing exit visas to foreign nationals in Iran,' he said.

'What do we have to do to get his help, especially given our present circumstances?' I asked.

Abu Ayad looked at both of us and replied, 'You have to buy him a nice gift; something not too big, but something expensive.' He made a big circle in the air with his hands, at the same time opening his eyes wide to further emphasise the point he was making. Then he added, 'You have to buy him something that he would consider to be worth his while, in case of any comeback.'

Following this statement, we wracked our brains to think of a suitable 'gift' that would be really impressive, and something that an Iranian Government official on the take would accept. As Abu Ayad said, it would have to be something expensive but not too big, so that it would not arouse anyone's suspicions. We had to think hard about what someone of high status would like to buy but could not afford. Something nice that he and his family would really appreciate... but not just anything. It had to be something that would be seen as being worthy of taking a big risk for. In other words, something that he would feel was so worth it that he would not renege on the agreement because he was not satisfied with the 'gift'.

The following day, Abu Ayad took us around Tehran to do some window shopping, especially at the stores that were only frequented by the very rich and elite of this society. We eventually arrived at a shop which he informed us was reputed to sell the best china and crystal ornaments and dinner services in Teheran.

'Well. What do you think? Should we go in and have a look?' Abu Ayad asked.

'I suppose there is no harm in looking, is there?' I commented.

Inside, there were so many beautiful items for sale, and it soon became pretty obvious that everything had a very high price tag to boot! There were stunning crystal chandeliers, gold inlaid vases, full dinner services and tea services, and so many fantastic items all over the shop. Mudhaffar and I were overawed at such expensive merchandise, especially as we had nothing like this back home in Iraq due to the current war situation. In fact, my wife often complained that the Orosdi-back – the biggest department store in Karbala at that time – had nice children's clothes and household items in the windows and on display, but every time you tried to buy something nice you were told it was 'L'il Urth Faquat' (just for show) and that none of these items were available to buy at that stage – or indeed, at any later stage. We had expected that life would be the same in Iran and that everyone would be suffering from shortages, as we did in Iraq. I remember that we once found some bananas on sale when we were on a trip to Baghdad, but when we asked the price, we discovered that only one banana was the equivalent of five British pounds. Carol insisted on buying one, which we cut exactly in half; Layla and Ramsay each received half a banana, while Carol and I were rewarded with just the smell of it!

So, we'd thought the Iranian people must be in the same dire situation as we were in due to the war and the subsequent restrictions on goods entering the country, but these luxury items were for sale and not just 'to look at'. How on earth could people afford to buy such luxuries?

In the end, we decided to purchase a full dinner service that had been imported from France. It was obviously one of the best quality items available in the shop, and cost the equivalent of approximately one thousand British pounds. Anyone looking at it would realise just how extremely expensive it was, and would immediately know it was well beyond the reach of the majority of the ordinary people. Before we paid for it, Abu Ayad asked the shopkeeper if this dinner service could be left in the store to be collected later.

The man responded that he would be more than happy to sell it to us and pack it up ready for collection whenever we wanted to pick it up, as long as we had the receipt. He was more than happy with this arrangement!

Abu Ayad informed the storekeeper that we would not collect the dinner service ourselves, but that someone else would come to the shop to pick it up. And he confirmed that this person would hand over the receipt to collect the goods.

'I should give it to anyone who comes to my store with the receipt?' the shopkeeper enquired.

'Anyone!' Abu Ayad answered, as we paid in cash and then left the shop.

The following morning, we went with Abu Ayad to the Department of Foreign Affairs. As we were climbing a flight of narrow stairs, Abu Ayad told us to leave all the talking to him. 'I can convince him,' he said, referring to the officer who would, hopefully, be issuing us with exit visas. 'I am pretty sure he will help you, so try not to worry.'

The corridor we came to was very dull and shabby looking. It appeared to be a dead end, except that there was one narrow door at the very end of the corridor. The door was open and there was one window letting daylight into an office that was stacked full of files and crammed with men chatting to each other in Farsi. Abu Ayad indicated his friend – a very tall, thin man, with short black hair that was combed straight back. He also sported a very neat beard and moustache that looked as though it had recently been professionally trimmed by a competent barber. Obviously, this man took great pride in looking immaculate and being professionally groomed. *Even the three stars on each shoulder were nicely polished,* I thought to myself.

'I hope that this captain will help us,' Mudhaffar whispered quietly.

We stood outside the office for a short while, and all the time Abu Ayad was looking straight at the officer, but he was too busy talking to the others in the room and did not pay any attention to us.

'We cannot enter straight away. I want him to look at me first,' Abu Ayad said, turning to us with a feeble smile on his face.

Eventually, the officer turned and looked at us, and Abu Ayad pulled the receipt from his pocket and waved it at him with a big smile on his face.

'Come in,' the officer beckoned with his hand, and Abu Ayad entered the office without any further hesitation.

The officer took the passports and the receipt from Abu Ayad, and they whispered together for a few minutes.

'See you tomorrow,' Abu Ayad said in his normal voice to the officer, while shaking his hand enthusiastically.

'Yes, I shall see you tomorrow morning,' the officer replied with a huge grin on his face.

The three of us left the office immediately after these proceedings, without either Mudhaffar or I uttering one single word to the officer. We did not speak at all until we left the building, and even then, we did not say very much. I think we were too scared to say anything in case we would jinx ourselves. We were also very worried that we had just lost a huge amount of money! We took a bus to the town centre and agreed to meet the following morning at 8am sharp near The High Commission of the Islamic Revolution Building.

Next day, at 7.45am, Mudhaffar and I were standing very close to the rendezvous point, wondering what time Abu Ayad would turn up, and at the same time cursing everyone and everything and bemoaning the fate which had brought us to that dangerous situation.

'Time passes very slowly in situations like this,' I said.

'Al salamu alaykum,' said Abu Ayad as he suddenly appeared from around a corner. He certainly had a voice that attracted attention. 'See, it is 7.55am, and

I am here as promised. I am on time. Today we should get your passports back as planned,' he said with a confidence that I had not heard in his voice before. 'We should rely on Allah for solving our intricate problems, so let us go.'

We smiled reluctantly, not knowing whether to believe him or not. After all, we had already invested a huge amount of money and we had no idea how much more money we would have to pay out – and whether it would be worth it in the long run. However, we knew that was part of the game of life - some you win, some you lose; everything in life is a big gamble.

We immediately went to get a taxi from the taxi rank two streets away. The journey to the Department of Foreign Affairs took around 10 minutes, during which time we discussed our next move, whether we were successful or not. Whatever happened, we needed to get our passports back; we should not be walking the streets of Tehran without them, in case we were arrested.

When we arrived at the building, we had mixed feelings but were cautiously optimistic. Abu Ayad ran up the stairs at a very fast pace while we followed slowly behind, dragging our feet.

'Just wait here!' he said, pointing to the middle of the half-lit corridor where a few people were wandering around with their heads down looking very miserable.

I could not resist the temptation. I was desperate to see what was going to happen and whether or not we were going to get that small, simple stamp on our passports which would give us the freedom we were looking for – that is *if* we got the passports back, and if they were stamped!

We walked quietly forward to peek into the room. The bureau drawer was opened. *That's a good start*, I thought; and yes, here come our two passports – hopefully opened at the correct page to get a visa stamped on it! My heart was pounding with the blood rushing to my head, and my legs started to quake with nervous apprehension!

I understood the officer when he said to Abu Ayad in Farsi, 'Here you are.' He had a smirk on his face that gave us the impression he felt he was doing us a great favour and being ever so kind to us. There was no mention at all of our 'gift' to him.

'Thank you very much,' our ginger-haired friend said, taking the passports in one hand and shaking the officer's hand with the other. 'Did you manage to get your gift all right, sir?' Abu Ayad enquired in a low whisper.

'Yes, thank you,' the officer replied, immediately lowering his head into a thick open folder on the desk in front of him, pretending to be too busy to keep up the conversation.

That was clearly his signal that the business was at an end and Abu Ayad should depart from his office. There was nothing else to be done or said.

'Khuda hafez agha,' (Allah protect you, sir) Abu Ayad said, then immediately turned away from the officer with a broad smile on his face. It was a smile that said 'success', because he felt he had managed to achieve a good result to the complex task he had been set.

'Oh my God! This is brilliant. He has done it,' said Mudhaffar in jubilation.

My own reaction was more muted. I would not believe it until I actually held my passport, with an exit visa stamped on it, in my own two hands.

Abu Ayad walked ahead of us and straight out of the building with our passports in his pocket. As we followed him outside, I sent up another silent prayer, *'Please, Allah, let that be us sorted out now. Please do not make us have to go back into that building again!'*

'Congratulations, both of you. Here you are, these are your passports with the exit visas stamped in them,' Abu-Ayad said. Then he continued enthusiastically, 'Right, let us get you to the travel agents. He is a friend of mine, and he should be able to book you on a flight bound for Syria as soon as possible.'

We both stared at our passports with utter disbelief and amazement. I could hardly contain my emotions; I was so excited to see the authentic official exit visa stamped on it!

'My passport expired a couple of months ago, therefore I can't travel unless a new extension to this old passport has been made,' I said.

'Mine, too,' said Mudhaffar.

'No problem. That is easily sorted,' Abu Ayad replied. 'There is a market here in Tehran called 'Kucha Arab' or the Arabic market (meaning the Black Market). They can do anything for money, even if you want new passports. They have the capability of forging any document and making it appear to be an exact copy of the original.'

As we followed our friend towards the Kucha Arab, we discussed this issue and concluded that we had to keep all our options open.

'Why don't we ask the people working in The High Commission of the Islamic Revolution in Iraq, as they might be able to do something about it?' I said.

There was no objection to this proposal, so we agreed to bring this issue up with one of the Mullahs in that building. Moreover, we personally knew Hassan who worked there, and he still owed me a big favour from the time when I helped him and his family before they managed to escape from Iraq. Perhaps now it was time for him to repay that favour by helping us to leave

Iran. We decided to return to the offices of the High Commission of the Islamic Revolution in Iraq, and try to get an appointment with the white-turbaned Mullah who had interviewed us only a few days earlier.

The next morning, we gathered up our courage once more, and went back to try to get yet another interview with the Sayed. As we walked towards the building, Mudhaffar said that having to enter that place was becoming a very unpleasant event, but that perhaps it was the better of two evils. I admitted that I felt very uncomfortable with the staff in that building, although so far they had not caused us any significant problems and had not cost us a huge amount of money, unlike the bent official at the Iranian Foreign Office.

We were allowed entry with no hassle whatsoever, and were able to wander around looking for a familiar face.

'Al salamu alaykum,' Mudhaffar said when he noticed our friend Hassan in the room adjacent to the one where we had been interviewed on our last visit.

'Wa alaykum al salam,' (Peace be upon you, too!) was the traditional reply from Hassan.

Formalities over, he asked us if we were progressing with our quest to get a legal exit visa, and whether there was anything at all that he could do to help us.

'Yes, and yes, to both of your questions,' I answered. 'We finally managed to get the exit visas from the Department of Foreign Affairs at the Iranian Home Office, but now we want to get our passports extended. Do you think there is any chance that we can get that done here?'

Hassan looked at us in silence for a few minutes before responding hesitantly, 'I am not entirely sure about extending passports legally. But because they can do so many things here, perhaps it would be better if you ask the boss.'

'That is why we came here again today,' Mudhaffar explained.

'Oh, by the way,' Hassan continued, 'if you have any relatives that are prisoners of war here in Iran, we could try to help you get in touch with them. I have lists here of the names and whereabouts of most of them.'

Mudhaffar gave him his cousin's name and age and, sure enough, Hassan searched through the lists on his desk and located someone of the same name and age.

'Would you like to see him?' he asked.

'Hmmh! Not under the present circumstances, thank you,' Mudhaffar responded without hesitation, 'but it is good to know that he is still alive at least.'

While we were in the middle of this conversation, the Mullah who had interviewed us appeared clutching his dark, finely woven abaya in his left hand and a bundle of keys in the other.

'Al salamu alaykum, Mullah,' Mudhaffar said to the man as he passed the door of the office we were in before going into his own office.

We got up from where we were sitting and went to the Mullah's office and waited outside until he entered it himself. The first thing he did when he got inside was to take off his white turban, revealing a very short haircut. He wiped the perspiration from his forehead with a gleaming white handkerchief then switched on the ceiling fan in the middle of the room.

'Come in and take a seat,' he said, looking at a thick file jam-packed with papers on the desk in front of him. 'So, how can I help you, my brothers?' he said.

He sat still, looking at both of us, waiting for us to broach the subject we needed to discuss with him. We were so apprehensive about speaking to him again that it was difficult to formulate the words, and nothing would escape our lips. Then we both started to talk at once, then both clammed up immediately, because it was neither professional nor polite to talk at the same time.

The Mullah rubbed his greying beard with his right hand, then supported his chin with his hand and rested his elbow on his swollen stomach as he waited patiently for us to finish our ramblings. Mudhaffar told him we had discovered that our passports were out of date and so we needed more help.

'Ah. It is an extension of your passports that you want, is it?' he asked with a puzzled expression on his face.

'Oh, yes please,' we both said simultaneously.

The Mullah said that was not a big problem. He told us to leave our passports with him for a day or two and he would get them sorted out and ready for us to collect. Then he immediately turned his attention to the file in front of him.

We thanked the Mullah profusely as we handed our passports over to him, shook his hand, and left the office. Once outside, we looked at each other in total disbelief. Was it really that simple? We could not believe that this was going to happen, and fully expected to be told to leave another expensive gift somewhere to be picked up at a later date.

'Do you honestly believe we are going to get our passports back with an extension on them?' Mudhaffar asked with growing apprehension.

Three days later, we again visited the offices of the High Commission of the Islamic Revolution in Iraq. We were immediately seen by the same Mullah, who took great delight in returning our Iraqi passports back to us. We looked closely at our passports, which were both stamped with a new stamp. This stamp had been issued by the Iraqi Embassy in London, and it stated that the passport had been extended for another three years! We were very pleasantly surprised at this, and thanked the Mullah from the bottom of our hearts.

When we got outside the building, we both jumped up and down with joy. We were amazed to discover that the stamp extending our passports was 100% identical to the official stamps issued at the Iraqi Embassy in London when we'd had to hand over our passports when there on official business.

Chapter 15

Our (mis)Adventures in Tehran continue...

A fortnight had passed since our arrival in Tehran, Iran. So far, we had only managed to get genuine exit visas stamped onto our passports, but no embassy officials were willing to speak to us. Having visited almost every foreign embassy building in Tehran, it was now clear that due to the Iraq/Iran war and various political issues in Iran itself, almost all the embassies were closed. There were only one or two staff barracked in the very few remaining embassies, and these officials would not speak to us, never mind allow us to come through the gates. We were in a hopeless situation now, and each day we despaired that we were stuck there for good.

'I have to get my glasses repaired,' Mudhaffar said, and suggested that I, too, would have to improve my image before I reached Heathrow Airport.

In our current situation, I was totally amazed that he could think like that, because he was a highly educated man and he could see our situation was becoming more precarious every day. Our money was being eaten up, and we were stuck in a horrible rut! How on earth would getting his glasses repaired improve his image?

However, I did not want to argue with my friend at that moment in time. He seemed to be quite content with his ideas, and I did not want to disillusion him any further. We strolled to the nearest market, which was just over a thirty-five minute walk from the hotel, and took us through an old bazaar. Most of the shops were small and crammed with local produce as well as things that had obviously been smuggled in from neighbouring countries. We managed to find an optician who was able to replace the broken lens in Mudhaffar's glasses while we waited outside.

On the way back to the hotel, I saw a shop selling men's clothes, and decided to buy a couple of shirts. 'How much is this shirt?' I asked the middle-aged shopkeeper who could not even be bothered to get up from his seat to greet his customers.

He raised his head slowly from the book that he was engrossed in, glanced briefly at us and the merchandise I was holding, then replied in Farsi that he did not sell one shirt at a time; I would have to buy a minimum of two! He did not even have a smile on his face when he said this to me.

'This is something unheard of in the Western world,' Mudhaffar moaned, turning away from the man and heading towards the shop door.

'Oh, okay. I will buy three of these, if the price is right,' I informed the man, and he immediately got up from his comfortable chair and walked towards me. After a brief haggle, we agreed on a suitable price and I bought three shirts.

Mudhaffar, who was still talking about how presentable he should be when we reached Heathrow Airport, came up with the idea that we should both buy a new, good quality suit. I did not see anything wrong with his idea, apart from the financial side of it.

However, I said, 'How much do you think this suit is going to cost us? Do you really think it is going to make any difference to the person I am going to talk to at the immigration office at Heathrow Airport?'

That afternoon, we decided to go for a walk and, at the same time, look for a tailor's shop that specialised in good quality suits, just to check out the prices. After a couple of hours walking around Tehran city centre, we spotted a nicely decorated shop that appeared to sell exactly what we were looking for. As we were looking in the shop window for some time, the owner came outside and asked us if we needed any help, which was totally different from the attitude of the other shopkeeper earlier that day. Probably this man was just eager to get people into his shop in the hope that he could get a good sale.

We both tried on a few suits and eventually settled on dark-coloured, two-piece suits that fitted us perfectly. Having bought the suits, we went straight back to the hotel.

We did not use the buses much at all in Tehran, as we were unsure of which bus to take and where to get off, and we were still not very good at speaking in Farsi. On the few occasions we did use the bus, we were with someone else who spoke the language, who knew where we were going, and who knew the best bus to take to get us there. The day our friend Abu Ayad took us to various travel agents was one such day.

The fare was very cheap, costing only a fraction of a penny. All the women on the bus were covered up from head to toe and sat at the rear end of the bus, and when any men got on the bus, they would not sit anywhere near the females! This was all part of the unspoken and unwritten rules of the Islamic regime in that country.

Abu Ayad thought we should try our luck with Swiss Air as that was the first travel agents we came to when we got off the bus. When we went into the travel agents, a middle-aged man looked up and asked us how he could help us. He was well dressed, wearing a two-piece suit without a tie, and was sitting in a comfortable-looking, leather chair. He looked surprised when we entered the premises, probably because we disturbed him as he was enjoying the cold air blowing directly towards him from the air conditioner.

'My friends would like to fly to London,' Abu-Ayad said to the man, pushing the two passports over the table to him.

'Where are the visas to London?' the manager asked in Farsi, while we just stood and looked at each other in dismay. We knew that was going to be the leading question, because who can travel anywhere without a valid visa? But this had been Abu Ayad's suggestion, not ours, and we knew it was totally wrong.

We left the Swiss Air office and headed on down the street towards another travel agency, which was only about five minutes' walk away.

'I know someone working in this shop,' Abu Ayad assured us, adding, 'He managed to issue many tickets to friends travelling to Syria; from there, they managed to travel to other places.' We looked at each other with both a glimmer of hope and some apprehension.

'Abu Ayad, my friend, how are you?' the gentleman behind the desk asked as soon as we entered the shop.

There were more than a dozen people all speaking in raised voices, rather than discussing their problems calmly with the other two travel officers who were working at small desks. Unfortunately, it is more normal for people to talk in loud voices in most Middle Eastern countries, unlike the British who do not tend to raise their voices in normal conversation. At first my wife used to think that people were arguing all the time until she became used to the normal raised voices that the Iraqi people used in everyday circumstances. She would say that she would hate to hear what it was like when people actually got angry and started shouting during an altercation! To us, it was just normal.

'Fine, thanks to Allah,' Abu Ayad replied with a huge smile on his face. 'I am here to assist my brothers who are planning to travel back to Britain to be with their wives and families. Is there any chance they can be issued with tickets? They have enough money to pay for them.'

'Can I see their passports?' the man asked.

The young travel agent scrutinized our passports thoroughly and looked at us attentively, with utter surprise. After his very thorough inspection of the documents in front of him, he had obviously missed the all-important piece of evidence required – the entry visa for the country we wanted to go to.

After a while, he handed our passports back to Abu Ayad, scratched the top of his head, and then rubbed his beard and moustache with his right hand. He stood looking at all three of us for some time – perhaps he was trying to think of a polite way of saying what he was about to say without upsetting us, and his friend Abu Ayad.

'Ah, as you know, we cannot sell travel tickets without valid visas,' he said eventually, 'and there is no visa, so do you think it would be possible to travel to London without one?'

'We had thought...' our colleague began, then hesitated for a second as he looked straight at his travel agent friend, 'that there were ways around it, if the money was right!'

'Sorry, this cannot be done.' The man's answer was immediate, and he looked angry. 'I can sell you tickets to Damascus, if you want. No visa is required, and you need to remember that it is the only country you can travel to' (as Arabs without any entry permit, he omitted to say) 'in your circumstances.'

I thought his advice was a combination of two things: he was trying to help us, and also benefit from the sale of the tickets. But I suppose it is natural for business people to resort to such tactics.

We looked at each other and ruminated on this proposal in our minds for a few minutes. 'Is there any other alternative?' I asked cautiously.

A sharp shake of the head clearly indicated that there was no chance of any other options. He again emphasised that the only way we could legally exit from Iran to another country was by travelling via Syria.

Although at that stage it seemed as though we were just going around in circles, at least we would be going to another Arab country and one where we could comfortably speak the language. Therefore, the decision was made there and then to book tickets to travel to Syria.

'When would you like to travel?' we were asked.

'As soon as possible, please,' said Abu Ayad, almost shouting over the noise of the busy office.

The travel agent looked at the computer screen and typed in a few details. 'A week today is the earliest I can offer you, travelling via the Airline of the Islamic Republic of Iran,' he replied. He knew that we had no other options available.

'Ok, come back in three days' time and your tickets will be ready to pick up,' he said, and held his hand out to Abu Ayad to collect the money for the tickets. We handed the money over, expecting to be given a receipt for the transaction, but he just reiterated that we needed to come back in three days' time and the tickets would be there ready for us to collect.

We thanked him for his assistance and left the travel agency empty-handed and feeling both apprehensive and a little disappointed. As we made our way back to the hotel, Abu Ayad assured us he would take us back to the travel agency to collect our flight tickets.

We spent the next couple of days doing very little apart from wandering around the streets near the hotel, and swearing at Saddam and the stupid Iraqi Government regime at that time.

On the third morning after paying for the flight tickets, Abu Ayad met us at the hotel as promised, just as the clock chimed nine o'clock.

'Right, are you ready, guys?' he said with yet another huge grin on his face. It was obvious that he was in remarkably good spirits, unlike us.

'Yes, we are ready!' we responded, although with much less enthusiasm than him.

We were unsure whether we had been conned yet again or whether the travel agent had been true to his word. If, and only if, he was genuine, then it would mean that our sojourn in Tehran was finally coming to an end and we could leave Iran and the Farsi-speaking people and travel to Syria, where the natives spoke Arabic, our mother tongue.

Abu Ayad hailed the first passing taxi, and fifteen minutes later we were at the travel agents. Immediately on entering the office, Abu Ayad was warmly welcomed by his friend. After the customary welcome greetings and warm wishes, the travel agent opened the desk drawer and retrieved our travel tickets, which he handed over to Abu Ayad.

'Here are the flight tickets for the Airline of the Islamic Republic of Iran,' he said.

Unbelievable! We actually had one-way tickets to leave Iran and fly to Syria in just four days' time. Now it was our turn to have huge grins on our faces as we thanked the man profusely.

When we left the travel agency, we told Abu Ayad that we needed to change most of our remaining money from Iranian Tomans into American dollars, if possible. Unsurprisingly, he said he knew someone who worked in a money exchange bureau. As he had lived in Iran for a number of years now, and because he worked for the Office of the High Commission of the Islamic Revolution in Iraq, he had made contacts in many different organisations.

We walked for around ninety minutes until we arrived at a small money exchange bureau, where it soon became obvious that Abu Ayad had dealt with one of the staff members on numerous occasions, and that worker knew the procedure very well. After the customary welcome and handshaking, the banker asked Abu Ayad, 'How much do you want to exchange, and do you want cash, travellers' cheques, or both?'

My briefcase was still fairly full of Iranian Tomans, as I had exchanged my Iraqi dinars into almost two million of them with the help of one of the Peshmerga. Knowing I still had a lot of money to be changed, I thought that the best way to safeguard it would be to buy travellers cheques', aside from some money to pay the hotel bills and for any unexpected expenditure over the next few days. The banker only had a small amount of American dollars and some Japanese yen, but he had plenty of Japanese yen travellers' cheques.

Soon my Tomans were exchanged for a mixture of Japanese yen and Japanese travellers' cheques. I had never seen Japanese yen before, so I was unsure if they were real or not.

'Japanese travellers' cheques!' I muttered, looking at my companions to see if they were as amused as I was. 'Yen,' I said a bit louder this time, and everyone looked at me with amusement. 'Well,' I went on, 'have you ever seen them before?'

Mudhaffar asked for some American dollars and some travellers' cheques, and we both hoped that the money and the documents we had received were genuine.

I was relieved to get rid of all those Tomans. I now had only a few pieces of paper and a small amount of dollars, instead of the vast amounts of money I had been carrying about for the last few weeks. I had made sure that I had enough Tomans to cover my living expenses for the next few days.

We headed back to the hotel in what was now the blazing heat of the day. After a stressful and tense morning, I was desperate to have a shower and relax in the air-conditioned room for a few hours.

It was during the last week of July 1988 that we were due to fly from Tehran to Damascus, the capital of Syria. As the flight was due to leave in the early afternoon, we checked out of the hotel in the morning. Our friend Abu Ayad had hired a taxi to take us to the airport.

'I want to see you getting on that flight to Damascus without any problems whatsoever,' he said with his customary huge grin. Along with a whole barrage of optimistic statements, he had some final advice for when we arrived at Damascus Airport.

'You need to put a US ten dollar note inside each passport, and do not let anyone see you doing this. It will help you get through security without any problems, but be careful as you know this is bribery and that is not allowed under Syrian Government laws. Therefore, you have to be careful when you do this.'

It was really good of him to accompany us to the airport and to give us as much moral support and advice as he could muster.

We stood in the queue for the check-in until my turn came, and the officer had a quick look at my passport and then threw it back at me.

'Your passport is expired, and you have to go and get it extended,' were his terrifying words. He did not comment that I did not have an entry visa to Iran on my passport, and obviously had no idea how we had managed to get into Iran in the first place.

'Excuse me sir, this is the extension to my passport. See, it is on this page,' I responded, opening the passport to the correct page with trembling fingers and my heart beating at an incredible speed.

He took a second look, stamped the page, then threw the passport back at me again. I do not know if he was in a bad mood generally, or just in a bad mood with me. Was it because I was an Iraqi travelling from Iran to Syria, or had he already dealt with passengers who had tried to pass old passports off as valid ones, so had to refuse them access? I had no idea. I only hoped that I could get on that plane and that everything would be okay at the other side.

'Now you can go to the gate,' was all he said before looking over my shoulder to serve the next person in the queue. It was, of course, Mudhaffar, who already had his passport open at the page with the extension notification in it. His passport was stamped immediately and handed back to him without any problem whatsoever!

Passing the extensive security checks was another big hurdle, since we had to go through several metal detectors and manual searches before we could reach the transit area. Once through all the security checks, we were pleasantly surprised when we arrived at the waiting area. It was fairly big and there was a prayer area off to one side of the space. The floor was covered with thick, dark red, high-quality carpets. We had to sit in the waiting area for a couple of hours, and found that the most comfortable place was actually in the prayer area. There, you could lie down, or just sit on the thick Iranian carpets that felt so lovely and comfortable.

Eventually, our long, nervous wait came to an end. It was just after lunchtime when the announcement went up that the gate was now open and we could finally board the Airline of the Islamic Republic of Iran's plane bound for Damascus!

Chapter 16

Our Stay in Syria

Having arrived at Damascus Airport late in the afternoon, we discovered that it was still very hot in Syria at that time of the day in July. Remembering the advice given to us by our friend, Abu Ayad, we inserted an American ten-dollar bill into our passports as we stood in the queue waiting for them to be scrutinised by the passport officers. It was a well-known fact that everyone in Damascus (both in the airport and in the country itself) was suspicious of everyone else.

My turn came and I handed my passport over to the officer, who inspected my face before hurriedly taking my passport from me. On opening my passport, he quickly placed it on a shelf below the table in front of him and surreptitiously slipped the ten-dollar bill into his pocket very quickly, without arousing any suspicion whatsoever. He looked at me again and then turned a few pages over in my passport, thoroughly scanning the contents carefully.

When he raised his head, he looked directly at me and said, 'You have to go to the Intelligence Office exactly one week from today to collect your passport.' Then he opened one of the drawers in front of him and threw my passport into it. As he closed the drawer, he added in a dismissive tone, 'You can leave now.' That brought our stilted conversation to an abrupt end, as he'd made it fairly obvious he had no intention of engaging in any further discourse with me.

Mudhaffar faced exactly the same treatment, with his American ten-dollar bill quickly disappearing into the security officer's pocket in an almost identical manner. He was also told to go to the Intelligence Office in one week's time to retrieve his passport. There was no acknowledgement from either security officer of the unexpected 'gift', nor did either officer smile as we were directed towards the baggage collection area.

We had hoped that the bribes would have smoothed our entry into Syria without any unexpected snags, but how wrong we were! Now we were twenty dollars down and had no passports with legal entry visas to Syria, and no identity papers to say that we had entered the country in a legitimate manner. In fact, we had no legal documents at all now, apart from the remains of our seat tickets for our flights into Damascus from Teheran. And they didn't prove anything at all – only that we had previously been in an Iranian country.

We had spent all that money and did not know if we would ever see our passports again. And if we were lucky enough to get them back, what then? Would we have legal entry visas to Syria? Or would we be arrested on some trumped-up charge? We did not have a clue what to do or where to go from here on our quest to get back to the UK.

We'd been told that we had to go to the Syrian Intelligence Office in one week's time, so we would have to pray that we could indeed retrieve our passports when we went there. We knew what happened to people who were summoned to the Intelligence Offices in Iraq, so we could only assume that the same things would happen at the Syrian Intelligence Office, if not 1000 times worse! What kind of questioning would we have to endure? And would their questioning involve some form of torture? Obviously, they wanted information, or something else, or they would not have taken our passports from us!

We were so disappointed and upset at this turn of events. We had hoped that leaving Iran legally and getting our entry visas to Syria legally stamped on our passports would be the beginning of a new episode in our lives when we could feel a lot safer and unthreatened. So, from being happy at the thought of getting one step nearer to returning to the UK we now felt despondent once more! Had we not suffered enough over the past few weeks? Were our problems never going to end?

We took stock of our surroundings and followed everyone else to the baggage reclaim area. Thirty minutes later, having retrieved our bags, we scoured the area to find the nearest exit doors. We were both still ruminating on what had just happened, what the consequences were going to be, and what on earth we were going to do next. Everyone else leaving the airport seemed happy, looking for their friends and relatives who were waiting to pick them up; we were both in a very sombre mood as we followed the others heading in the general direction of the exit doors.

We were unsure whether to take a taxi to Damascus city centre or go by bus, which would presumably be a lot cheaper. While walking towards the exit in discussion about the best way to get to the town, a short, thin, young man approached us.

'I couldn't help but hearing from your dialects that you are Iraqis,' he said, 'and it seems that this is your very first time in Syria. Am I correct?'

Although we looked almost the same as the indigenous population, it was obvious to anyone overhearing us that we were not locals. So, we told him the truth that we were Iraqis on our first ever visit to Damascus. He immediately volunteered his assistance and guided us towards the bus stop just outside the arrival area. How kind of him to do this to strangers. Thankfully, this was an era when you could still trust people – unlike today, when you have to be very wary everywhere when people offer their services.

We did not have to wait long for the bus to arrive, and when it did, there were suddenly lots of people rushing forward to get on board. Our new friend hurried to secure his place by putting his small bag onto one of the seats to reserve it, then came back to help us carry our bags; we followed him onto the bus like lost sheep.

Unfortunately, we had not thought about changing some money into the local currency (the Syrian Lira) because of the problems with our passports. We explained we had not had a chance to change any money into Lira, but our new companion, who introduced himself as Bilal, was more than happy to step in and pay for our fares without any hesitation whatsoever. He insisted that he would pay for us in the same way that he would pay for any guests who had come from abroad to visit him. We had the same custom in Iraq and, as far as I am aware, this custom was observed in many Arabian countries at that time.

On the bus, Bilal explained that he had been waiting in the airport for a friend of his who should have been on the same flight as us from Tehran, but something must have gone wrong as he had not arrived.

The bus did not take long to reach Damascus city centre, but by this time it was already late in the evening and the streets were buzzing with people. Bilal again volunteered his services to us. He was only carrying a small bag, which was light and easy to carry, but we had to drag our suitcases along bustling streets, not knowing where we were or what hotel we could afford to stay at to help us eke out our money as much as possible.

First, Bilal took us to an exchange bureau where we were able to change what we felt would be enough money to keep us going for a few days at least, as we could not afford to waste any money.

He then accompanied us to what looked like a very nice hotel, not far from the bus station. It was not at all what we had expected to find in Syria, because it was a poor country even though there was no war situation at that time. When I asked the young blonde girl at the reception desk if there were any vacancies in the hotel, at first she did not confirm whether there were any rooms available. Instead, she asked me, 'Are you Arabs?'

I thought that was a really peculiar question to ask, because I had spoken to her in Arabic and not in English or any other language! Obviously, we were Arabs, as we looked like Arabs and we spoke Arabic to her. Perhaps she was mistaking us for foreign, non-Arabs attempting to speak Arabic. But how likely was it that a foreigner could speak rapid, un-halting Arabic as well as any native person did?

'Yes, we are Arabs and we are from Iraq,' I replied in Arabic, and continued with an obvious look of surprise and disdain on my face, 'Is that a problem?'

'No, there is no problem whatsoever,' she said, 'and yes, we have vacancies. But I have to charge you in US dollars, not in Syrian Lira, if you want to stay in this hotel. It is $50 per person per night, no matter which room you take.'

We were astonished and dismayed at her response, and I could not resist asking her, 'Why do you insist that we, or any other non-Syrian Arabs, have to pay in American Dollars and not Syrian Lira?'

Her reply was simple and to the point. 'You are not Syrians, so consequently you are foreigners! We charge all foreigners who wish to stay here, and who are not Syrian, in American Dollars rather than Syrian Lira.'

I tried to argue with her that we were Arabs just like her, and that the management should not be allowed to discriminate between Arabs, no matter which country we originally came from. But she turned her face away and pretended to be busy dealing with administrative work.

We were both absolutely furious at this blatant disrespect to foreign Arab guests, and felt we had no other option but to walk out of that hotel.

We walked further along the same street for another fifteen minutes until we arrived at the next hotel. By this time, it was already dark and we were beginning to feel really tired, hungry and desperate to find somewhere to sleep.

Bilal volunteered to go inside and enquire whether there were any vacancies in that hotel. We were right behind him when the young gentleman confirmed that they had vacancies and agreed that we could pay for the room using Syrian Lira and not American dollars. The charge for the hotel room was fairly reasonable, and we asked if we could stay for one night at a time, which the young receptionist was quite happy for us to do. We paid for one night's accommodation and were given the room keys and rough directions. When we got to the room, it was a lot better than I had expected for the price, which I felt was well within our budget. Leaving our belongings in the room, we went downstairs again to thank Bilal for his help and said we hoped to see him again the next day. He replied that he would meet us the following morning and show us around his beloved city.

We soon discovered there were many shops and small restaurants in the close vicinity of the hotel. And immediately we stepped outside, the enticing smell of lamb tikka from a nearby restaurant was irresistible. We went inside and found an empty table in an open area in front of the small eatery. The place was very shabby-looking, with aluminium chairs and dirty seat pads with many of the straps hanging down from the metal framework. But the place was busy, so we assumed that it must be popular. And if it was that popular, then the food must be fresh enough, and the state of the furnishings was fairly unimportant.

We were very hungry and eventually managed to attract the waiter's attention. We could not see any menus, and he did not have a pad in his hand to take our orders.

'What do you want to eat?' he asked, without giving a hint as to what was available.

'Can we both have two shish of your lamb tikkas with bread and salad, please?' I asked, hoping that he would not fire any other questions at us.

His next question was to ask us how much meat we wanted, and whether we wanted a half a kilogramme or one kilogramme of meat each. I found it rather strange to be asked how much weight of meat we wanted to eat. I replied that we would have half a kilogramme of meat between us, as I felt that was quite a lot of meat for two people to consume in one sitting.

When the skewers were brought to our table, the dish was served with a pile of salad and some Syrian flat bread, and there was also a big jug of water. Having not had anything to eat since breakfast time that morning, we were ravenous, and the meal was absolutely delicious.

On our second day in Damascus, we ventured outside the hotel and waited in the shade of one of the nearby buildings hoping that our new friend Bilal would appear. The city was buzzing with people going about their daily business, and it was approaching ten o'clock in the morning when he finally appeared around the corner. Although he was apologetic, we assured him that we were not in any hurry because we were not going to be doing anything important. It was obvious that he had other things on his mind, and we soon found out that he wanted to get us out of that hotel and into private accommodation. He said it would be a lot cheaper for us in the long run, especially as we had spent a lot more money that we'd expected since leaving Kurdistan, twenty-seven days before.

Bilal led the way through the narrow streets and souks of Damascus city centre until we came to a narrow road that was less than two meters wide, and with old houses lining both sides of the road. We followed him down this road for another five minutes, not knowing where we were going. Eventually, he stopped outside one of the houses and knocked on an ancient wooden door, which was slightly ajar. A middle-aged woman, wearing a black headscarf and a long black dress, appeared at the door; behind her, a young girl stood watching us. We later discovered that this young girl was the woman's daughter.

'Sabah al khayr (Good morning),' Bilal said to the lady in an open and friendly manner.

She replied in the same manner, 'Sabah al noor (your morning is bright).' This is the typical response to someone wishing you a good morning.

She had a mildly surprised expression on her face as she pondered why there were three strangers standing outside her door. 'Can I help you?' she asked.

Bilal replied, 'My friend told me that you have a room to let, is that correct?'

'Yes, that is correct, I do have a room to let,' she replied, pushing her daughter gently aside to open the door fully and we rather hesitantly entered.

'This is the room,' she gestured, with a big smile on her face.

The room was in a small extension on the left-hand side of the house. It had a very low ceiling, which gave Mudhaffar – at six feet tall in his stockinged feet – a clearance of only a few centimetres. In the corner of the room there was one single bed, which was quite high off the ground (leaving very little space between the bed and the ceiling). Along the other wall there was one doshek, but at least it was a very thick, albeit narrow, fabric-covered sponge which was long enough for one person to lie on.

There were no wardrobes or drawers for our clothes, nor were there any chairs or a mirror – in fact, there was nothing else whatsoever in that room. However, we agreed that we could live there for the next week or two until we retrieved our passports from the Intelligence Office.

Bilal discussed the rent and conditions with the woman on our behalf and managed to negotiate a really good price for us, especially as would be paying the rent one week in advance. The room, although tiny, was sufficient for our current needs, as it was really just a stop-gap for a week or two at most – all being well. The cost was reasonable, but I cannot remember now how much it was, but it was cheaper than forking out money for a hotel room.

The lady was also kind enough to offer us the use of her fridge if we wanted to keep any small perishable items. As she gave us one single key for the main door, we thanked her for her kindness in agreeing for us to stay there with no questions asked. Bilal then took us back to the hotel to collect our belongings, then helped us to get our bearings as we returned to the house once more.

We spent the next two days wandering around the streets of Damascus. During this time, Bilal took us to the Sayyidah Zaynab Mosque, which was purported to be the burial site of Zaynab, the daughter of Imam Ali and his wife Fatima (according to Shia Muslims). According to Sunni Muslims, however, it is believed that Zaynab is buried in a mosque of the same name (Sayyidah Zaynab Mosque) in Cairo, Egypt! Whatever the truth of the story, the tomb in Damascus has become a centre for Shia religious studies in Syria, and it is a well-known destination for mass pilgrimages by Shia Muslims from across the Muslim world.

We soon discovered that many travellers had their passports confiscated by the security services at Damascus International Airport. We were told that people would stand outside the Intelligence Office every day of the week to listen for their names being called.

We spent the next five days wandering the streets of Damascus, interspersed with going to the Intelligence Office and standing with the rest of the crowd outside, hoping that our names would eventually be called out and we would get our passports back. Every day we hoped against hope that we would be amongst the lucky ones who retrieved their passports, then we would be free to plan our next steps towards returning to the UK.

Exactly seven days after our passports were taken from us at the airport security check, we stood outside the Intelligence Office building, watching as the officers shouted out people's names and threw their passports into the air for them to either catch or to scrabble around the ground to pick up before they were trampled on.

Suddenly, our names were shouted out. But instead of throwing our passports into the air, when we shouted out that we were there, the man gestured for us to follow him into the building. The other people standing there gave us strange looks before dispersing as quickly as their legs could carry them. I turned around to see if anybody was still hanging around, but the area was empty. Within seconds, Mudhaffar and I were the only two people left outside the Intelligence Office building. That really scared the living daylights out of us!

The sun was burning above us, and the fear of the unknown started to take hold. We looked at each other but said nothing, simply because there was nothing to say. We had no clue why we had been singled out from everyone who had been standing there waiting for their passports to be thrown at them.

No matter what was to happen, we had no option but to follow the man into the bowels of the Intelligence Office. It was more like a single-storey house built in typical Arabic style, with a number of rooms surrounding a central space that was open to the sky. The officer we were following was fairly young, with a 'short back and sides' military-style haircut. He wore a grey suit and blue tie in spite of the fact it was so hot at that time of the year.

He indicated that I should enter a small side room first, while Mudhaffar was told to wait a few metres away in the middle of the central courtyard.

'Sit down,' he ordered, pointing to a rickety old chair that groaned and creaked as I sat on it.

He sat down on an almost identical chair behind an ancient desk. I looked around and noticed that there was a single bed in one corner of the room, with a very thin mattress, one pillow, and a sun-bleached cover. I was unsure whether the man worked and slept there, or whether this office was used for some nefarious purpose. This was definitely an odd arrangement, and I dreaded to think about what might have happened in that room.

However, I was in no position to ask any questions, so kept my mouth shut. I could only hope that he was sleeping there rather than using the room for long-term interrogation procedures. The regime in Syria had as bad a reputation as the Iraqi regime, and I knew that many people had been tortured in rooms like this in many buildings throughout Iraq. There was even a small building only two streets away from our family home in Karbala, and I had personally heard screams coming from inside the offices there. Carol had also spoken to me about sometimes hearing terrified screams emanating from the building when she passed to go to the market.

To my relief, the first question I was asked was about my reasons for travelling to Syria. My interrogator had a notepad in front of him and a pen in his hand, ready to write down all the answers I gave him. I was totally honest in my reply, as I had nothing to hide.

I explained that I only wanted my passport back, and that there were no untoward reasons for me being in Syria. This country was only a means to an end in my quest to return to the UK. We had hoped that it would be easier for us to return to the UK to be reunited with our wives and children if we travelled from Syria, rather than travelling from Iran, mainly because of the Iraq-Iran war and the lack of a fully-staffed British Embassy to provide us with visas. I explained that both our wives were British, and could no longer stand the austerity in Iraq due to the long-term effects of the sanctions, so they felt they could not survive the struggles of daily life there any longer. I said this was true more now than before because we had been living in Erbil, in the north of Iraq – an area which had been really badly affected by the war, the actions of the resistance fighters, and the deepening effects of rationing.

He scribbled down a few sentences on his notepad and then raised his head to look at me again, perhaps preparing his next question. 'What qualifications do you have, and do you have any proof of them?' he asked.

I explained that I held a PhD in Chemistry and that this involved the synthesis of organic chemicals in search of cures for illnesses. I further explained that I intended to return to the UK to work in either a university or in an industry to find cures for cancers and other life-threatening illnesses.

His next statement took me totally by surprise. 'We would like you to work for our Syrian Intelligence Organisation,' he said. 'There are so many Iraqis here in Syria, and we want to know if they are planning anything to cause us problems, or to bring the Syrian regime down. What do you think of that?'

That question was totally unexpected; it was not something I would ever have imagined that I would be asked. As it had never crossed my mind at all, not even fleetingly, I was totally unprepared on how to reply.

Sometimes we have to say or do things immediately or impetuously without thinking things through thoroughly. Instead, we have to think on our feet and do what we must to survive. Therefore, I replied without hesitation that I would be happy to let them know if I heard anything subversive that would affect the stability of the Syrian people or the country of Syria. I tried my utmost to be as convincing as possible, and managed to keep a straight face as the officer watched my every movement and facial expression.

He seemed to be very pleased with the outcome of his interrogation and pulled open one of the drawers in the desk in front of him, retrieved a piece of paper, and passed it to me. I had a quick look at the slip of paper, which had a name written in Arabic on it. I raised my eyes and looked at him and was just about to ask him about it when he said, 'This is your new cover name.

If you have any information to pass on to us, just use this name and we will take it from there.'

The situation was totally surreal and I was sure that my body was shaking all over. There was no way I would ever consider spying on anyone, and I would never, ever, think of becoming an agent for any regime anywhere in the world. But I did my best to not let him see the fear I felt, and I pretended to be more than happy to help them and to accept this preposterous proposal!

He then opened another drawer in the desk and pulled out my passport, which he handed to me with a big smirk on his face. I can only assume that he had believed every word I had said to him. I took my passport and the slip of paper with my 'code name' on it in my left hand, and then shook his hand, willing myself to stay calm and collected and not show the turmoil I felt in my guts at that moment.

With my passport in my hand, I walked calmly through the doorway and over to Mudhaffar, who was standing ashen-faced in the courtyard. I gave him a thumbs-up with my passport held visibly over my chest, and at the same time, I screwed up my face to try to warn him to be careful.

I waited patiently in the courtyard while Mudhaffar took his turn with the same intelligence officer. Forty minutes later, he emerged from the room. He looked white-faced and exhausted, but bemused and very happy to have his passport back in his hands.

'Right! Let's go and have lunch to celebrate,' I said, as it dawned on us that we were okay and nothing sinister had happened. We felt as though we had just survived a big battle against our enemies.

After lunch, we went to one of the phone booths in the street and took turns to phone our wives at home in the UK. They assured us that throughout the duration of our journey from Iraq, they had continued their search for any legal way to help us to get back to the UK. They had literally left no stone unturned. Carol told me that she had spoken to her local Member of Parliament in Dundee and had also been in contact with a Cabinet Minister in the House of Commons. Both had said they would do their best to help get me back to the UK, but they could only help if we managed to get to Cyprus where there was a fully operational British Embassy, unlike in most of the Middle East at that time.

Mudhaffar told me that his wife had been in contact with her local MP, and had also received the same advice. As we were still in Damascus, it meant we had to really try hard to get from Syria to Cyprus by any means possible.

Both wives informed us that we had to get appointments with the British Embassy staff in Nicosia as soon as we arrived in Cyprus. And, once we managed to get to the embassy, there should be letters from the MP and the Cabinet Minister instructing the staff to assist us both by giving us entry visas to the UK.

This information gave us both such a boost, and a much-needed glimmer of hope that we would eventually succeed in returning to the UK. Feeling much more optimistic, we hailed a taxi and asked the driver to take us to the Cypriot Embassy, wherever that was. Fifteen minutes later, the taxi pulled up and the driver pointed the building out to us.

At the door of the Cypriot Embassy, a middle-aged man wearing civilian clothes was refusing everyone entry to the building. We politely asked if we could possibly enter the building, as we needed to discuss an important issue with the staff there.

'You cannot enter this building at all,' he said simply.

We now knew from experience that we had to bribe him if we wanted anything done. So, we discreetly passed him an American ten-dollar bill.

'How can I help you, gentlemen?' he asked with a slight hint of a smile on his face. What a difference ten dollars made!

'We both need to get a visa to Cyprus,' I explained to him as he pocketed the money without acknowledging it.

'No problem, just wait here and I will bring two application forms out for you. Bring the filled forms back to me and I will make sure they come to the attention of the officer in charge,' he said.

We both filled the application forms in as quickly as possible, stating that we only required visas for a very short stay in Cyprus. Then we returned to the Cypriot Embassy with the completed application forms and our passports, and handed everything to the gentleman we had spoken to earlier. He took the documents and went into the building, returning less than ten minutes later to inform us that we should come back to the embassy the following morning to collect our passports.

By ten o'clock the following morning, we were standing nervously outside the door to the Cypriot Embassy in Damascus. The middle-aged man who had been on guard the previous day recognised us immediately, and asked us to wait there while he went to retrieve our passports. We could not wait to get our hands on them to see if we had been lucky enough to get that elusive entry visa to Cyprus stamped on our passports or not.

It did not take long for the guard to come back holding our passports, which he handed over to us with neither a smile nor a frown on his face. We were both excited and apprehensive at the same time, but on checking through our passports, we both gave whoops of delight to see we had been granted a two-week visa to Cyprus! Un-be-lieve-able! We had a genuine visa to Cyprus, wa-hey!

Two weeks there should give us ample time to sort out our affairs for the final leg of our journey to Britain. We were so relieved that we could have kissed that guard, but instead, we both shook his hand and thanked him profusely for his help, then walked smartly away as fast as we could. We were so sure that he would call us back at any minute to tell us that they had made a mistake or had changed their minds and wanted to take the visas back!

Finally, on 8th August, 1988, we had visas to Cyprus stamped in our passports! Hallelujah!

We immediately took the minibus to visit the Sayyidah Zaynab Mosque and offered up a prayer of thanks, as is customary in our religion when we have had something fantastic happen to us. Being given the visas to Cyprus was synonymous with a personal miracle.

After we visited the mosque and performed our prayers there, we went to one of the nearby restaurants and ordered kebabs, rice, bread and salad for our lunch. Although the restaurant was not very big, it was good and the chefs prepared the food in front of diners, baking bread in the tanoor (clay oven) while the customers sat and waited. That meal was fantastic; probably because we were so ecstatic at the idea of getting yet another step closer to Europe, and eventually to the UK. As we ate, we discussed our next steps, and how soon we would be able to get our travel arrangements sorted out so that we could continue our journey.

After lunch, we went straight to the nearest travel agency to ascertain when the next available flight to Cyprus was due to leave, and whether there were any seats available. The travel agent informed us that we were in luck as there was a Syrian Airways flight going to Limassol on the 13th of August, and there were still a few remaining seats. However, there were no flights due to go to Nicosia in the near future.

'Ok. That is fine. Can you please book the two of us onto that flight?' I asked, starting to feel excited at the prospect of leaving Damascus behind and getting another step closer to our families in Britain.

Turning towards Mudhaffar, I suggested to him that we would be better to take a taxi from Limassol to Nicosia. He nodded his agreement with a big smile on his face.

We paid for two single tickets in cash, and as soon as the travel agent took our details and the money, he immediately handed over the two airline tickets. *Great*, I thought! *Not one, but two fantastic pieces of good luck in one day. Surely we could finally believe that miracles can and did happen!*

Early in the morning, two days later, we bade farewell to our landlady and her daughter. Outside the house, Bilal waited to give us a hand with the small amount of possessions we had, and dropped us off at the airport some three hours before the flight was due to depart for Limassol in Cyprus.

We said goodbye to Bilal and gave him the Syrian money that we still had in our pockets. Waving what we prayed was a final goodbye to him and to Syria, we went into the transit area. We were both exhilarated and extremely apprehensive at the same time.

We got through the security and baggage checks with no problems whatsoever, and were waiting to board our flight when it was announced that the flight was delayed. Ninety minutes after our expected departure time, though, we finally boarded our flight to Limassol.

Within ten minutes of the doors closing, we were finally taxiing down the runway. But it was only once the flight was in mid-air that we could both let out deep sighs of relief.

Finally, it was actually happening. We were leaving the Arab-speaking countries behind, and were on our way to a new adventure in Cyprus.

Chapter 17

Our Flight and Subsequent Sojourn in Cyprus

Once we had cleared the airport and were up in the air, I felt that we could relax a little, so I looked around us at our fellow travellers. There were two fairly young gentlemen in the seats directly in front of us, and at first glance they appeared to be normal travellers with short, close-cropped hair, wearing nice suits, and having normal interactions with each other.

I thought nothing more of them until later on in the flight when one of them bent down to tie his shoelace and I noticed the fairly obvious bulge at the back of his jacket. As he bent down further, I was shocked to realise that he was carrying a handgun in his trouser belt. I did not really think that he was a terrorist, as neither he nor his companion appeared apprehensive or showed any signs of agitation. Neither of them had spent any time in the toilet, or walking up and down the aeroplane, or reaching into any overhead luggage since getting on the flight. So, he must have worn the gun through the security checks without any problems, which meant they were probably intelligence officers.

It must have been standard practice for armed intelligence officers to fly on board the Syrian Airways planes at that time. Certainly, I knew that armed Israeli intelligence officers, known as Air Marshalls, travelled on all El Al Airways flights, because the Israeli authorities were worried about the possibility of hijackers. However, I had no idea that other countries had the same arrangements for armed intelligence officers on international flights!

After that, I did my best not to look anywhere near these two men in case they thought that I was paying too much attention to them. I did not see them leaving the plane when everyone else left, so I can only assume that they stayed on board and returned back to Damascus on the next flight back. We, however, got off the plane with everyone else and did our best to be near the front of the queue.

When our turn came to go through the immigration channels, the immigration officer checked our passports and our visas, which clearly stated that we were allowed to stay in Cyprus for two weeks. However, he scored the 'two weeks' out on both our visas and changed it to 'one week', before signing the visa page on our passports. We were so glad to get through that process that we did not argue or demur at this – we were just happy to have finally arrived in Cyprus.

We collected our belongings and then looked around to find somewhere to change some of our money into Cypriot pounds. There was a kiosk just inside the exit doors of the airport, so we both exchanged some money then walked out of the airport into the heat of a hot August afternoon. Pulling our cases behind us, we headed straight to a line of taxis waiting to pick up weary travellers. After some negotiation with a taxi driver, we agreed on a price for him to drive us to Nicosia, the capital of Cyprus.

The journey lasted slightly less than one hour, and the driver dropped us off in the city centre. After wandering around for some time, we managed to find a hotel where the receptionist was happy to give us a room for the night. Once we were signed in, we put our belongings into our room, then went out in search of food. It was getting late in the afternoon and we were hungry.

Only a short distance away from the hotel, we spotted a small restaurant which had a display of chickens being roasted on a spit outside the entrance door. The smell was so enticing, our stomachs were rumbling at the thought of that delicious looking roasted chicken. We had not had a meal like that for a long time now. I have to admit, it felt lovely to think that we were back on European soil and were about to eat a meal of roasted chicken once more, instead of minced lamb kebabs.

We both ordered roast chicken and cans of coca cola. When the food was brought to our table the waiter put down two plates in front of each of us. The first two plates consisted of a half a roast chicken and two portions of pitta bread, while the other two plates held huge servings of fresh salad coated with loads of olive oil. This meal was so different from our recent menu, which had consisted of mince kebab, rice, and glasses of water!

As we sat there, we both remarked on how good it was to eat and drink the type of food we were once used to back in the UK. It felt as though we were finally getting closer to our goal of enjoying meals like this with our wives and families. After leaving the restaurant, we wandered around the vicinity for the rest of the evening, finally returning to the hotel with the intention of having a quick look at the news on the television before going to bed.

We had just sat down in the reception area to watch the television, when we noticed that there were several fairly young girls walking about in the foyer and the corridors wearing what we felt were very revealing clothes and they all seemed to be very heavily made-up. We could not differentiate where these young women were originally from, as they seemed to be speaking to each other in either a Syrian or a Lebanese dialogue.

Whilst watching these comings and goings, a man came and sat down beside us in the reception area. Judging by his appearance, he was an Arab, and he sat down next to me looking anxious and watchful. When he thought the coast was clear, he began to warn us in halting English, 'Please to be careful with them girls, as these are prostitutes and they skin you live. So be warned and avoid them if here you are on holiday, and you don wanna get busy with these sorta womans.' He maintained a serious expression on his face the whole time he was speaking these words.

I was not sure why he felt he had to advise us about this issue. Had he suffered as a result of some involvement with these young girls? Had he lost a substantial amount of money during his stay in that hotel? We had no idea what gave him the urge to warn us, but we just wanted him to go away and leave us in peace. We were not stupid young men, and we were definitely not in the slightest bit interested in the comings and goings of the other hotel residents.

However, we politely thanked him for his advice and reassured him that we were not at all interested in getting involved with any of these females as we had enough problems of our own to deal with. We also informed him that we would be looking for a different hotel the very next day. Then we promptly got up from the seats and bade him goodnight before going upstairs to our room.

The following morning – Tuesday, 16th August, 1988 – we left the hotel before 8am and hired a taxi to take us to the British Embassy in Nicosia. As the Embassy was still closed when we arrived, Mudhaffar and I enjoyed a short stroll around the area then stood in the shade of a few nearby trees to wait patiently for the doors to open. By then, there were a few people already hanging around waiting.

When the doors eventually opened, we went over to the building and formed an orderly queue, hoping that we would all be seen by the embassy officials in due course. When my turn came, I handed my passport over to the young lady sitting behind the safety glass.

'How can I help you?' was her opening statement.

'I would like to apply for a visa to return to the UK,' was my simple answer.

She went to the other side of the office and brought back an application form that consisted of a few pages. Then she handed my passport back to me with the application form and asked me to fill it in and bring it back later.

I went outside again and filled in the form, before returning to wait in the queue once more. Eventually, I was seen by the same lady, who scrutinised the contents of the visa application form and my passport, then got up from her chair and left the office to go and see someone else. It was a hair-raising scenario. Why on earth did she take my passport and the application form and then leave the room? What on earth was going on? Was I in some kind of trouble? Was I going to get arrested? Should I just run away and hide somewhere? I was quaking in my boots, and all the time I was thinking to myself, 'Oh my God, I am so near to my goal. I just need one more visa and one more flight and I will be back with Carol and my children. Home safe and sound! Please, Allah. Please give me the strength to get through this!'

Although only five minutes passed before she returned to her desk again, to me it seemed like an hour. The lady sat down and looked up at me before handing me back my passport and a slip of paper. As she handed them over to me, she said, 'The Ambassador will see you tomorrow morning at 9am on the dot.' She looked deadly serious when she said that, which made me feel even more anxious.

However, I kept my cool and politely thanked her for her assistance, even though my mouth was dry as I stumbled out the words. But inside, I was thinking about how many times I'd had problems when trying to get a visa. Would it never end?

I went outside and waited under the trees for Mudhaffar to appear. When he finally came over to me, he informed me that he too had an appointment the next morning with the British Ambassador. Neither of us knew what was happening, and we were both naturally very apprehensive. At the same time, we hoped against hope that our wives had managed to get some strings pulled to help us get visas to the UK. We would just have to wait and see what would happen tomorrow! Only time would tell!

We got up early the next morning in anticipation of our meeting with the British Ambassador to Cyprus. In all honesty, neither of us had slept well, worrying about what was going to happen at our appointments. Once again, we took a taxi to the British Embassy and arrived there by 8.15am. The weather was absolutely glorious at that time of the morning as the sun was shining bright in a cloudless blue sky, but it was not yet too hot. We heard a multitude of birds singing in the trees and parks near the Embassy, but couldn't help but wonder if we would still be free to listen to the birds later that day, or whether we would be incarcerated or what on earth was going to happen. There were so many scenarios running through our heads and none of them were good – probably due to the experiences we had already endured.

Although we had been told by our wives that the Embassy was supposed to have received information from the House of Commons regarding our case, we were still doubtful that anyone would have passed any information on, particularly when no money had changed hands to facilitate any assistance from anyone. Over the past six weeks or so, since we first escaped from Iraq, we had come to realise that the majority of people in authority did not do anything for anyone unless there was something in it for them. So why would a British MP, or a senior member of the House of Commons for that matter, do anything to help us?

Carol had already confided in me that she felt her local MP was not in the least bit interested in helping, so why would someone else in the House of Commons be any different? So far, we had been coerced into paying out hundreds of pounds in bribes and 'fees', and had received almost nothing in return for all our efforts. So why should it be any different this time?

Mudhaffar and I stood under the shade of the trees close to the British Embassy building counting the minutes until our appointments. During that short time, we hardly uttered a word to each other, but just held on like grim death to our passports and the various documents that we hoped might help us. Slowly but surely, other people began to arrive and wait near where we were standing, each with their own problems and requests.

As it got nearer to 9am, we formed an orderly queue in front of the door of the building, waiting for it to open. Exactly on time, the door opened and Mudhaffar and I were first in the queue to walk into the building and towards the cubicles we had visited the previous day.

When I was signalled to come forward, I went into a cubicle where a well-dressed young lady sat at a big desk. I was holding my documents tightly in my right hand and staring at her intently.

'How can I help you?' she asked, with her hands outstretched to take my documents from me.

'I have an appointment with the Ambassador at 9 o'clock,' I said to her in what I hoped was a confident manner.

She responded by asking, 'What is your name, and how do you spell it?'

She wrote my details on a slip of paper and disappeared out of the door with it – presumably going to speak to someone in another office. A few minutes later, she reappeared and waved for me to go to a door at the end of the corridor. By the time I got there, she was already waiting for me, and said, 'Please follow me. The Ambassador will see you now.'

She walked me through another short corridor to a smart office, where a secretary was sitting at an expensive-looking desk waiting for us. I greeted her politely and she gestured for me to sit down. She then rose from her seat, knocked gently on the Ambassador's office door, and waited. When she heard his response, she opened the door to let him know that his 9am appointment was here waiting for him.

Although the door was already open, I still knocked gently on it and waited until I was invited to enter. The Ambassador was a gentleman in his mid-thirties, wearing a grey suit and tie. He got up from a lovely, dark coloured, plush leather chair and walked forward a few steps, thrusting his hand out to shake mine. He then invited me to sit down on a leather settee just off the centre of the room.

Once I was seated, he sat next to me, giving me the impression that he wanted to have a formal chat with me regarding my case.

'Tell me what brought you to Cyprus?' was his opening question – one which I had already anticipated I might be asked.

I gave him a very brief summary of my adventures so far, without going into all the trivial details. He listened intently but did not write anything on the pad in front of him.

'I have to contact the Home Office again today and inform them that I have interviewed you, that I am satisfied with your case, and have no problem in issuing you with a visa to the UK. However, I still have to ask them for permission to grant you the visa. I should have an answer for you at some stage tomorrow, but I suggest you come back the following day instead, in case the answer does not arrive until late afternoon. Hopefully, everything will be okay, as I can see no reason for your visa application to be rejected.'

He appeared fairly confident as he stood up and held his hand out to shake mine as a signal that the meeting was terminated. As I turned to leave the office, he added, 'Good luck and all the best, and no more adventures like these. And definitely no more riding on mules up mountains!' This was all said with a broad smile on his face.

'Thank you so much for your help,' I said. And I left that office feeling more optimistic than I had done for a good few weeks.

I left the coolness of the British Ambassador's office and walked straight outside into the sunshine. In fact, I was so excited that I did not even pay attention to Mudhaffar and must have passed him in the corridor as he waited for his interview with the British Ambassador. I was just far too excited and bemused to think about anything at that moment in time!

It was only when I came to a halt under the trees across from the Embassy Building that I realised that Mudhaffar was not beside me. I began to calm down as I waited for him to come outside.

The next two days were the longest of our lives as we anxiously waited to find out whether we would be granted visas to travel to the UK or not. Early on the morning of Friday, 19th of August, we made our third – and what we hoped was our last – trip to the British Embassy, and joined the few people waiting in the queue.

When my turn came, I handed my passport to the lady behind the glass barrier and she examined it carefully then looked at some documents on her desk. She again looked carefully at me to make sure it was definitely my photo that was on the passport. Satisfied, she then opened a desk drawer and took a rubber stamp out which she proceeded to apply to my passport. Having stamped it, she stood up and left the room with my passport in her hands, then returned a few minutes later and pushed my passport under the glass partition.

As I picked up my passport, she smiled at me and wished me luck.

'Thank you so much for your help,' I said to her with a beaming smile and a huge sigh of relief.

I took my passport, left the building with a spring in my step, and headed straight to the comfort of the shady trees while I waited for Mudhaffar to appear. As I waited, I opened my passport and double-checked the page that held the stamp and the signature of the British Ambassador to Cyprus. I just could not believe it! I had to keep telling myself that this was not a dream and that my struggles would soon be over. I would soon be back in the UK with my wife and children; back home, safe and sound in a comfortable environment. It was what we had been praying for, for so long, and we were another huge step nearer to it. All we had to do now was get a flight back to the UK.

As my mind whirled at the prospect of finally being reunited with my wife and children, I lost track of the time until Mudhaffar came rushing towards me waving his passport in the air. He was as excited as I had been with the outcome, and we ended up hugging each other and jumping up and down with happiness.

That afternoon, once we had calmed down and got used to the fact that we both had visas to allow us entry to the UK, we found a travel agency fairly close to the hotel where we were staying.

After a short discussion with the travel agent, we were offered business class tickets from Limassol to Heathrow Airport on a British Airways flight. It was scheduled to leave Limassol International Airport shortly after 8am the following morning, which meant we had to leave our hotel around 4am, but we didn't care.

We paid for the tickets, then headed straight back to the hotel to pack our belongings and settle our bill at the reception. We both decided to try to get an early night so that we would be refreshed in the morning to tackle the – hopefully – final leg of our journey. But it was difficult to get to sleep when we were so excited.

We asked for an alarm call at 3.15am to give us enough time to get washed and dressed and out of the hotel by 4am, but I hardly slept a wink as I kept checking my watch every half hour or so until the phone rang with our wake-up call.

With no time to waste, we both washed and dressed as quickly as possible, before dragging our suitcases down the corridor and out to the reception area. The taxi, which the receptionist had booked for us, arrived quickly and we were soon heading towards Limassol and the airport.

When we reached the airport and checked in for our flight, there were no problems whatsoever and we were ushered through to the transit area. As we had business class tickets, we were shown to the business lounge to wait on our flight being called. We were delighted to find that there was free tea, coffee, and biscuits on offer, so we helped ourselves and relaxed on the comfortable leather settees. In fact, we were so relaxed that we were almost sleeping when our flight was called, and we had to quickly walk the short distance to the terminal gate.

Our flight bound for Heathrow Airport departed on time, and we were comfortably seated in the first row in the first-class section of the plane. What luxury! Within minutes, the stewardess approached us to ask if we would like a glass of wine or a soft drink, then returned with our two glasses of orange juice. Less than five minutes later, the same stewardess appeared with two bags of goodies, including flight socks, earphones, and an eye mask. Around 9.30am, a cooked breakfast of scrambled eggs, toast, marmalade, and yoghurt was served, along with offers of more tea or coffee. And around 10.30, another stewardess brought around a tray of snacks.

I felt really pampered on that flight, but my emotions were still a mix of euphoria and apprehension. Although we had been successful so far, I was still terrified in case we would be turned back at Heathrow Airport. And if we did manage to get through passport control and security, what next? Would I manage to get a job and be able to support my wife and family? After all, the reason I had found myself in this predicament in the first place was because I could not get a job in the UK and was so indebted to my relatives that I had to return to Iraq to get work.

In fairness, I had loved being a lecturer in Iraq, but would I be able to get a position as a lecturer in Britain? And if not, what would I do to support my wife and children? I had not seen them for so long, and so many things had happened. Would my wife and children still want me? Had they changed too much since we were last together? Had *I* changed too much because of what I had been through? Could we really make our marriage work once again? So many questions and not a single answer!

I would have to pray that we could sort out any differences and continue our lives as a happy family.

Chapter 18

Back in the UK at Long Last

Due to the time difference, we finally arrived at Heathrow Airport late in the morning of 20th August, 1988. The queue of people waiting to get through and past the immigration officers was long, as per usual. Eventually, my turn came, and I found myself talking to a smartly-uniformed immigration officer who seemed to take her job very seriously. From her demeanour and the expression on her face, it would appear that she felt she, rightly, had an extremely important role to play within the department. I handed my passport over to her and she scrutinised it meticulously, page by page, looking for any irregularities.

'Where did you come from?' she asked, her puzzled blue eyes looking from me to my open passport and back.

'I have just arrived here from Limassol in Cyprus,' I replied politely.

I had answered her question truthfully, as we had just arrived off a plane from Cyprus. However, she looked at me as if I was an idiot and again asked me where I had come from. Again, I said we had arrived from Cyprus.

Then she said to me, 'No! I mean, where are you originally from?'

This time, she placed her hands on the open pages of my passport and leaned over to me. She looked at me with a pained expression, as if she was speaking to an idiot and she did not have time to waste on idiots. I immediately got the impression that I was going to be in trouble if I did not give her a speedy, truthful answer.

'I am originally from Iraq, and as you can see, this is my Iraqi passport in front of you. I have a visa from the British Embassy in Cyprus allowing me entry into the UK,' I answered, with a confidence I did not feel. I wanted this over and done with; I had been through enough over the past seven weeks, and had thought that having an entry visa to the UK on my passport would be more than enough proof that I was a genuine traveller.

'I know that, and I can see that this is an Iraqi passport. But how did you manage to get here, especially as there is a ban on Iraqis travelling out of that country?' She continued to question me, eventually asking me if I had any other documents to support my case.

I opened my briefcase and pulled out my MSc and PhD degree certificates, but she glanced at them and passed them back to me, showing no interest in these documents. I looked over to my left, where Mudhaffar was in the process of having his passport checked by another immigration officer. Within seconds, he was allowed to pass through the channel to the other side, where his wife was already standing waiting just outside the barrier.

Obviously, the immigration officer who checked his passport was lenient; either that, or my friend had managed to convince him that he was not just any old asylum seeker coming to the UK for financial gain or some such, but was a man who wanted to come to the UK to join his British wife. No matter what, he was free and on his way over to embrace his wife.

I informed the immigration officer that my wife was British and was waiting on me phoning her to tell her exactly what time I would arrive at Edinburgh Airport, so that she could travel to Edinburgh from our home in Dundee to meet me with our two children.

I found it really difficult to speak by this stage, as my mouth had become so dry. I felt that she did not want to believe me and did not trust a single word I said. I was petrified that I was going to be deported. It was obvious that she was not satisfied with the information to hand or my explanation, and she clearly thought there was something fishy going on. She made me stand aside then went off to speak to another officer, and they both returned to speak to me.

'Please come with me, sir,' the second officer waved for me to follow her, and we walked along a few corridors of Heathrow Airport and through several security doors until we reached a small office. In this office, there was only room for one small table and two chairs. It was claustrophobic, and I estimate that it was no more than 1.5 metres by 1.5 metres in size. There was nothing else in that small space apart from a telephone.

I was told to sit down and, once seated, she was kind enough to ask me if I needed a cup of water, to which I gratefully answered, 'Yes, please.' She left me alone in the office while she went to a water dispenser and soon came back with a cup of cold water for me. After I had taken a few sips of water, she started to interrogate me.

This interrogation lasted for over fifty minutes, although to me it felt more like several hours. Eventually she asked me once again what my wife was called, and whether she was waiting for me at Edinburgh Airport and, if not, then where would she most likely be. I told her that if she was not at Edinburgh Airport by that time, then she would be *en route* there to meet me off the plane.

The officer left me alone in the room once more, but this time she was only gone for a minute or so. When she came back in, she picked up the phone and dialled a number. I heard her asking the person she spoke with to put a message over the public announcement system asking for a Mrs Carol Khalaf to present herself at the Immigration Office at Edinburgh Airport. She informed the officer on the other end of the phone that he/she should speak to my wife and check up on whether our relationship was *bona fide* or whether this was just a ruse to get me into the country. She said that she would wait on a return call from the Immigration Officer.

Ten minutes later, another member of staff knocked on the door and asked the immigration officer to step outside for a brief discussion. All that time I was sitting in the office not knowing what was happening. Shortly afterwards, the immigration officer came back into the room with a notepad. Picking up my passport, she said, 'Ok, you can come with me now. I will do the paperwork, and I am going to issue you with a one-year permit to say in Britain.'

On hearing this, I felt slightly more relaxed and followed her all the way back to the same desk where I had been spoken to by the first immigration officer. The second officer who had interviewed me stamped my passport and took me through to the baggage area. My luggage had just been left abandoned several metres away from the conveyor belt.

I thanked the immigration officer for her help and then left the area, dragging my suitcase behind me. I still had to get another flight to Edinburgh Airport, so I had to go looking for the standby desk to try and book a one-way ticket on the next available flight. Thankfully, there was a British Airways flight leaving for Edinburgh in two hours' time, and I managed to get a seat on it.

Nearly three hours later, my plane landed at Edinburgh Airport. My wife and children were there waiting for me, along with my brother-in-law Andy, who had driven them to the airport to meet me off the plane and was waiting to drive us all back to Dundee. That was a truly wonderful reunion I had with my family. The sense of achievement at finally reaching my desired goal, especially after all the struggles I had been through and all the terrifying events I had endured, was unsurpassable.

*****

Carol's story:

At last, my husband was back where he belonged – with me and our two children. I was so happy to see him down on his knees hugging Layla and Ramsay, but I could not believe it was all over. For weeks now, I had been living in a state of limbo. Both the children had missed their father so much, and words could not explain how I felt at long last. The past few weeks had been an uphill struggle for me, and I was under such stress on my own with two young children, not knowing if my husband was alive and well, or whether he had been captured as an illegal immigrant somewhere, or whether he was dead and lying in a hole somewhere.

I did my best to be both mother and father to the kids, but it was a very hard struggle. From the minute I received the very first phone call from Abed to say he was travelling to Karbala in two days' time, my nerves were on edge. Saying that he was travelling to Karbala was the code phrase to tell me that he had made all the arrangements and was going to be smuggled out of Iraq two days later.

In reply, I warned him to watch all these wrecked cars that were lying at the side of the desert. This was me trying to tell him to be careful, because we knew the stories about the people smugglers who had stolen all the belongings of people they were supposed to be smuggling out of Iraq, but along the way they had either killed the people or the people had fallen from the mountains. Sometimes, the stories went, it was because the people had not obeyed the 'rules' and had refused to supply any more money, or they had been arrogant and treated the smugglers with contempt. Sometimes, it was truly because of a horrific accident on the treacherous mountain slopes. However, I always say that there is no smoke without fire, and we knew just how ruthless the smugglers and Peshmerga could be.

Anyway, when the telegram arrived to say he was in Iran, I set about doing what I could from this side of the world. I researched to see if there were any organisations that could help to ease Abed's exploits. There was a charitable organisation I found out about, and I contacted their offices in London. They were sympathetic about our story, but said the best they could do would be to ask the International Red Crescent to try to find out where he was and to let us know that he was safe. There was little else they could do. I thanked them for their advice but declined their assistance as it sounded as though there was nothing they could really do to help us.

I contacted my local MP although he was difficult to get hold of and seldom returned my calls. When I did manage to speak to him, he was not very forthcoming and said he would phone back, but he never did. Instead, he would get one of his underlings to return my call, and I then felt I was just being passed from pillar to post with no help whatsoever.

On receiving that first telegram, I had phoned Mudhaffar's wife, who had not received any correspondence from her husband. From that day on, we were constantly on the phone to each other to see if either of us was making any headway in getting assistance from anyone in power or authority. She informed me that her MP was useless, but that she had been in contact with one of the Ministers in the Home Office, who said he would look into this further and try to help if he could.

That spurred me on, so I wrote to the then Minister of State, Tim Renton. I explained that I was unemployed at present as I had two young children under the age of five. I then explained in my letter about our predicament. I wrote that my husband was in transit from Iraq – having fled from there because of the political situation – and was trying to make his way back to the UK to be with me and our children. I explained that he had a PhD in Science, and that he was a good lecturer and a fantastic husband and father. I said that if he could find any way of helping us, then we would be forever in his debt. If my husband came to the UK, we would not live off the state but would get a job. If hubby could not get a job, then he would be the chief babysitter and bottle-washer, and I would get a job and support our family.

Within ten days, having not had any success with our local MP, I was amazed to receive a letter with the Parliamentary logo on it. I did not think it would give me any hope for the future but was amazed to read that the Honourable Gentleman would try to help my husband, provided he managed to get to a British Consulate. Unfortunately, during that period of time, most of the consulates had been closed in the Middle East because of the instabilities in these regions.

However, the letter went on, if he managed to get to Cyprus, then the Minister would do his best to help him to get an entry visa for the UK! Wow – that was fantastic news – but how could I get this information to Abed and

Mudhaffar? I phoned Mudhaffar's wife and asked if she had heard any news. She had not heard anything from her husband or anyone else, so I read my letter out to her. This was the first promising news that either of us had heard for a number of weeks.

Meanwhile, until we heard from either of our husbands, life had to go on. Each morning, I would get the children up and ready for school. Sometimes my sister would come over and we would take the bus into the town just to go window shopping, and occasionally buy some new clothes for the children in the sales. One afternoon, after sending Layla back to school after lunchtime, I was walking along the road to the bus stop and stopped when I heard someone crying. It sounded so sad and distressed – I ran towards the noise and it was Layla. Some idiot had hit her on the head with a brick in a bag!!!

Once I had comforted her, I marched her into school to speak to the headmistress. Thankfully, she was really super about the incident and helped locate the perpetrator, who was an older pupil in the school and came from a very deprived family. It took some persuasion to encourage Layla to go back to school on a daily basis after that, but I succeeded, and she was a very studious pupil. Even in Iraq, I would sit with the two children every day and read stories from their Jack and Jill books I had taken with us, and I had them both reading and writing and counting, much to the amazement of some of our friends.

Late one afternoon, I received a call from Abed. Although the call did not last long, it was long enough for me to tell him he had to get to Cyprus and, once there, he should get help from the British Ambassador to Cyprus. That phone call brightened us both up, but even then, I did not pin any hopes on him getting any help. I mean, why should a stranger help us? Especially a stranger who worked in Parliament and must have had a very stressful position and more to think of than helping us - a mere mixed-marriage family. But at least it bolstered Abed's feelings and gave him some hope for the future.

Suffice to say, it was amazing when Abed managed to phone and say that he now had a visa to the UK on his passport! The next hurdle would be getting to the UK.

I thought that, once here, it was a foregone conclusion that he would be allowed entry with no questions asked. How wrong could I have been? It was so scary when I was sitting in Edinburgh Airport waiting on Abed and the allotted time passed and he did not come through the gates. What on earth could have happened? Was he ill? Did he not get on the flight? Had he been intercepted somewhere and ghosted away? Had he had second thoughts and felt he was better off where he was and without the added burden of a wife and family?

Three flights from London had arrived with still no sign of him. My brother, who drove me to the airport, had asked if we should just go back to Dundee but I didn't want to give up – not yet! Then suddenly, my name came over the PA system, asking me to go and speak to an immigration officer. I was escorted into a small room and asked what felt to me like a thousand questions. Was I really married to an Iraqi? When did we get married? Was it a marriage of convenience? Where did we meet? How long had we been married? What was his full name and date of birth? What qualifications did he have, and did he have a job to come to?

I answered every question as thoroughly as I could, and ended by saying that if my husband was allowed to join me and the children, we would get jobs – either one or both of us – and we would not claim any benefits from the Government. It was not just a marriage of convenience – for pity's sake, we have two children! Look at them, I said. It was obvious they were children from a mixed marriage, and they were made from love and not just to cause problems for anyone! I felt I was begging for my husband, my children, and my own future life...

*****

Carol told me later that she had decided it would be better if she headed straight to Edinburgh Airport so that she could be there waiting on my flight landing from London. But she had been really worried when she could see on the announcement boards that several flights had arrived from Heathrow Airport and I was not amongst the passengers. Then she had been shocked to hear her name coming over the public announcement system asking her to present herself at the Immigration Office immediately. Leaving the children with her brother, she had gone in search of the Immigration Office, which turned out to be a 'pokey little hole'.

When she informed a member of the Immigration Office staff who she was, the immigration officer asked her, 'Are you Mrs Khalaf; Mrs Carol Khalaf?' Of course, Carol replied in the affirmative.

The next question was, 'Are you still married to Mr Khalaf?' He was trying to find out whether we were still together or whether we had separated. 'Yes, of course we are still married,' my wife responded.

'What is his full name?' was the next question. So my wife replied, 'Abedawn Ibrahim Khalaf Al-Shimmery Toga is his full name, but he only goes by the name on his passport which is Abedawn Ibrahim Khalaf.'

'What is his date of birth?' Carol immediately answered this, too.

'Do you still want him to enter this country, or should we return him back to the country that he came from?' was the next question.

'Of course I want my husband here, and his children want their father, too,' she responded.

This was followed by, 'Does he have a job and, if not, how will he support his family?' Carol informed the officer that I did not have a job at present, but that I would do my best to get one. She also explained that she was not working because our children were too young.

Then she said, 'However, if you let my husband come back to me, even if he does not get a job then he will stay at home and look after the children and I will get a job. We have no intention of scrounging off the State and sticking our hands out asking for Social Security.'

Carol said that her final words to the officer were, 'Surely it is better for children to live in a two-parent household rather than to live with only one parent. Let my husband come home and we will work it out. It is better that he is here and we make a proper life together. He will get a job and he will contribute to society. He was a lecturer in Iraq, and a good one at that. Hopefully, he will manage to get a post as a lecturer here!'

Obviously, my wife must have made a very good impression on the Immigration Officer that day. Thank heavens she did!

Chapter 19

Getting Back to Normal Life

Although it was absolutely wonderful to be back in the UK and living with my wife and children, I soon found it extremely difficult being unemployed and living in a council flat. Being out of work was the reason I had left Dundee in the first place, and now, after everything that I had been through, I felt that I was back to square one, with no job prospects in sight.

To stay true to her word, Carol managed to find a place on a Government training course which led to a job working in a garage. This barely paid enough money for the four of us to survive and to pay the rent, etc., so we lived on simple foods like rice and lentils or tuna and pasta to try to ensure we kept our finances in the black. Due to her austerity measures, we were succeeding... but only just!

We bought a small portable typewriter and Carol helped me update my CV and covering letters, then I applied for each and every vacancy going in the chemical industry or in academia. I applied for literally hundreds of positions, and received rejection letters from maybe a few dozen; more often than not, I did not get any responses from the companies or the universities I had applied to.

I remember during this time I received rejection letters from two different companies, both stating that they 'already had their quota of foreigners' working for them! These letters were worse than the straightforward rejections and the no responses.

I did manage to get a handful of interviews, but they were mostly in industries in Durham and Manchester, and I also had an interview for a position at King's College, London. However, no matter how good my CV looked on paper, by the time I had been through the interview process there were still no offers of a job. I was never sure whether my failure to gain successful employment was down to my age (by now I was in my mid-thirties), my abilities, my suitability for the post in question, because English was not my mother tongue, or whether some of it was purely due to racial discrimination because I am from the Middle East.

I even contacted my old supervisor and other colleagues from my days as a student at the University of Dundee. Unfortunately, they all told me that they did not have enough funding to offer me a position, but said if they did succeed in getting any funds, they would all be delighted to offer me a position and would not hesitate to contact me if anything turned up.

*****

Carol's story:

While Abed was trying to get some form of employment, and I was very proud of him persevering, there had been very little contact with his family back in Iraq. Eventually, he did get through to speak to his sister, only to discover that his mother had died seven days after he had started on his travels to get out of Iraq. Nobody had wanted to tell him that she was dead because they did not want to upset him. It was exactly the same when his father died while Abed was studying for his MSc. It took months for him to find out his father had died of a heart attack, because the family had not wanted to upset him.

Abed managed to speak to one of his best friends and was informed that, because he had left Iraq without authority, there was a bounty on his head. This meant that if he ever went back to Iraq while the present regime was in control, he would be shot on sight! He was also told that all those scientific books he had translated from English to Arabic while he was a lecturer at Salahaddin University had been removed from sale until his name had been deleted from the books! Abed felt as though he had been totally obliterated.

Another huge cause of consternation was when he took a phone call from his niece one evening. The conversation started off as normal and I could understand the gist of the phone call. Having left the room for a minute, I came rushing back in when I heard the most horrific sound coming from Abed. After trying to sound normal on the phone, his niece told him that her brother had been killed by the Iraqi regime. Apparently, he had been sitting in a café with friends when they were suddenly surrounded by Intelligence Officers. They were arrested and charged with committing acts of treason against the Iraqi Government. Within ten days, he was hanged in Abu Ghraib prison, and his sister was told to come and collect his remains. She was warned that the family should not mourn his death, and they were not allowed to perform the normal funeral procession rituals of taking the body around the mosque nor the usual forty days mourning, or all the family would be arrested.

*****

Three months after I arrived back in Dundee, I was sitting in a library sifting through the job advertisements in scientific magazines when I saw an advert for a post-doctoral research fellow at the University of Strathclyde in Glasgow. The post was for one year in the first instance, with the possibility of an extension of up to two more years, depending on the progress of the research project. I decided to apply for this post and on 24th November, 1988 I received a letter from Professor Colin Suckling OBE, from the Department of Pure and Applied Chemistry, stating that he had written to my referees and would be back in touch once he had received their responses.

The following month, I had an interview with Professor Suckling and the late Dr George Proctor. They explained the proposed research they wanted done, which involved organic synthesis and some biological assays. I must admit that I had never heard of that kind of work before, but I was desperate for a job and was prepared physically and mentally for any challenges that would lie ahead if I was successful. However, I wasn't confident of success, due to my previous track record and, as I said above, because I had never been involved in work like that before.

At the end of the second week of December, I received a letter offering me one year's employment in the Department of Pure and Applied Chemistry at the University of Strathclyde, Glasgow. The letter stated that, if I accepted the job, I could start work on the 16th of January, 1989.

I was over the moon when I received that job offer and accepted it immediately. Although it was only for a twelve-month fixed term contract in the first instance, I was just so grateful for any job. Admittedly, I was apprehensive as this work was in an area I was not familiar with, and it was also in a town I had never even visited before. The position meant that I would have to commute between Dundee and Glasgow, or I would have to find somewhere to stay in Glasgow and travel home to my family at weekends. I was desperate for the job, and would just have to find out what was the best option for all concerned.

Monday, 16th January, 1989 – my first day of work in my new research career in the Organic and Medicinal Chemistry Laboratory, Department of Pure and Applied Chemistry, University of Strathclyde, Glasgow.

For the first few weeks in post, I commuted to Glasgow five days a week. It involved me leaving our flat by 4am to take a bus to the centre of Dundee, and then another bus to Glasgow to be at the department for 9am. In the evenings, the earliest I arrived home was 9pm, and it was often later than that. I found it exhausting, especially after a day's work in the laboratory.

After only two months of exhausting commuting, we decided that I should rent a flat in Glasgow and only come home at the weekends. Neither of us wanted me to become unwell due to exhaustion, and we also had to consider the cost of travelling backwards and forwards from Mondays to Fridays.

I began searching for accommodation that would not be too expensive, and we had to decide whether the cost of renting in Glasgow would be offset by only having to pay the cost of transport over the weekend rather than for five days a week.

I soon found a bedsit to rent in Glasgow's Buccleuch Street, which was not too far from the Department. This meant that I lived in Glasgow during the week and only saw my family at weekends. To help eke out the money a bit, I took food from home to last me for a few days and then had to buy enough food to keep me going for the rest of the week. However, it was still slightly more expensive than the cost of daily transport to and from Dundee.

Although this new living arrangement cost a bit more money than the previous one, we agreed that it was far healthier for me as it was better than me being unable to cope due to exhaustion. Carol also said it was less disruptive for the children, because they sometimes woke up when I left the flat in the early hours of the morning and she then struggled to get them back to sleep.

Within four months of starting the research work, everything seemed to be going so well that Professor Suckling informed me that the indications were that the contract would be extended for three years in total, which was fantastic news. Around the same time, my wife started having problems with some of the neighbours in the tenement close, who were shouting racist remarks when they were under the influence of alcohol. At one stage she actually had a fist fight with a female who lived across the road. The obscenities were getting worse, and my wife was fed up with the situation but did not want to involve the police.

While this was happening in Dundee, I had struggled to contact my family back home in Iraq. My friends had tried to contact me, but I had not managed to speak to any of my relatives as they all seemed to be unavailable when I tried to phone.

Due to the news about my position being extended to three years, and because of the problematic neighbours, we decided to get a mortgage and purchase a house in Glasgow. One of the lab ladies told me about new houses that were going to be built beside her daughter who lived in the first phase of a fairly new estate in Garthamlock. The new houses were to be in phase two of this estate.

I arranged to visit the site and met with the lab lady's daughter. That weekend, I discussed everything with my wife, who said that we should just go for it, especially as the houses being built had two bedrooms and a box room. It would have one room more than we had in the flat, and there would be a front and back garden – ideal for the growing children.

We applied and were approved for an endowment mortgage and, as the houses were not yet built, we started paying the endowment premiums on a monthly basis until the house was completed. Unfortunately, the builders seemed to have problems with the construction site on more than one occasion, which held the process up. As the house was not completed on time, we were subsequently informed that the costs had risen and so the house price had increased.

We tried to argue the case that we had a contract with the building company, but they were adamant that the costs had increased and there was nothing we could do about it so we would just have to pay the extra costs. Although I complained to them on a number of occasions about how long it was taking for the house to be completed, their response was that the weather conditions had adversely affected the construction work but they were doing their best to get it completed as soon as possible.

We eventually moved into our new house in February, 1990. We knew it was an incredible gamble, but it was one that we were both more than willing to take. In Dundee our daughter was in Primary Three at school and our son was in Primary Two. However, the Glasgow primary school we enrolled them in informed us that they would be held back a year to ensure they were able to keep up with the rest of the class. Although we were not happy with this, that school was the nearest to our home so we just had to agree to this. It soon turned out that our two children were more advanced than the children in their new classes.

We were still struggling financially, especially as our bank was charging us an extra 1% on top of the original mortgage cost because we were first-time buyers. However, as before, my wife made sure we were able to pay all our bills and we lived on simple foods to try to eke out our money as much as possible.

Within weeks of moving to Glasgow, Carol started applying for all the part-time jobs she could find, and six weeks later she was successful in securing a part-time job as a secretary/administrator for the Portering Services Manager in a nearby mental health hospital. This helped us so much, as it was a big support both financially and psychologically.

Carol worked from 10am to 3pm, so she was able to take the children to school in the mornings, and in the afternoons the children were looked after by a couple who worked in The Play Barn, which was an after-school activity centre for local children. At last, things were starting to look up a little, and we were now able to put some money aside towards a rainy day. The children were well looked after, and during the school holidays, they were taken on day trips with the other children who attended the Play Barn.

When the three-year project I was working on was nearing its end, more research projects with the same supervisor in the same department followed. Sometimes the contract was only for two months at a time; sometimes it was a six-month contract; at other times the projects were two or three years long. My research projects all went extremely well, and we kept moving from one project to another. As a team, we were able to publish a large number of research papers and we also filed five patents in the field of medicinal chemistry (see the appendix for more information).

In 2013, while still working for the Department of Pure and Applied Chemistry, a member of staff from the Royal Society of Chemistry had discovered a bit about my life history, my escape from Iraq and how I had managed to get back to the UK. I was subsequently contacted by one of the press officers and informed about a project they were doing called the '175 faces of Chemistry' wherein they were printing articles on 175 chemists to celebrate 175 years since the establishment of the Royal Society of Chemistry. They had already interviewed a number of scientists from around the world who had achieved something amazing, or who had gone the extra mile to push chemical knowledge forward in spite of the obstacles they faced in life.

I felt truly honoured and privileged to be asked if they could print an article about me, with a very brief account of my life. The article was published in January 2014, alongside articles about many incredibly distinguished scientists who worked hard for chemical sciences, education, and related subjects.

As Sir Isaac Newton is reported to have said in 1675: 'If I have seen further than others, it is by standing upon the shoulders of giants.' Those academics and supervisors whom I worked with over the years were certainly giants and pillars of wisdom in the scientific community, and I am forever indebted to them for their help and support over the years.

*

Photo courtesy of the Royal Society of Chemistry
© Royal Society of Chemistry/ Anne Purkiss

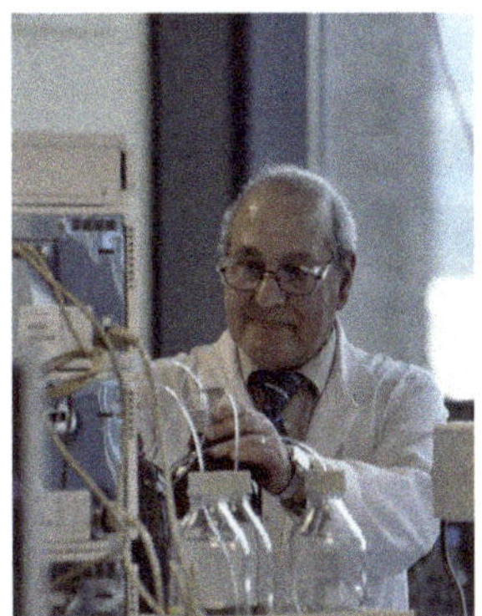

Photo courtesy of the Royal Society of Chemistry
© Royal Society of Chemistry/ Anne Purkiss

Courtesy of the Royal Society of Chemistry
© Royal Society of Chemistry/Anne Purkiss

Two of the patents that we produced were licenced by the University of Strathclyde to a small pharmaceutical company called 'MGB Biopharma Ltd', who had an office in Glasgow. One specific drug that this pharmaceutical company was interested in was a broad-spectrum antibiotic which I named in my research books as 'MGB-BP-3'. MGB Biopharma adopted this name during their Phase I clinical trials – which were trials on healthy volunteers.

Eventually, on 14th March, 2018, Dr Miroslav Ravic, the CEO of MGB Biopharma, announced that they had been *awarded a £2.78million grant from Innovate UK – the UK's Innovation Agency – under its Biomedical Catalyst programme. This grant was allocated to facilitate the Phase IIA trial* of the oral formulation of MGB Biopharma's MGB-BP-3 drug for the treatment of *Clostridium difficile* infection. These Phase IIA trials were to be conducted on people suffering from *C diff*. It was hoped that the company would start the trials on sick patients by the summer of 2018.

My wife Carol was also my pillar, and she stood by me throughout these years while I worked in the Department of Pure and Applied Chemistry. She progressed from working part-time to full-time when the children were old enough to look after themselves more. During this time, in addition to bringing up our children and working full-time, she embarked on a course of study with the Open University, graduating with a BSc in 1997. Following her graduation, she decided to extend her studies and completed a Post Graduate Certificate in Business Management with the topic 'Management in the NHS'.

By the summer of 2006, Carol felt that she wanted a new challenge, so she successfully applied for a secretarial post in the Department of Pure and Applied Chemistry. She still works in the same department now, as a research administrator.

Both of our children went on to study pharmacy, and our daughter Layla graduated from Robert Gordon University, Aberdeen, with an MPharm degree in the summer of 2004. Our son, Ramsay, graduated a year later, with an MPharm degree from the University of Strathclyde.

Carol and I both worked in the same department, although she was in her own office and I was in the laboratory, but it meant we could travel to and from work together on a regular basis.

Things went fairly smoothly until one day in 2007 when I had been out having lunch with fellow students and researchers to celebrate one of them passing his viva that morning. I went to the toilet and, as I had not come back to the table for some time, one of the researchers came looking for me and found me collapsed in the bathroom.

They took me to Glasgow Royal Infirmary by taxi, and I was eventually diagnosed as having paroxysmal atrial fibrillation. It was explained to me that tiredness or too much stress could trigger an episode of this. Obviously, all those times in the past when I had felt my heart beating too fast or felt that I was going to collapse, had been a symptom of this paroxysmal atrial fibrillation. I was informed that I should just lie down and relax for a little while and things should go back to normal – something that I strictly adhered to.

Life was then fairly uneventful for some time until I started suffering from breathlessness in 2015. I attended a cardiology appointment and was informed by the consultant that there was nothing wrong with my heart, so I was referred to a lung specialist at the respiratory clinic. Again, I was told there was nothing wrong with my lungs, so I was referred back to cardiology.

The cardiologist arranged for an echocardiograph, and I was given the treadmill test. Once again, I was informed that there was nothing wrong with my heart. The cardiologist must have been right, and it must have been my imagination, I was told.

When I told the cardiologist that my wife and I wanted to go abroad on holiday, she told me that was fine because she was discharging me from her care.

As I still did not feel right and was still suffering from bouts of breathlessness, I visited my GP. The doctor told me that I had been discharged from the hospital as there was nothing wrong with me, so I should just go off on holiday and enjoy myself.

A week later, on 29th September, 2015, Carol and I flew to Tenerife for a week's holiday. The flight was fine, and we had a lovely first day wandering the streets of Puerto de la Cruz. The following day started off well, and we did all the normal touristy things. But that night, I was really unwell and was experiencing horrific chest pains.

The paramedics and a medical doctor were called to my hotel room and I was taken to one of the private hospitals in Puerto de la Cruz. After a few hours there, I asked the staff to send me to a general hospital because they had refused to treat me without advanced payment being secured on a credit card, and they wanted €2000 security deposit. I did not have that kind of money, and we did not even have a credit card; we only had debit cards because we did not want to overspend.

In the early hours of the morning of 30th September, 2015, I was driven by ambulance to the University Hospital in Santa Cruz, the capital of Tenerife. I was kept in the emergency department until morning, when I was seen by three cardiology consultants. They managed to stabilise me, and over a few days performed a whole plethora of tests, including an angiogram. Meanwhile, my wife visited me every single day, twice a day.

Eventually Carol was informed that I needed a heart bypass, and when she asked how long I would be in hospital, she was told it would take three months before I could even think of travelling back to the UK. Carol was cracking up! She said she could not go back to the UK and leave me there, but she had to work! She asked if they could just patch me up the best they could, enough to get me back home to the UK to be treated there instead. However, she was soon put in her place, and the consultant said that they would run more tests and see what they could do. Two days later, when my wife came to visit me on the ward, she was informed that at that very moment they were operating on me as I was very unwell. I had four stents inserted into my coronary arteries, and we were told later by the medical staff that I was very lucky to still be alive.

September 2015, recuperating after four stents were inserted into my coronary arteries.

I must admit that the staff in the hospital were absolutely amazing to me throughout my stay there. Even the bed I was in was state-of-the-art and I was not even allowed to sit up without assistance. Once I was feeling much better, Carol told me that the holiday insurance we had taken out was worthless and the company were refusing to pay out. She said she had handed over the European Health Insurance Card (EHIC) at the emergency desk and they had, thankfully, accepted that in the first instance.

While I was in hospital, Carol stayed in the same hotel that we had originally booked into, and she took me back there after I was finally discharged. There was another big drama when I was discharged from the hospital, though. I had been given one week's worth of most of the tablets which had been prescribed by the hospital consultants, but there was only two days' supply of one particular tablet. This tablet was called 'Brillique' (also known as Ticagrelor), which is a platelet aggregation inhibitor, and we were told by the medical staff at the hospital that they were not allowed to give me more than two days' worth of tablets to take home with me. But they said I had to have this medication, otherwise I would definitely die!

Carol subsequently made enquiries and discovered that the only way to get this medication was to go to the island's Central Medical Centre, the Casco Botanico, and get a prescription written up from there. We took a taxi to the Casco Botanico and were told by one of the receptionists that we needed an interpreter and would not be seen without one.

There was one very well-dressed man standing beside the reception area, and I asked him if he understood English. He did, and fortunately was able to interpret for us. He informed the receptionist that I was just out of hospital and needed a special medication, so urgently needed to see a doctor. We were eventually seen by a lovely medical doctor who understood English. She took the discharge letter and list of medications, read them thoroughly, and then asked us how she could help us.

We explained about the small supply of medication I had been given on my discharge, and that we needed to get Brillique as we had only been given two days' supply and I only had another two tablets left. We emphasised that I had been informed I would die if I did not take this medication.

Unfortunately, she informed us that none of the medical doctors on the island were allowed to prescribe that medication because it was extremely dangerous. Only the island's Medical Director was allowed to approve a prescription for this, so she immediately typed up a letter which she told us had to be faxed to the Medical Director, who would decide whether we would get permission to buy this medication or not. She explained that if the Medical Director agreed we could get it, we should go to a pharmacy the next day to get the prescription made up.

We took the letter to the main reception area and persuaded a receptionist to fax it through to the Medical Director. The fax took ages to go through, but eventually, she gave us the thumbs up and told us to go! There was no explanation whatsoever, so we did not know if we had to go to a specific pharmacy or even when we should go.

The following morning, Carol climbed the hill to the nearest pharmacy and spoke to the pharmacist on call who, thankfully, spoke good English. He asked for my EHIC card and said we would have to pay 50% of the costs of the medication. For that one day alone, Carol paid over €160 for some of the medication – but said she would have paid hundreds to ensure that she got the medication I needed.

Over the next couple of weeks, we paid out a lot more money for medication until we were able to fly home to the UK and get to our own GP.

*****

Carol's story:

I never thought that we would have any more problems, because I felt we had had enough for a lifetime due to everything we had been through. I had managed to make myself understood to the natives of Iraq, and now here I was in another foreign country with another set of problems, but this time I did not speak the lingo. When Abed told me he was having a lot of pain in his heart, I assumed it was normal heartburn and it would go away in an hour or so. But this time it was different.

He was in agony, and as soon as I realised that, I phoned the reception desk asking them to call a medical doctor. It seemed like hours, but was less than thirty minutes, when a medical doctor and two paramedics arrived in the hotel room. It was very scary watching them checking his vital signs, and he was hooked up to a portable ECG machine. After ten minutes, it was obvious that this was serious, and the paramedics got Abed onto a stretcher and he was whisked away in an ambulance. They would not let me go with them, so I had to follow behind in a taxi. After sitting in that private hospital for a number of hours, I was eventually allowed to see him.

Abed explained that he had insisted on going to a general hospital because we could not afford private treatment. I practically begged the ambulance driver to let me go with them this time, as I did not have a clue where they were taking him. I did not understand a word that was said to me, and I didn't have one of these fancy word translators either! Suffice to say, I have never been as scared in my life. Even when Abed was trying to escape from Iraq, I could at least speak to someone, but here in Tenerife, who could I talk to?

Thankfully, another patient's visitor was able to explain a bit about the procedure. We were not allowed to visit the patient until we had spoken to the consultant; only after that meeting were we allowed to visit the patient. The rest is history now, thank heavens.

*****

We ended up staying in Puerto de la Cruz for just over three weeks, and our son had to help to get us on a flight home to the UK. The spokeswoman from

Thomson, the travel company, said that they could not help us because we had paid for a package holiday and it was not their fault we did not get our original flight home. Ramsay came to the rescue and bought seats on a flight leaving from Tenerife South. He also arranged for transport to pick us up near the hotel. Luckily enough, Carol was able to pay the hotel bill, and we were eventually on our way to the airport.

During that EasyJet flight home, she kept asking me every few minutes if I was ok. I think she was more scared of something happening to me than I was. We got home at 4am on Thursday, 22nd October, and by 8.30am she was on the phone to our GP's surgery. We managed to get an appointment for that morning, and when we finally got to the surgery, our GP was amazed at what had happened.

Although the GP wanted me to take a few months off work to recuperate, I wanted to go back to work as soon as possible. I had already been off work for four weeks and I felt that was long enough. I started back at my post the following Monday.

My GP referred me back to cardiology, and when I finally got my appointment, it was with the cardiologist I had originally seen. I was told that what had happened to me in Tenerife was 'just one of these things' and we should put it behind us and just move on!

I continued working in the lab for the next two years until I had to retire from work due to ill health caused by allergic reactions to the chemicals in the labs. As I had worked with various chemicals for almost 29 years, my body had started to become sensitised to the chemicals. This led to me having to take time off work because my face and hands would swell up as soon as I came into contact with a specific chemical. I did return to work for a few weeks, but soon found that more and more chemicals were causing adverse reactions; at one stage, it was so bad that I was hospitalised overnight.

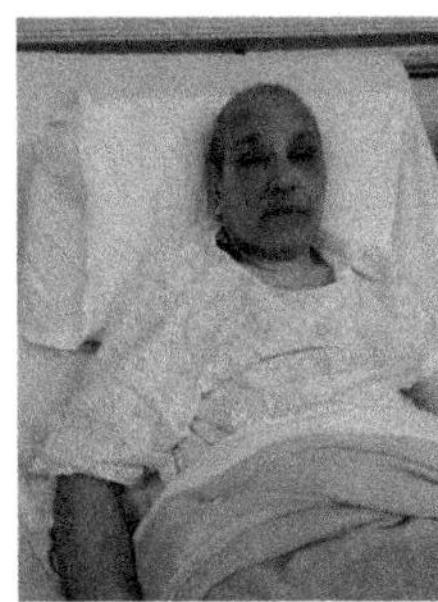

Admitted to hospital overnight due to allergic reaction – February 2017.

Regretfully, my own GP insisted that I had to retire for my own sake. Subsequently, I retired from the post of Research Officer on 17th November, 2017.

I am now formally retired, but I still receive emails and phone calls from former students asking me for help and advice. Although I cannot go anywhere near a laboratory, I still do my best to explain to them how to go about synthesising different compounds, and offering advice and encouragement. I also help many academics from Arab countries, including Iraq, Saudi Arabia, and Libya, to name a few.

In November 2018, I spoke on the telephone to one of the students who graduated the previous year. He reminded me that I had helped him when he was struggling with his studies, and the time he had promised me he would plant trees in his village when he got home, as a thank you for all my assistance. He told me he had planted two fruit trees which were now growing strong; he planted them near a river so he did not need to water them every day, as they were able to get enough water from the ground. He said that as soon as the trees bore fruit, the villagers would be able to help themselves to them and they would offer up prayers of thanks for the kindness that had resulted in them being planted! He finished the call by saying he intended planting more fruit trees as an offering of thanks because I am still helping him when he needs advice.

Carol on her graduation day in May 1997 (with our two children, outside our house).

On Carol's BSc graduation day, we visited Glasgow's Botanical Gardens to take photos to send back to Iraq.

Since retiring from my post at the University of Strathclyde, I have tried to keep myself busy. I go for long walks on a daily basis, and volunteer with different organisations twice a week. On Tuesdays, I visit a language exchange and help people – mostly refugees – to improve their English, as well as helping British people who want to learn Arabic. I also sit with a group of people who are cancer survivors, and we go for a long walk on Saturdays and discuss various things. I get a lot out of sitting and walking with this group, as they are so upbeat about their circumstances.

*

Layla's MPharm graduation in summer 2004.

Ramsay's MPharm Graduation in 2005.

My brother, Abu Zoher (Abd-Alhussain), who was approximately six years older than me, woke up complaining of feeling unwell on the morning of Sunday, 30th December, 2018. His wife telephoned for an appointment with his GP, which was arranged for 4pm that afternoon. My brother decided to do some work at his orchard and returned home at lunchtime. After having a simple lunch, he announced to Umm Zoher that he was going to take a short nap, and lay down on the doshek. Within ten minutes, his wife heard him making strange noises and thought that he was having a bad dream, so she went to shake him awake but could not get any response. She shouted on her sons to come and see to their father, and they subsequently phoned for an ambulance.

His two sons went in the ambulance with him and Umm Zoher went to the hospital by taxi. She arrived in the ward just as the doctor was examining her husband. Having tried unsuccessfully to find a pulse, and having carried out one or two other procedures, the doctor just put a sheet over my brother's head. Umm Zoher started shouting at him, and her sons had to inform her that their father had passed away.

Due to the heat in Iraq, Abu Zoher was buried the following day (Monday, 31st December, 2018 – Hogmanay). In his will, he had written that he did not want any people to be paid to cry at his wake. Instead, he wanted the money to be given to the poor – and his family obeyed his wishes.

Following the death of my brother Abu Zoher and because I had not seen my family for many years, we managed to arrange a four-day trip to Istanbul in February 2019. Travel permits were secured for my sister, Umm Amira, and her daughter and grandson, Sejad, for the same time so we were able to spend a few days together. It was wonderful to see these relatives after so many years. Carol had not seen my sister for over thirty years, and she could not believe how old and frail she had become in the intervening years. We had such a tearful welcome and saying goodbye was the worst thing on earth for all of us as we know it is highly unlikely that we will ever see them again.

Unfortunately, I have not seen Mudhaffar in person since the day we parted at Heathrow Airport. We have had sporadic contact since then and he has settled into a happy life with his wife and daughter in South Wales, where he runs his own business.

Life seems to have come full circle for me. When we married, I was a student and Carol helped support me emotionally and financially. Now, I am retired and once again I am suffering heart problems and, yet again, Carol is by my side helping to support me as much as she can. I have so much to be grateful for, but still suffer from bouts of Post-Traumatic Stress Disorder, and I am now just taking each day as it comes.

Dr ABEDAWN I. KHALAF
BSc, MSc, PhD, CChem, MRSC

LIST OF PUBLICATIONS

83 Selective in vitro anti-cancer activity of non-alkylating minor groove binders

Authors: Ryan Nichol; Abedawn Khalaf; Kartheek Sooda; Omar Hussain; Hollie Griffiths; Roger Phillips; Farideh Javid; Colin Suckling; Simon Allison; Fraser Scott

Journal: *submitted to MedChemComm,* **2019**

82 Novel Minor Groove Binders cure animal African trypanosomiasis in an in vivo mouse model

Authors: Giordani, Federica; Khalaf, Abedawn; Gillingwater, Kirsten; Munday, Jane; de Koning, Harry; Suckling, Colin; Barrett, Michael; Scott, Fraser

Journal: Journal of medicinal Chemistry, **2019**, 62, (6), 3021-3035.

DOI: 10.1021/acs.jmedchem.8b01847

81 Development of a derivatisation method for investigating testosterone and dehydroepiandrosterone using mass spectrometry in saliva samples from young professional soccer players pre- and post-training

Authors: Mansour A Alzahrani, Ghareeb O Alshuwaier, Khalid S Aljaloud, Colin Gibson, Abedawn Khalaf, Aliyah S Alhawiti, David G. Watson

Journal: Scientia Pharmaceutica, **2019**, 87(2), 11, 1-16

DOI: 10.3390/scipharm87020011

80 Synthetic analogues of the parasitic worm product ES-62, reduce disease development in *in vivo* models of lung fibrosis

Authors: Colin J. Suckling, Sambuddho Mukherjee, Abedawn I. Khalaf, Ashwini Narayan, Fraser J. Scott, Sonal Khare, Saravanakumar Dhakshinamoorthy, Margaret M. Harnett, William Harnett

Journal: Acta Tropica, **2018**, 185, 212-218.

https://doi.org/10.1016/j.actatropica.2018.05.015

79 Chartered Status: advance your career in Science (Royal Society of Chemistry)

http://www.rsc.org/learn-chemistry/resource/download/res00001021/cmp00001664/pdf

78 *175 Faces of Chemistry: Celebrating Diversity in Science* (Royal Society of Chemistry)

Words by Jenifer Mizen Images © Anne Purkiss / Royal Society of Chemistry Published January 2014

http://www.rsc.org/diversity/175-faces/all-faces/dr-abedawn-khalaf-cchem-mrsc

77 Minor Groove Binders for DNA as Antitrypanosomal Agents: the Veterinary Context

Authors: Colin J. Suckling, Abedawn Khalaf, Fraser J. Scott, Kirsten Gillingwater, Liam Morrison, Harry de Koning, Federica Giordani and Michael Barrett

Journal: 3rd International Electronic Conference on Medicinal Chemistry; 1-30 November 2017

76 Why Antibacterial Minor Groove Binders Are a Good Thing

Authors: Colin J. Suckling, Abedawn Khalaf, Fraser J. Scott, Nicholas Tucker, Leena Niemenen, Kimon Lemonidis, Iain S. Hunter

Journal: 3rd International Electronic Conference on Medicinal Chemistry; 1-30 November 2017

75 Evaluation of Minor Groove Binders (MGBs) as novel anti-mycobacterial agents, and the effect of using non-ionic surfactant vesicles as a delivery system to improve their efficacy

Authors: Lerato Hlaka, Michael-Jon Rosslee, Mumin Ozturk, Santosh Kumar, Suraj P. Parihar, Frank Brombacher, Abedawn I. Khalaf, Katharine C. Carter, Fraser Scott, Colin Suckling, Reto Guler

Journal: *Journal of Antimicrobial Chemotherapy*, **2017**, 72(12), 3334-3341.

https://doi.org/10.1093/jac/dkx326

74 An evaluation of Minor Groove Binders as anti-fungal and anti-mycobacterial therapeutics

Authors: Fraser J. Scott, Ryan J.O. Nichol, Abedawn I. Khalaf, Federica Giordani, Kirsten Gillingwater, Soumya Ramu, Alysha

Elliott, Johannes Zuegg, Paula Duffy, Michael-Jon Rosslee, Lerato Hlaka, Santosh Kumar, Mumin Ozturk, Frank Brombacher, Michael Barrett, Reto Guler, Colin J. Suckling

Journal: *European Journal of Medicinal Chemistry,* **2017**, 136, 561-572.

http://dx.doi.org/10.1016/j.ejmech.2017.05.039

73 Four pyrrole derivatives used as building blocks in the synthesis of minor-groove binders

Authors: A. R. Kennedy, A. I. Khalaf, F. J. Scott and C. J. Suckling

Journal: *Acta Crystallographica* Section E, 2017, E73, 254-259.

https://doi.org/10.1107/S2056989017001177

72 A method for the analysis of sugars in biological systems using reductive amination in combination with hydrophilic interaction chromatography and high resolution mass spectrometry

Authors: Sami Bawazeer, Ali Muhsen Ali, Aliyah Alhawiti, Abedawn Khalaf, Colin Gibson, Jonans Tusiimire, David G. Watson

Journal: *Talanta:* 2017, 166, 75–80.

http://dx.doi.org/10.1016/j.talanta.2017.01.038

71 DNA Minor Groove Binders-Inspired by Nature

Authors: Abedawn I. Khalaf, Ahmed A. H Al-Kadhimi, Jaafar H. Ali

Journal: *Acta Chimica Slovenica,* 2016, 63, 689–704.

DOI: 10.17344/acsi.2016.2775

70 An Evaluation of Minor Groove Binders as Anti-Lung Cancer Therapeutics

Authors: Fraser J. Scott, Mireia Puig-Sellart; Abedawn I. Khalaf; Catherine J. Henderson; Gareth Westrop; David G. Watson; Katherine Carter; M. Helen Grant; Colin J. Suckling

Journal: *Bio-organic and Medicinal Chemistry letters,* 2016, 26(15), 3478–3486.

http://dx.doi.org/10.1016/j.bmcl.2016.06.040

69 Selective Anti-malarial Minor Groove Binders

Authors: Fraser J. Scott, Abedawn I. Khalaf; Sandra Duffy; Vicky M. Avery; Colin J. Suckling

Journal: *Bio-organic & Medicinal Chemistry Letters,* **2016**, 26, 3326–3329.

http://dx.doi.org/10.1016/j.bmcl.2016.05.039

68 An evaluation of Minor Groove Binders as anti-Trypanosma brucei brucei therapeutics

Authors: Fraser J. Scott, Abedawn I. Khalaf, Federica Giordani, Pui Ee Wong, Sandra Duffy, Michael Barrett, Vicky M. Avery, Colin J. Suckling

Journal: *European Journal of Medicinal Chemistry*, **2016**, 116, 116-125.

DOI: 10.1016/j.ejmech.2016.03.064

67 Synthesis and Characterization of Some Novel Isatin Azo–Imine Dyes

Authors: Ahmed A. H Al-Kadhimi, Nuhad K. E. Al–Azzawi and Abedawn I. Khalaf

Journal: *Journal of Chemical, Biological and physical sciences*, **2015**, 6(1), 138-152.

66 Quantum Chemical Study of Molecular Structure, First Order Hyper Polarizability and Vibrational Properties of 3-Halofulvenes Molecules (Fluoro, Chloro, Bromo, Iodo, and Stato Fulvenes)

Authors: Jaafar H. Ali and Abedawn I Khalaf

Journal: *Journal of Chemical, Biological and physical sciences*, **2015**, 5(4), 3729-3739.

65 Quantum Chemical DFT study of the fulvene halides molecules (Fluoro, Chloro, Bromo, Iodo, and Statofulvenes)

Authors: Jaafar H. Ali, Shaymaa I. S. Zuafurni, Khulood O. Kzar and Abedawn I Khalaf

Journal: *Journal of Chemical, Biological and physical sciences*, **2015**, 5(3), 2738-2745.

64 Crystal structure of N,N-dimethyl-2-[(4-methylbenzyl)sulfonyl] ethanamine

Authors: Alan R. Kennedy, Abedawn I. Khalaf, Fraser J. Scott and Colin J. Suckling

Journal: *Acta Crystallographica* Section E, **2015**, E71, 757–759.

DOI: 10.1107/S2056989015010233

63 Facile synthesis of Schiff and Mannich bases of isatin derivatives

Authors: Ahmed A.H. Al-kadhimi, Nuhad K.E. Al-azzawi and Abedawn I. Khalaf

Journal: *Journal of Chemical, Biological and Physical Sciences*, **2015**, 5(3), 2338-2349.

62 Prophylactic and therapeutic treatment with a synthetic analogue of a parasitic worm product prevents experimental arthritis and inhibits IL-1b production via NRF2-mediated counter-regulation of the inflammasome.

Authors: Justyna Rzepecka, Miguel A. Pineda, Lamyaa Al-Riyami, David T. Rodgers, Judith K. Huggan, Felicity E. Lumb, Abedawn I. Khalaf, Paul J. Meakin, Marlene Corbet, Michael L. Ashford, Colin J. Suckling, Margaret M. Harnett, William Harnett

Journal: *Journal of Autoimmunity*, **2015**, 60, 59-73.

http://dx.doi.org/10.1016/j.jaut.2015.04.005

61 Modified Dowex-50 W-promoted synthesis of chalcones containing hydroxyl and nitro groups

Authors: Ahmed A.H. Al-Kadhimi, Abedawn I. Khalaf, Khalid M.M. Al-Janabi, Suad A. Jameel

Journal: *Karbala International Journal of Modern Science*, **2015**, 1, 60-65. http://dx.doi.org/10.1016/j.kijoms.2014.12.001

60 Small molecule analogues of the immunomodulatory parasitic helminth product ES-62 have anti-allergy properties

Authors: Justyna Rzepecka, Michelle L. Coates, Moninder Saggar, Lamyaa Al-Riyami, Jennifer Coltherd, Hwee Kee Tay, Judith K. Huggan, Lucia Janicova, Abedawn I Khalaf, Ivonne Siebeke, Colin J. Suckling, Margaret M. Harnett and William Harnett

Journal: *International Journal for Parasitology*, **2014**, 44, (9), 669-674.

DOI: 10.1016/j.ijpara.2014.05.001

59 Recognition of the DNA Minor Groove by Thiazotropsin Analogues

Authors: Hasan Y. Alniss, Marie-Virginie Salvia, Mykhailo Sadikov, Igor Golovchenko, Nahoum G. Anthony, Abedawn I. Khalaf, Simon P. MacKay, Colin J. Suckling and John A. Parkinson

Journal: *ChemBioChem*, **2014**, 15, 1978-1990.

DOI: 10.1002/cbic.201402202

58 Structure based design and synthesis of antiparasitic pyrrolopyrimidines targeting pteridine reductase 1

Authors: Abedawn I. Khalaf, Judith K. Huggan, Colin J. Suckling, Colin L. Gibson, Kirsten Stewart, Federica Giordani, Michael P. Barrett, Pui Ee Wong, Keri L. Barrack and William N. Hunter

Journal: *Journal of Medicinal Chemistry*, **2014**, 57(15), 6479-6494.

DOI: 10.1021/jm500483b

57 Designing Anti-inflammatory Drugs from Parasitic Worms: A Synthetic Small Molecule Analogue of the Acanthocheilonema viteae Product ES-62 Prevents Development of Collagen-Induced Arthritis

Authors: Lamyaa Al-Riyami, Miguel A. Pineda, Justyna Rzepecka, Judith K. Huggan, Abedawn I. Khalaf, Colin J. Suckling, Fraser J. Scott, David T. Rodgers, and William Harnett

Journal: *Journal of Medicinal Chemistry*: **2013**, 56, 9982-10002.

DOI: 10.1021/jm401251p

56 Oligoamides of 2-amino-5-alkylthiazole 4-carboxylic acids:anti-trypanosomal compounds

Authors: Stuart Lang, Abedawn I. Khalaf, David Breen, Judith K. Huggan, Carol J. Clements, Simon P. MacKay, Colin J. Suckling

Journal: *Medicinal Chemistry Research*: **2014**, 23, 1170-1179.

DOI: 10.1007/s00044-013-0723-0

55 Thiazotropsin aggregation and its relationship to molecular recognition in the DNA minor groove.

Authors: Marie-Virginie Salvia, Fiona Addison, Hasan Y. Alniss, Niklaas J. Buurma, Abedawn I. Khalaf, Simon P. Mackay, Nahoum G. Anthony, Colin J. Suckling, Maxim P. Evstigneev, Adrián Hernandez Santiago, Roger D. Waigh, John A. Parkinson

Journal: *Biophysical Chemistry*: **2013**, 179, 1-11.

DOI: 10.1016/j.bpc.2013.04.001

54 Design, Synthesis and Antibacterial Activity of Minor Groove Binders: The Role of Non-Cationic Tail Groups

Authors: Abedawn I. Khalaf, Claire Bourdin, David Breen, Gavin Donoghue, Fraser J. Scott, Colin J. Suckling, Donna MacMillan, Carol Clements, Keith Fox, Doreen A. T. Sekibo

Journal: *European Journal of Medicinal Chemistry*: **2012**, 56, 39-47.

DOI: 10.1016/j.ejmech.2012.08.013

53 Rationalizing Sequence Selection by Ligand Assemblies in the DNA Minor Groove: The Case for Thiazotropsin A

Authors: Hasan Y. Alniss, Nahoum G. Anthony, Abedawn I. Khalaf, Simon P. Mackay, Colin J. Suckling, Roger D. Waigh, Nial J. Wheate and John A. Parkinson

Journal: *Chemical Science:* **2012**, 3, 711-722.

DOI: 10.1039/C2SC00630H

52 Catalytic antibodies (abzymes): From concept to application

Author: Abedawn I. Khalaf

Journal: Trends in Heterocyclic Chemistry: **2011**, 15, 89-98.

51 Amide isosteres in structure-activity studies of antibacterial minor groove binders

Authors: Abedawn I. Khalaf, Nahoum Anthony, David Breen, Gavin Donoghue, Simon P. Mackay, Fraser J. Scott, and Colin J. Suckling

Journal: *European Journal of Medicinal Chemistry:* **2011**, 46(11), 5343-5355

DOI:10.1016/j.ejmech.2011.08.035

50 Small molecule analogues of an immunomodulatory helminth product provide a novel approach to dissecting macrophage signal transduction pathways

Authors: L. Al-Riyami, J. Rzepecka, A. Khalaf, C. Suckling, M. Harnett & W. Harnett

Journal: *Immunology,* **2010**, 131 (Suppl. 1), 164

49 Photocyclization of Stilbenes and Stilbenoids

Author: Abedawn I. Khalaf

Journal: Trends in Photochemistry & Photobiology, 2010, 12, 65-75.

48 Ranking ligand affinity for the DNA minor groove by experiment and simulation

Authors: Wittayanarakul K, Anthony NG, Treesuwan W, Hannongbua S, Alniss H, Khalaf AI, Suckling CJ, Parkinson JA and MacKay SP

Journal: *Med. Chem. Lett.* **2010**, 1(8), 376-380.

47 Minor Groove Binders: Recent Research in Drug Development

Author: Abedawn I. Khalaf

Journal: *Current Trends in Medicinal Chemistry:* **2009**, 6, 53-63.

46 Photochemistry and free radical stabilisation of the captodative centre

Author: Abedawn I. Khalaf

Journal: *Trends in Photochemistry & Photobiology*, **2010**, 12, 7-15.

45 2,2,2-Trifluoro-N-(5-isoquinolinylmethyl)acetamide

Authors: Alan R. Kennedy, Abedawn I. Khalaf and Colin J. Suckling

Journal: *Acta Crystallographica*, Section E, **2010**, E66, o135.

44 The influence of aryl-aryl interactions in the photochemistry of some 1,3-diarylpropanes

Authors: Abedawn I. Khalaf, Clive E. Badman, Marcus P. Ennis, William M. Horspool, and Qaisar Sultana

Journal: *Trends in Photochemistry & Photobiology*, **2010**, 12, 1-5.

43 A detailed binding free energy study of 2:1 ligand-DNA complex formation by experiment and simulation:

Authors: Witcha Treesuwan, Kitiyaporn Wittayanarakul, Nahoum G. Anthony, Guillaume Huchet, Hasan Alniss, Supa Hannongbua, Abedawn I. Khalaf, Colin J. Suckling, John A Parkinson, Roger D. Waigh and Simon P. Mackay

Journal: *Physical Chemistry Chemical Physics*, **2009**, 11, 10682-10693.

42 A new synthesis of alkene-containing minor-groove binders and essential hydrogen bonding in binding to DNA and in antibacterial activity:

Authors: Nahoum Anthony, David Breen, Gavin Donoghue, Abedawn I. Khalaf, Simon P. Mackay, and Colin J. Suckling.

Journal: *Org. Biomol. Chem.*, **2009**, 7, 1843-1850.

41 Comparison of DNA complex formation behaviour for two closely related lexitropsin analogues:

Authors: John A. Parkinson, Abedawn I. Khalaf, Nahoum G. Anthony, Simon P. Mackay, Colin J. Suckling, Roger D. Waigh

Journal: *Helvetica Chimica Acta*, **2009**, 92, 795-822.

40 Selectivity in the Antibacterial Activity of Minor Groove Binders, Derivatives of the Natural Product, Distamycin

Authors: Colin J. Suckling Abedawn I. Khalaf, David Breen, Elizabeth. M. Ellis, Iain S. Hunter, Samuel Nyabam.

Journal: Drugs of the Future, **2008**, 33(Suppl. A): page 16: [L27].

[XXth Int Symp Med Chem (Aug 31-Sept 4, Vienna) 2008].

39 Structure and Selectivity in the Binding of Small Ligands to DNA and their Consequences

Authors: Colin J. Suckling, Abedawn Khalaf, David Breen, John Parkinson, Gavin Donoghue, Roger Waigh, Simon Mackay, Nahoum Anthony, Elizabeth Ellis, Iain Hunter, Curtis Gemmell, and Keith Fox

Journal: 2-7 July 2007 Faro, Portugal XI European Symposium on Organic Reactivity (ESOR). Abstract of Plenary Lecture

38 Antimicrobial Lexitropsins Containing Amide, Amidine, and Alkene Linking Groups

Authors: Nahoum Anthony, David Breen, Joanna Clarke, Gavin Donoghue, Allan Drummond, Elizabeth Ellis, Curtis Gemmell, Jean-Jacques Helesbeux, Iain Hunter, Abedawn I. Khalaf, Simon Mackay, John Parkinson, Colin J. Suckling, Roger D. Waigh

Journal: *Journal of Medicinal Chemistry*, **2007**, 50, 6116-6125. DOI: 10.1021/jm070831g

37 M4 agonists/5HT7 antagonists with potential as antischizophrenic drugs: Serominic compounds

Authors: Colin J. Suckling, John A. Murphy, Abedawn I. Khalaf, Sheng-ze Zhou, Dimitris E. Lizos, Albert Nguyen van Nhien, Hiroshi Yasumatsu, Allan McVie, Louise C. Young, Corinna McCraw, Peter G. Waterman, Brian J. Morris, Judith A. Pratt, and Alan L. Harvey

Journal: *Bioorg. & Med. Chem. Lett.*, **2007**, 17 (9), 2649–2655.

36 3-Nitro-1-(triisopropylsilyl)-1H-pyrrole

Authors: Alan R. Kennedy, Abedawn I. Khalaf, Colin J. Suckling and Roger D. Waigh

Journal: *Acta Crystallographica*, Section E, **2006**, 62 (18), o3282-o3284

35 DNA sequence recognition by an imidazole-containing isopropyl-substituted thiazole polyamide (thiazotropsin B)

Authors: A. J. Hampshire, H. Khairallah, A I. Khalaf, A. H. Ebrahimabadi, R. D. Waigh, C. J. Suckling, T. Brown, K. R. Fox

Journal: *Bioorg. Med. Chem. Lett.*, **2006**, 16 (13), 3469-3474.

34 Ethyl {[(1Z)-2-nitro-3-oxo-1-propenyl]amino}acetate

Authors: Alan R. Kennedy and Abedawn I. Khalaf,

Journal: Private Communication (1078), Cambridge Crystallographic Data Centre, summary of Data CCDC 275865. 2005.

33 2-(1-Piperidinyl)-1,3-benzothiazole

Authors: Recardo G. Alvarez, Alan R. Kennedy, Abedawn I. Khalaf, Colin J. Suckling and Roger D. Waigh,

Journal: *Acta Crystallographica* Section E, **2005**, 61 (3), o569-o570.

32 Steps towards a practical synthesis of macrocyclic bisbenzylisoquinolines

Authors: Yusuf Al-Hiari, Stephen J. Bennett, Brian Cox, Robert J. Davies, Abedawn I. Khalaf, Roger D. Waigh and Alan J. Worsley.

Journal: *Journal of Heterocyclic Chemistry*, **2005**, 42, 647-659.

31 Methyl 2-amino-5-isopropyl-1,3-thiazole-4-carboxylate

Authors: Alan R. Kennedy, Abedawn I. Khalaf, Colin J. Suckling and Roger D. Waigh

Journal: *Acta Crystallographica* Section E, **2004**, 60 (9), o1510-o1512.

30 Ethyl 2-amino-4-isopropyl-1,3-thiazole-5-carboxylate

Authors: Alan R. Kennedy, Abedawn I. Khalaf, Colin J. Suckling and Roger D. Waigh

Journal: *Acta Crystallographica* Section E, **2004**, 60 (7), o1188-o1190.

29 DNA sequence recognition by an isopropyl substituted thiazole polyamide

Authors: Peter L. James, Elena E. Merkina, Abedawn I. Khalaf, Colin J. Suckling, Roger D. Waigh, Tom Brown and Keith R. Fox

Journal: *Nucleic Acids Research*, **2004**, 32(11), 3410-3417.

28 Short Lexitropsin that Recognises the DNA Minor Groove at 5'-ACTAGT-3': Understanding the Role of Isopropyl-thiazole

Authors: Nahoum G. Antony, Abedawn I. Khalaf, Simon P. Mackay, John A. Parkinson, Colin J. Suckling, and Roger D. Waigh

Journal: *Journal of the American Chemical Society*, **2004**, 126(36), 11338-11349.

27 Synthesis and Antimicrobial Activity of Some Netropsin Analogues

Authors: Abedawn I. Khalaf, Abdolrasoul H. Ebrahimabadi, Allan J. Drummond, Nahoum G. Anthony, Simon P. Mackay, Colin J. Suckling, and Roger D. Waigh

Journal: *Org. Biomol. Chem.*, **2004**, 2 (21), 3119 – 3127.

26 Distamycin Analogues with Enhanced Lipophilicity: Synthesis and Antimicrobial Activity

Authors: Abedawn I. Khalaf, Allan J. Drummond, Breffni Pringle, Ian McGroarty, Graham G. Skellern, Roger D. Waigh, Colin J. Suckling

Journal: *J. Med. Chem.*, **2004**, 47, 2133-2156. DOI: 10.1021/jm031089x

25 DNA binding of a short lexitropsin

Authors: Nahoum G. Antony, Keith R. Fox, Blair Johnston, Abedawn I. Khalaf, Simon P. Mackay, Ian S. McGroary, John A. Parkinson, Graham G. Skellern, Colin J. Suckling and Roger D. Waigh

Journal: *Bioorg. Med. Chem. Lett.*, **2004**, 14(5), 1353-1356.

24 The Thiazotropsins Antimicrobial DNA Minor Groove Binders

Authors: Khalaf AI, Parkinson JA, Suckling CJ, Anthony NG, J-Helsebeux J, Mackay SP, Waigh RD and Fox K

Journal: *Drugs of the Future*, **2004**, 29 (suppl. A), 159.

23 Ethyl 5-oxo-2,5-dihydro-4-isoxazolecarboxylate hydroxylamine salt

Authors: Alan R. Kennedy, Abedawn I. Khalaf, Colin J. Suckling and Roger D. Waigh

Journal: *Acta Crystallographica* Section E, **2003**, 59 (9), o1410-o1412.

22 Minor Groove Binders Substituted By Lipophilic Groups

Authors: Suckling CJ, Waigh RD, Khalaf AI, Parkinson J and Hunter IS

Journal: [*19th International Congress on Heterocyclic Chemistry Abstracts*, **2003**, page 98].

21 Ethyl 2-aminooxazole-5-carboxylate

Authors: Alan R. Kennedy, Abedawn I. Khalaf, Colin J. Suckling and Roger D. Waigh

Journal: *Acta Crystallographica* Section E, 2001, 57 (9), o832-o833.

20 Unexpected Dealkylation During Nucleophilic Substitution: Synthesis of 2-N,N-Dialkylamino Benzoxazoles and Benzothiazoles

Authors: Abedawn I Khalaf, Ricardo G Alvarez, Colin J Suckling, Roger D Waigh

Journal: *Tetrahedron,* **2000**, 56, 8567-8571.

19 The Synthesis of Some Head to Head Linked DNA Minor Groove Binders

Authors: Abedawn I Khalaf, Andrew R Pitt, Colin J Suckling, Martin Scobie, John Urwin, Roger D Waigh, Robert V Fishleigh, Stephen C Young and Keith R. Fox

Journal: *Tetrahedron,* **2000**, 56, 5225-5239.

18 On the Specificity of Reactions Catalysed by the Antibody H11

Authors: Abedawn I Khalaf, Sabin Linaza, Andrew R Pitt and Colin J Suckling

Journal: *Tetrahedron,* **2000**, 56, 489-495.

17 3-Acetoxycyclohex-4-ene-1, 2-dicarboxylic acid anhydride

Authors: Alan R Kennedy, Abedawn I Khalaf, Colin J Suckling

Journal: *Acta Crystallographica C,* **2000**, C56 (6), e265-e266. IUC0000131.

16 DNA Binding, Solubility, and Partitioning Characteristics of Extended Lexitropsins

Authors: Robert V Fishleigh, Keith R Fox, Abedawn I Khalaf, Andrew R Pitt, Martin Scobie, Colin J Suckling, John Urwin, Roger D Waigh and Stephen C Young

Journal: *J. Medicinal Chemistry,* **2000**, 43(17), 3257-3266. DOI: 10.1021/jm990620e

15 Synthesis of Novel DNA Binding Agents: Indole-Containing Analogues of Bis-Netropsin,

Authors: Abedawn I Khalaf: Andrew R Pitt, Colin. J Suckling, Martin Scobie, John Urwin, Roger D Waigh, Robert V Fishleigh, Stephen C Young and Keith R Fox

Journal: *J. Chem. Research (S),* **2000**, 264-265;.J. Chem. Research (M), 2000, 751-770.

14 Methyl 2-Amino-4-(methoxymethyl)thiazole-5-carboxylate

Authors: Alan R Kennedy, Abedawn I Khalaf, Andrew R Pitt, Martin Scobie, Colin J Suckling, John Urwin, Roger D waigh and Stephen C. Young

Journal: Acta Crystallographica C, 1999, C55, Part 7, CIF-ACCESS PAPERS [WWW.iucr.org/], IUC9900072.

13 2,8-Dimethylphenoxathiin 10-Oxide

Authors: Stephen R Bennett, Alan R Kennedy, Abedawn I Khalaf and Roger D Waigh

Journal: *Acta Crystallographica C*, 1998, C54, 1511-1513.

12 Azabenzocycloheptenones. Part 20. Synthesis and utilisation of 4-amino-1,2,3,4-tetrahydro-1(1H)-benzazepines

Authors: Kevin I Booker-Milburn, Ian R Dunkin, Frances C Kelly, Abedawn I Khalaf, David A Learmouth, George R Proctor and David I Scopes

Journal: *J. Chemical Society Perkin Transaction* I, 1997, 21, 3261-3273.

11 N,N-Diacetyl-2,5-dimethyl-6-nitroaniline

Authors: Alan R Kennedy and Abedawn I Khalaf

Journal: *Acta Crystallographica C*, **1997**, C53, 744-746.

10 Synthesis and chemical reactivity of benzothiazol-2-yl hydrozonyl chlorides

Authors: Hikmat H Alnima, Abedawn I Khalaf, and Walid F Hammady

Journal: *Indian Journal of Chemistry*, **1995**, 34B, 736-739.

9 A Catalytic monoclonal antibody with unexpected esterase activity

Authors: William H Stimson, Laura M Bence, June I Irvine, Abedawn I Khalaf, George R Proctor, M Catriona Tedford and Colin J Suckling

Journal: *J. Clin. Lab. Immunol.*, **1994**, 43, 167-175.

8 Catalytic antibodies: designed and accidental

Authors: Colin J Suckling, William H Stimson, George R Proctor, Laura H Bence, Linda Brooks, Abedawn I Khalaf, Catriona M Tedford, Sabin Linaza, Iain McGilp, Raymond Maguire, and June Irvine,

Journal: *Biochemical Society Transactions*, **1993**, 21, 1099-1102.

7. Remarkably efficient hydrolysis of a 4-nitrophenyl ester by a catalytic antibody raised to an ammonium hapten

Authors: Abedawn I Khalaf, George R Proctor, Colin J Suckling, Laura H Bence, June I Irvine and William H Stimson

Journal: *J. Chem. Soc. Perkin Transaction I*, **1992**, 1475-1481.

6 Catalytic antibodies: a new window on protein chemistry

Authors: Colin J Suckling, Catriona M Tedford, George R Proctor, Abedawn I Khalaf, Laura M Bence and William H Stimson

Journal: Catalytic Antibodies, Wiley, Chichester (CIBA Foundation Symposium 159) 1991, pp. 201-210.

5. Influence of wavelength on the Photochemistry of triarylbenzofurodioxin derivatives

Authors: William M Horspool and Abedawn I Khalaf

Journal: *J. Chem. Soc. Perkin Transaction I*, **1989**, 1147-1152.

4. A novel method for the preparation of β-γ unsaturated carbonyl compounds

Authors: Abedawn I Khalaf, Mohammad S Mustaffa, Jaafar H Ali, Ju'ma R Al-Dulaymi, and A K Hashem (in part)

Journal: J. *Iraqi Chem. Society* **1988**, 13(1), 159-172.

3. Preparation and photolysis of 1,3-diarylpropanols and the study of the validity of Hammett equation

Authors: Abedawn I Khalaf, Jaafar H Ali, and William M Horspool

Journal: *J. Iraqi chem. Society*, **1987**. 12 (2), 9-25.

2. The influence of aryl-aryl interaction in the photochemistry of some 1,3-diarylpropanes

Authors: Abedawn I Khalaf and William M Horspool

Journal: *J. Iraqi Chem. Society*. **1986**, 11 (2).

1. Substitution and wavelength effects in the photochemistry of 5,6,7,8-tetrachloro-3a,9a-triarylfuro(2,3-b)(1,4)benzodioxin derivatives

Authors: William M Horspool and Abedawn I Khalaf

Journal: Tetrahedron Letters, 1983, 24(35), 3745-3748.

Patents Published

5. Margaret. Harnett, William Harnett, Colin J. Suckling, Fraser J. Scott, Judith Huggan, Abedawn Ibrahim Khalaf

New substituted aryl sulfonyl compounds are TNF-alpha modulators, useful for modulating immune response and treating rheumatoid arthritis, asthma, Type I diabetes mellitus, systemic lupus erythematosus, psoriasis and multiple sclerosis. Patent Number(s): WO2014023934-A1

International Patent Application No PCT/GB2013/051988 (2014)

4. Abedawn I. Khalaf, Colin J. Suckling, Roger D. Waigh

Heterocyclic carboxamide derivatives as minor groove binders of DNA and their preparation, pharmaceutical compositions and use in the treatment of bacterial, fungal and other microbial infections: PCT Int. Appl. (2008), 117pp. WO 2008038018 A1 20080403

3. Ernst Wülfert, Colin J Suckling; Abedawn I Khalaf, Simon P Mackay and Blair F Johnston:

Hunter Fleming Patent Application

Preparation of tricyclic cytoprotective compounds comprising an indole residue: Brit. UK Pat. Appl. (2006), 44pp. GB 2422828 A

2. Abedawn I. Khalaf, Colin J. Suckling, Roger D. Waigh

Preparation of oligopeptide DNA minor groove-binding compounds: PCT Int. Appl. (2003), 150 pp. WO 2003059881 A2 20030724

1. Abdullah Tuncay Demiryurek, Kathleen Ann Kane, William John Kerr, Abedawn Ibrahim Khalaf, Derek Charles Nonhebel, William Ewen Smith, Roger Wadsworth, Cherry Lindsey Wainwright

Preparation of Amino acid and peptide free radical scavengers as Drugs

PCT Int. Appl. (1996), WO 9627370 A1 19960912

www.ingramcontent.com/pod-product-compliance
Ingram Content Group UK Ltd.
Pitfield, Milton Keynes, MK11 3LW, UK
UKHW062309290726
14090UKWH00018B/971

9 781916 136809